NATIVE TONGUES

NATIVE TONGUES

an african hip-hop reader

edited by

p. khalil saucier

AFRICA WORLD PRESS

TRENTON | LONDON | CAPE TOWN | NAIROBI | ADDIS ABABA | ASMARA | IBADAN | NEW DELHI

AFRICA WORLD PRESS
541 West Ingham Avenue | Suite B
Trenton, New Jersey 08638

Book and cover design: Saverance Publishing Services

Front cover photo:
Magee McIlvaine/http://www.mageemcilvaine.com/

Back cover photo:
Noelle Theard/http://www.noelletheard.com/

Permission to use these photos is gratefully acknowledged.

Library of Congress Cataloging-in-Publication Data

Native tongues : an African hip-hop reader / [compiled by] P. Khalil Saucier.
    p. cm.
Includes bibliographical references and index.
ISBN 978-1-59221-837-0 (pbk.)
1. Rap (Music)--Africa--History and criticism. 2. Rap (Music)--Africa--Social aspects 3. Hip-hop--Africa. I. Saucier, Paul Khalil, 1976-
ML3531N38 2011
782.421649096--dc22
                    2011009107

table of contents

acknowledgements

While the editing of this book has not occupied me for very long, the subject is one which for many years has furnished the theme of constant thought and discussion with friends and colleagues sharing the same interest in hip-hop. In mentioning a few names, I am conscious of the manifold intellectual debts incurred in the process. This book was inspired in many ways by the writings, analyses, and cultural criticism of Tricia Rose, Craig Watkins, Mark Anthony Neal, Greg Tate, and countless other intellectuals who have expanded the range of hip-hop studies. However, Murray Forman probably had the greatest influence upon the general approach adopted in this work. His contemplative questions, serious scholarship, support, and advice over the years have all helped in the completion of this book. I appreciate the constant support and encouragement I received from my editor Angela Ajayi and all those at Africa World Press and The Red Sea Press, especially Kassahun Checole. I thank them for having believed in this project from its earliest stage. I also owe a debt of gratitude to all the contributors and translators of this collection. I thank you for your enthusiasm, work, and patience in seeing to that this project become a reality. In addition, I would like to acknowledge Noelle Theard and Magee McIlvaine for their wonderful photos that help bring balance to the book. I would also like to thank Emmett Price, Geoff Ward, Alan West-Duran, and Murray Forman, all members of the now defunct Northeastern University Hip-hop Studies Collective, for our lively discussions served as inspiration to bring together a book of essays on African hip-hop. Special thanks to Thomas Gesthuizen and others at Africanhiphop.com for keeping the world up to date on the history and recent achievements of hip-hop across Africa. Thank you to my colleagues at Rhode Island College for supporting my intellectual curiosities. I am grateful for the support and encouragement of my friends and academic interlopers like Corey D.B. Walker, Kumi Silva, Adam Haupt, James Manigault-Bryant, Rhon Manigault-Bryant, and others. Lastly, many thanks to my cherished partner, Jasmine, for her unwavering love, editorial skills, endurance, and support of my academic pursuits.

foreword

MURRAY FORMAN

> Born to a throne, stronger than Rome
> but Violent prone, poor people zone,
> But it's my home, all I have known,
>
> When I get older, I will be stronger,
> They'll call me freedom, just like a Waving Flag,
> And then it goes back, and then it goes back,
> And then it goes back
>
>   – K'naan, "Wavin' Flag"

As I write this, the news is still swirling that a refugee from war-torn Somalia, displaced from his home and raised in Canada, will provide one of the theme songs of the 2010 FIFA World Cup football tournament in South Africa. The song, "Wavin' Flag" by K'naan, is an uplifting anthem that cites Africa's royal legacy and its post-colonial adversity, turning toward an appropriately global theme of hope and optimism. Apart from its selection for a sports event of such magnitude, the song was also earlier selected in another realm of considerable magnitude (7.0 on the Richter Scale): a remixed version was recorded by Young Artists for Haiti, a celebrity-studded Canadian campaign for Haitian earthquake relief.

K'naan's rise over for the past several years is interesting in its own right; a product of the lively and talented Toronto/T-dot hip-hop scene (that also nurtured Kardinal Offishall and Drake), he has emerged as a sophisticated MC whose astute lyrics and tight rhyme style distinguish him from many aspiring rappers. Yet his hybrid cultural identity is nothing new in the T-dot and in many ways he is an apt signifier of the relatively liberal and progressive potentials of Canada's most "multicultural" city. Within the current global condition K'naan's world-wide profile also makes sense. He is frequently called upon for commentary about Somali society and politics and to address issues pertaining to the status of refugees, global migration, or international human rights.

If representin' is something we do and take seriously in hip-hop then K'naan represents the world (even if he temporarily does so under the imprimatur of FIFA and Coca-Cola, the sponsors of the international World Cup Tour). That's no small thing for a brother from Mogadishu who bolted under dire and deadly circumstances. Tours with Youssou N'Dour, Talib Kweli and Mos Def, Stephen and Damian "Jr. Gong" Marley, and appearances with Nas present fascinating transcultural, diasporic collaborations (Dakar Senegal, Kingston Jamaica, NYC, Mogadishu/Toronto), a point acknowledged by Damian Marley in his comments about K'naan: "we are definitely players of the same team in terms of our mission in life and in terms of schooling people to what's really going on locally and going in our own countries and in our own culture."

This important collection of essays, thoughtfully "curated" by P. Khalil Saucier, has several similarities with K'naan. For one, it writes hip-hoppers and rappers from throughout Africa back into the narrative of global hip-hop. In doing so it corrects an often-glaring absence in the field of hip-hop studies. The circulating images and tales of African urban existence infrequently convey the fact that in the mid-1980s hip-hop was taken up by the youth of Africa's larger metropolitan areas, just as it was in many other locales around the world. Hip-hop in Africa engages with many of the same issues that disenfranchised youth confront anywhere, emerging as a strategic factor in negotiating conflicts of power, authority and repression.

Hip-hop in Africa is, under the current conditions of deterritorialization, transcultural "flows," and intersecting "scapes," a full-fledged global phenomenon and its dialogical character contributes to its richness. The hip-hop artists and activists touted in this text simultaneously cite their pre-colonial cultural heritage and their thoroughly contemporary cosmopolitan practices. The essays describe in detail the artists' deployment of postmodern digital technologies in the manifestation of a joyfully radical remix culture. As the authors here go to great lengths to explain, the youth of the African continent adopt hip-hop as a mode of expression, resistance, and fun and in the process they have transformed it on the ground where meanings are made.

While Africa has long been defined as hip-hop's "ground zero," the original site of the drum and dance from which hip-hop was born, there was until quite recently a surprising paucity of research and writing on pan-African hip-hop. In the least convincing arguments, Africa is cast as the wellspring of an innate black cultural aesthetic that reverberates across time and the diaspora, producing a single essentialist cultural continuum that is unproblematically traced through the creative arts. The essays here aren't having any of that; they stand as a testament to the sophisticated analytical research that fully addresses hip-hop within Africa's diverse local, regional, and national contexts, positioning hip-hop expressivity within an array of distinct aesthetic forms. Indeed, as hip-hop studies have evolved, the theoretical complexity of the research has also intensified which is clearly evident within these pages.

Of course the rampant differences that are characteristic of hip-hop in Africa are also mirrored in the research. The contributors from different national settings take up and extend the analytical project within hip-hop studies by drawing on critical race theory, post-colonial theory, and theories critiquing neo-liberal trends and global media influences. They addresses specific historical moments in order to tease out significant evolutionary factors and they accommodate varied experiential realities when they explore differences in ritual practices, social conventions, political regimes, or everyday factors such as infrastructural discrepancies (technological, economic, educational) that intersect with aspects of age, class, gender, or race. The urgent reminder that "it's bigger than hip-hop," expressed by the U.S. artists dead prez and others, is altogether relevant in this regard and scholars in Africa and around the world -- as well as researchers across the disciplines -- will surely benefit from the new approaches and applications to deeply important issues addressed here.

The authors place an emphasis on the historical, linguistic, or socio-political idiosyncrasies that are in effect across the continent and within separate regions. By reinforcing the culturally specific nuances and subtleties we see how different conditions give rise to multiple creative cultural strategies within which hip-hop is both interpreted and mobilized as a communicative medium. Lest anyone forget, hip-hop, too, is a multi-faceted cultural phenomenon and among its greatest virtues are its incredible versatility and the endless capacity for reinvention displayed by its core artists and producers. Hip-hop scholars share that inventiveness and, as I have suggested in prior instances, hip-hop writing and research and the act of generating knowledge are also fundamental elements of hip-hop.

In an earlier moment, perhaps twenty-five years ago, it might have seemed appropriate to simply enunciate that African hip-hop had, in a sense, arrived, that it was on the map. But thinking metaphorically, if there is an aspect of cultural cartography relating to global hip-hop then this collection serves as an advanced GPS system guiding our navigation through the fascinating intricacies of hip-hop across Africa.

INTRODUCTION
hip-hop culture in red, black, and green

P. Khalil Saucier
In October 2009 during their
annual Hip-Hop Music Awards,
Black Entertainment Television (BET), paid tribute to hop-hop's
formative years and future with a video featuring a freestyle
cipher. In order to create a sense of nostalgia for hip-hop's past,
the video was filmed in black and white. Encapsulating those
participating in the cipher were quickly executed graffiti tags that
read, "self-expression," "be true," and "peep your passion." With
an old school drum beat lopped by legend DJ Premier, emcees,
wearing the most up-to-date elements of hip-hop fashion, gave
the millions watching a lesson in verbal improvisation. While
Mos Def, Black Thought, Eminem, and KRS-One were the most
identifiable members of the cipher, the least known member was
Gsan, a Tanzanian emcee from the group X Plastaz. However,
rapping in Swahili, Gsan does not skip a beat, flowing effortlessly
over the DJ Premier provided beat, telling all viewing and listening of his struggles and affection for hip-hop. More importantly,
Gsan calls out the cities and countries known for vibrant hip-hop
scenes, two of which are located on the African continent. At
that moment, Gsan identifies the transnational and global nature
of hip-hop, while simultaneously positioning African hip-hop
within a complex and vibrant genealogy of hip-hop. This is not
to say that Gsan's appearance at the BET Music Award's marks

the beginning of African hip-hop. Rather, what I think it marks is the shifting nature of African hip-hop from the margins to the center of the hip-hop world. In other words, African hip-hop has now entered the cipher.

Since its arrival in many African countries in the early 1980s, rap music and hip-hop culture in Africa has experienced slow and steady growth and popular success. Many African's were seduced by the affective qualities of the music by the Sugar Hill Gang, Grandmaster Flash, and Afrika Bambaataa. Vibrant hip-hop communities developed in Capetown, Dakar, Lagos, Accra, to name more than a few places. Meanwhile, hip-hop in these early places crossed borders influencing youth throughout the rest of Africa. The impact and visibility of the late North American rappers Tupac Shakur and Biggie Smalls serve as wonderful examples. Both Tupac and Biggie became legends across the vast continent. There was no major city in Africa one could go to in the late 1990s and not see images of both Tupac and Biggie or hear youth reciting them. Today, hip-hop is arguably the fastest growing component of African youth culture. It can be heard in vibrant and chaotic urban areas and desolate and pastoral rural areas of Africa. It can be heard in both private and public spaces, while piped through loud speakers or one's personal music device.

Over the last decade, as hip-hop has become more prominent in Africa, it has become a powerful means of cultural expression, a means by which old identities are deconstructed and new identities are established. For many African youth, hip-hop has become the voice of change and represents a future of promise and hope, Pan-African unity, and national growth. For others, it has become a source of tragic consequences; the spread of hypermaterialism and the end of "traditional" Africa. On the one hand, African hip-hop addresses HIV/AIDS, moral corruption, exploitation, and neocolonialism. It speaks of kleptocracy and social misery. Hip-hop is part of a youth project of modernity as well as a means to return to the sources of African cultures. On the other hand, it also represents cultural imperialism and postcolonial forms of subordination and domination. In the 1990s, for instance, rap music was exploited by Sierra Leone rebels, particularly the West Side Boys, a splinter faction of the Armed Forces Revolutionary Council. In fact, Tupac t-shirts often served as uniforms (Presholt, 2009).[1] In short, hip-hop in Africa illustrates the back and forth between the neocolonial, the oppressive, and the liberatory.

Furthermore, African governments have recognized the power of hip-hop in its ability to reach and communicate with audiences. Africa's less democratic leaders often fear the political potential of a youth movement spurred by it, and have tried to censor the more politically charged artists and marginalize its youthful listeners. Others have embraced the popularity that can be gained by supporting artists in their countries, using hip-hop's influence to spread party propaganda and to make sure their messages reach a mass audience. Hip-hop has become a tool to win votes in local and national elections. For instance, Alexis Sinduhije, a 2010 presidential candidate in Burundi, teamed up with record label Nomadic Wax to release a hip-hop complication, entitled "Democracy in Burundi: Open Source Mixtape Volume One."[2] Young rappers assisted in the election of Senegalese president Abdoulaye Wade in 2000. Other examples include the Togo Hip-hop Awards which were established in 2003 by the Minister of Culture and the government sponsored Gabao Hip-Hop festival, also started in 2003, recently featured artists such as Jay Z and Fat Joe. Similarly, in October 20-21, 2005 the United Nations launched the first African Global Hip-hop Summit in Johannesburg, South Africa.

Since hip-hop dominates much of the popular cultural landscape of Africa, many hip-hop festivals, aside from the political, in and of themselves have become important regional and continental cultural events. Hip-hop receives copious media coverage. Hip-hop awards festivals are set up as public events similar to sporting events. Burkina Faso known throughout the world for its Ouagadougou Pan-African Film & Television Festival, an event that has taken place every two years since 1969, is home to one of the most popular hip-hop festivals on the continent, the Wada Hip Hop Festival. The Wada Hip Hop Festival, approaching its eighteenth year, has been featured in cities throughout Burkina Faso such as Ouagadougou, Bobo-Dioulasso, Pô, Ouahigouya, and Koudougou.[3] Other hip-hop festivals have been established in Guinea-Conakry, Senegal, South Africa, and elsewhere. Many of these festivals feature poetry slams, rap competitions, and b-boy and b-girl battles, while also featuring seminars on music production and music industry rules and regulations. Hip-hop also is often prominently featured in the MTV Africa Music Awards (MAMAS). And, African hip-hop videos are widely accessible through Youtube.com and Africanhiphop.com. As one can easily access American hip-hop videos, one can easily access African hip-hop videos.

As a result of its growing popularity and socio-cultural impact, enterprises related to hip-hop such as recording, clothing, and promotions are increasing in popularity. For instance, while many African youth may fancy American name brand clothing like Rocawear and FUBU, they also fancy local hip-hop clothing by Mau Mau University Clothing, Fundi Frank, Kina Clothing,[4] and Gangwe Wear, a clothing brand created by the popular Tanzanian hip-hop group Gangwe Mobb in 2001. Today, hip-hop in Africa dominates award shows, magazines, videos, radio play, and sales charts. By extension hip-hop is serious business for producers, rappers and studio owners. For example, in places like Nigeria, Kenya, South Africa, Senegal, Cape Verde, and Uganda the top club and radio playlists have been dominated by hip-hop since the early 1990s. Many young artists who would have once entered the music scene through traditional music genres have become hip-hop artists and have contributed to the evolution of the musical form in Africa. In other words, in post-colonial Africa hip-hop has impacted national and local economies by creating industries and by giving economic opportunities for many African youth unavailable to them in the past.

Since hip-hop has become such a significant social and cultural phenomenon in Africa it has attracted the attention of scholars of ethnomusicology, media studies, African Studies, and popular culture. Yet, despite the importance, centrality, vibrancy, and achievements African hip-hop has shown over the last couple of decades, academically and intellectually speaking, more attention needs to be paid to African hip-hop. While several books, monographs, and journals have dedicated space to hip-hop culture, little has been dedicated to African hip-hop. African hip-hop artists and practitioners are important, however, they are often ignored not only by parents, grandparents, policy makers, but ignored by the academy. Paying closer attention to hip-hop on the continent allows us to better understand a multitude of social phenomena and processes. More specifically, it allows us to better understand the socio-cultural realties of Africa, youth identity construction, and African modernities created by local and global processes. It allows us to explore the contradictions inherent in African societies. Accompanied by a thick bass line, colorful and surreal street murals, headspinning and acrobatic youth, hip-hop symbolizes the uneven and complex trajectory of an Africa in search of its own rhythm and identity.

african youth coming to voice

Youth have emerged as one of the central concerns of those interested in the African continent. Over the years, Africanists have become preoccupied with African youth.[5] Young Africans can be seen as searching for a narrative that provides a territory for the free play of their imagination and political consciousness; a space for their coming of age in a neo-colonial Africa.

In this sense, hip-hop is more than entertainment in Africa. It provides a space where African youth voice their opinions and participate in open, public discourse in ways that are often not possible through more traditional avenues of political and cultural participation. Echoing hip-hop legend Grandmaster Flash, hip-hop in Africa has allowed its youth to speak about anything. In other words, hip-hop has allowed many subaltern groups, who find themselves similarly affected by the weight of neo-colonialism and free market capitalism to speak with one voice; it provides them with a space to speak about the crush of neo-liberal politics and corruption. Many African rappers consider themselves modern day equivalents of the traditional African artist such as the griot and the oral storyteller where art is valued for its functional role in matters of state and civil society as well as for its essential beauty and emotive qualities. They have a sharp awareness of the internal dynamics of their society as well as the larger world with which it interacts. For instance, they are cogently aware of privatization programs that benefit a small minority and World Bank structural adjustment programs.

Hip-hop offers African youth opportunities for entry onto the world stage. It is a space for neocolonial struggle. It is a new modality of and for action. Since the early 1980s, hip-hop particularly rap music, has gripped the hearts and minds of African youth and by extension has strongly influenced the possibilities of their political imagination. It is an important source of affective investment. According to Mwenda Ntarangwi, "Hip-hop is...a forum through which East African youth, often left out of the important socioeconomic and political commentaries and decision-making processes, attain agency... (2009: 3)."[6] Hip-hop, in many ways, is doing its part in constructing a new language of human emancipation that has the capacity to project a new vision for society. It helps shape youth subjectivities. Hip-hop, as part of a counter hegemonic movement, nevertheless faces considerable challenges. While it can be, and is liberatory, it can also be home to the rhetoric of freedom, the ethos of male sexual aggressiveness and abjection, and the mores of capitalistic consumption. While rappers often and explicitly critique free market capitalism and state intervention, they have benefitted from both. They ironically desire their destruction and continuation. There is an intense avowal of consumerism and disavowal of capitalism. Nonetheless, hip-hop in Africa forces us to move beyond the simple binary of capitulation and resistance, into a space of proliferating agency; an act of self-assertion and differentiation.

global and local articulations

Hip-hop knows no boundaries. It is simultaneously aspatial and spatial. In other words, it is attuned to the local and national, while also disregarding local and national boundaries. As already mentioned, Africa is home to many thriving hip-hop scenes that are simultaneously global and unmistakably local. However, the process of indigenization, or rather the Africanization of hip-hop was not always a reality, for many young Africans were simply imitating the beats, styles, and aesthetics of North American hip-hop. For example, many emcees, despite using other languages for everyday use, would rhyme in English and utilize many of the same social and cultural frames used by North American emcees. A simple chronology of hip-hop in Africa would mark the 1980s as a period of mimicry and appropriation, while the mid-1990s to the present has been a period of ingenuity, re-appropriation, and hybridization.

Today, hip-hip in Africa is fully Africanized and ever evolving. Many songs and videos highlight local issues, incorporate regional languages, dialects, traditional storytelling, and proverbial oratory. Traditional musical styles are often sampled. Both the *kora* and *balafona* are often heard in many popular hip-hop songs as are other traditional African musical instruments. In Ghana, hip-hop has merged with the highlife music scene, creating hiplife.[7] Similarly, *bongo flava* and *lugaflow* have been created in Tanzania and Uganda respectively, while in South Africa *kwaito* has developed among township youth. Many emcees can now be heard rhyming in Twi, Wolof, Swahili, and other African languages along with English, French, Arabic, and pidgin.

To this end, African hip-hop allows us, as Diouf (2003) suggests, to understand how African youth are "situated in a temporality [that is] both indigenous and global."[8] That is hip-hop in Africa illustrates a certain set of modalities of passage from the autochthonous to the universal or global. However, hip-hop is seen by many African youth not so much as a loss of culture and tradition than as an addition. Like many things in Africa, things appropriated from the outside are forever resignified and reconfigured in locally meaningful ways (Piot 1999).[9] Hip-hop lyrics are reauthored by local values and histories. Hip-hop illustrates creative re-appropriations. Based on a North American template, hip-hop in Africa was taken up, studied, and practiced. And then revised, repurposed, and remade, thus allowing for the reinvention of national identities and collectivities and by extension has the potentiality to produce new socialities, new cultures, and new meanings. In short, African youth simultaneously partake in a global hip-hop culture, but they also live in a day-to-day world that is distinctly African.

outline of the volume

Native Tongues is an anthology of essays and interviews on hip-hop in Africa. However, it by no means is intended to be a comprehensive text, although it addresses many important areas concerning African hip-hop. It grapples with many of the key issues and debates confronting hip-hop in Africa today in that the reader examines issues of cultural imperialism, the integrity of local cultures, corporate culture, local economies, and more, while simultaneously working through global and local concerns. The topics herein engage with issues central to all disciplines within the social sciences and humanities. To this end, this reader is devoted to introducing the reader to a more organized account of African hip-hop. With the exception of Mwenda Ntarangwi's *East African Hip-hop: Youth Culture and Globalization* no one has analyzed, in book form, the complex interior/exterior of African hip-hop. The essayists in this book address this deficiency. *Native Tongues* plugs a gap in the literature, which surprisingly has not been filled up until now. This is especially perplexing given the popularity of hip-hop studies.

Yet, a study which sets out to present an integrated and variable account of African hip-hop cannot hope to satisfy those who look for a comprehensive study of such a diverse social and cultural phenomena on such a vast and variable continent. Africa is too large. It is too complex. Further, *Native Tongues* is not intended to rival the work and labor of scholars who have examined in detail one particular corner of the field. The task of assembling so many different essays and interviews under general heading imposes limitations of which I am only too conscious. It is pertinent, to state at the outset, that *Native Tongues* is not proposed here to do more than indicate the general trajectory of the cultural and social phenomena under review. This project is intended to bring together work that, up until now, has been commonly treated separately. For my part as editor, I only claim the extent of familiarity with the subject which is required to distinguish what is relevant from the boundless data circulating in piecemeal fashion. The principal of selection may perhaps be thought to have resulted in a degree of compression unusual in a work intended to investigate something as broad as African hip-hop. Since this volume is overly concerned with rap music, more attention needs to be paid to documenting and analyzing the other elements of African hip-hop culture. Many African youth expend a great deal of intellectual and creative energy on deejaying, graffiti art, and b-boying/b-girling and as result more work needs to be completed.

The title of this book has a double meaning. First, it takes its inspiration from The Native Tongues, a collective from late 1980s and early 1990s of hip-hop artists known for their positive, good-natured Afrocentric lyrics. Its principal members were the De La Soul, A Tribe Called Quest, and the Jungle Brothers. The collective was also closely tied to the Universal Zulu Nation. While in high school these groups ignited my interest in rap and hip-hop culture more generally. Second, the native in *Native Tongues*, speaks to the glocalized ways in which African youth have and continue to negotiate and reinvent hip-hop culture on the continent.

Native Tongues is divided into four parts. In the first part, "African Noise: Mapping African Hip-hop from East, West, and South," hip-hop is used as a frame for a critical analysis of contemporary social, cultural, and political forces. In other words, we examine hip-hop as an alternative mode of social and political discourse as well as a form of gainful economic activity and social upward mobility. Other essays in this section examine the "hip-hop wars," that is, the conflict between underground hip-hop and mainstream hip-hop, while others look at the processes of identity formation particularly in South Africa. "We Are Africans:" African Hip-Hop Beyond the Motherland" then reveals some of the African manifestations in the diaspora, particularly in Europe. Many scholars have tended to focus on hip-hop within specific countries, ignoring cross-border exchanges and collaboration. These essays focuses on hip-hop artists from the African diaspora, some of whom have never set foot on African soil, yet they get inspiration from their African heritage. Thus, rather than fix African hip-hop to a specific country and to the African continent itself, the current volume shows youth engagement with hip-hop through a lens of transnationalism. Part three "The Rap-Up: Conversations and Interviews" features an interview with several members of the Tanzanian hip-hop group X Plastaz and a cross-generational conversation between two South African hip-hop practitioners, activists, and scholars. Finally, "Who Shot Ya? African Hip-Hop in Focus" features photos by Noelle Theard and Magee McIlvaine, thus enhancing this collection that brings together the foremost experts on the pop culture explosion of hip-hop in Africa. In the end, my hope is that *Native*

Tongues, building on the enormous popularity and potency of hip-hop in Africa, will draw people to become engaged in writing and researching about hip-hop in Africa as it evolves.

notes

1. Jeremy Prestholt. "The afterlives of 2Pac: imagery and alienation in Sierra Leone and beyond." *Journal of African Cultural Studies* Volume 21, Issue 2, (December 2009), pp. 197-218.
2. See http://nomadicwax.bandcamp.com/track/democracy-in-burundi-mixtape .
3. See http://www.wagahiphop.com/ for more information. Also consult the documentary *Ouaga Hip Hop* (2003) by Benny Malapa
4. Juma4. "Tanzanians are supporting homegrown brands more than ever before." http://www.africanhiphop.com/. December 9, 2009.
5. See for example Cati Coe. 2005. *Dilemmas of Culture in African Schools: Youth, Nationalism, and the Transformation of Knowledge*. Chicago: University of Chicago Press; Nadine Dolby. 2001. *Constructing Race: Youth, Identity, and Popular Culture in South Africa*. Albany: State University of New York Press; Mwenda Ntarangwi. 2009. *East African Hip Hop: Youth Culture and Globalization*. Chicago: University of Illinois Press; Jay Straker. 2009. *Youth, Nationalism, and the Guinean Revolution*. Bloomington: Indiana University Press.
6. See also Adam Haupt. 2008. *Stealing Empire: P2P, Intellectual Property and Hip Hop Subversion*. Cape Town: Human Science Research Council.
7. For more information see *Living the HipLife* (Director, Jesse Weaver Shipley, 2007) and *Homegrown: HipLife in Ghana* (Director, Eli Jacobs-Fantauzzi, 2009).
8. M. Diouf. 2003. "Engaging Postcolonial Cultures: African Youth and Public Space." *African Studies Review* 46 (1): 1-12.
9. C. Piot. 1999. *Remotely Global: Village Modernity in West Africa*. Chicago: University of Chicago Press.

PART I

african noise: mapping african hip-hop from the east, west, and south

CHAPTER 1
rappin griots:
producing the local in
senegalese hip-hop

CATHERINE APPERT More than thirty years ago, hip-hop music and culture sprang to life in the Black and Latino neighborhoods of New York City, as minority youth drew on interconnected musical and socio-economic histories to create a music that was both strikingly innovative and grounded in the past. Stemming from a lineage of Afro-diasporic music that encompasses Southern oral traditions, Jamaican sound system culture, the blues, disco, and funk music, hip-hop's genealogy is etched in histories of oppression and migrations, cultural movements such as the Harlem Renaissance and the Black Arts Movement, political movements for Civil Rights and Black Nationalism, and socio-economic struggle. In the three-plus decades that have elapsed since hip-hop's now almost mythical emergence from the postindustrial ashes of the South Bronx, the music and culture have spread like wildfire throughout the globe. Responding both to hip-hop music and to the histories of struggle it evokes, youth on every inhabited continent create distinct hip-hop cultures that speak to the intersections of local experience and globalizing flows of people, capital, and cultural production.[1]

Dakar, Senegal hosts a hip-hop culture that is simultaneously grounded in the local and in a transnational network of music and ideas. Dakar youth began experimenting with hip-hop only shortly after its inception in New York, initially rapping in English but quickly indigenizing the music through language use and the incorporation of local musical elements. Today, Dakar's thriving hip-hop scene includes over 3,000 groups, whose often political messages build on complex histories of racial disenfranchisement in Africa and the United States. While operating in an explicit relationship to the African diaspora, Senegalese rappers continue to indigenize hip-hop both musically and discursively, incorporating local musical elements and claiming that hip-hop is rooted in the indigenous *griot*, or bardic, performance tradition.[2] In their music and performance, processes of musical and discursive indigenization centering on the griot intersect with performative identifications with U.S. hip-hop and the communities of the diaspora. The intersections of music, lyrics, and discourse in Senegalese hip-hop can be read as instances of strategic and multi-layered intertextuality that are simultaneously traditionalizing and transformative, allowing Senegalese youth to position themselves and their music in a transnational network of hip-hop practitioners while grounding themselves in localized identifications with Senegalese music and culture.[3]

performing intertextuality

Scholarly inquiry into African hip-hop is the latest chapter in a growing body of research on African popular music (and popular culture more generally) that often takes as its focus the novel cultural forms that have developed through a blending of elements of indigenous and Western music.[4] But rather than creating new musical forms via a hybrid fusing of indigenous and Western music, Senegalese hip-hop practitioners strategically mobilize distinct performance genres in a way that draws on and emphasizes, rather than altering, the generic characteristics of each. By constructing – musically, lyrically, and discursively – an intertextual relationship linking U.S. hip-hop and griot performance, Senegalese rappers define their music in relation to both local practice and global cultural flows.

At the level of everyday language use, intertextuality indicates a process through which two (or more) texts derive meaning from their interdependent relationship to each other.[5] To describe the relationship between African American and Senegalese hip-hop as intertextual suggests that these musics take on meaning for Senegalese youth largely through how they are perceived to relate to each other. Intertextuality, however, is not only relational but performative, embedded in and enacted as practice. In examining Senegalese hip-hop as instances of performed intertextuality, I draw largely on the work of Richard Bauman and Charles L. Briggs, who describe verbal performance as a multi-staged process in which performers remove texts from an original context and transform them through re-contextualization. This process is transformational because the text is not exactly reproduced – it carries meaning from its earlier contexts but also acquires new meaning, form, and function in the process of recentering. The continuous decentering and recentering of texts illuminates processes of traditionalization, which create a discursive continuity with a past that is meaningful in some way (Baumann and Briggs 1990; Briggs and Bauman 1992).

While drawing on this textual approach, in looking at instances of intertextuality in Senegalese hip-hop I go beyond a text-based understanding of interconnectedness in performance to consider not only particular songs but also genres, musical performance styles, language, and discursive practices as texts that are performed and received. Framing Senegalese hip-hop as performed, dynamic intertextualities highlights the imbrication of music, lyrical content, and the discourses surrounding cultural production. Considering the ways in which musical and social characteristics of griot performance are self-consciously decentered from their original context and transformed in hip-hop reveals multi-layered processes of indigenization that operate through performed intertextuality at the musical, discursive, and social levels. In drawing on the figure of the griot, Senegalese rappers decontextualize traditional music, speech genres, and personae and re-contextualize them in hip-hop.[6] At the same time, a multi-tiered intertextual relationship to U.S. hip-hop places the griot as an indigenized and indigenizing practice in dialogue with African diasporic cultural production.

The idea of intertextuality is thus particularly suited to hip-hop studies because it allows for a dynamic interrelatedness of lyrical and musical levels of performance, rather than the divorced or reflective relationship between music and "text" that characterizes so much of the scholarly work on hip-hop music and culture. At the same time, an intertextual framework incorporates the discourses surrounding hip-hop performance as an integral element of that performance. Senegalese youth engage hip-hop from within its generic parameters to discursively and musically position hip-hop in an intertextual relationship with griot performance. In this process, the socio-cultural histories of hip-hop and griot performance are brought into meaningful dialogue with each other, as Senegalese rappers draw on hip-hop's characteristic intertextuality to construct a music that is at once local and transnational, indigenous and diasporic.

rappin griots indigenizing hip-hop

In the U.S. and elsewhere, hip-hop's inextricable musical and socio-cultural histories are consistently invoked in the practice of self-conscious musical and lyrical intertextuality. Hip-hop's first musical tracks were built from the instrumental breaks of existing funk and disco music looped on turntables, a foundational technique that later evolved into the practice of sampling musical excerpts from the genre's musical predecessors. As hip-hop developed and its repertoire expanded, young artists incorporated musical quotations from earlier hip-hop songs as well, making musical intertextuality a foundational aspect of hip-hop production. Within this musical framework, rappers practice lyrical intertextuality in several ways: by repeating, signifying on, or responding to the lyrics of other rappers; through sampling and lyrically playing off of the vocals to preexisting songs; or in citing the words of historic Black figures, either through direct audio-sampling or verbal quotation.[7] As a musical and speech genre, then, hip-hop is defined by intertextuality, drawing on distinct yet overlapping music and histories to create music that is always in dialogue with other artists, genres, and eras. Senegalese rappers operate within these generic parameters to musically and discursively indigenize hip-hop, refiguring the griot as both a social figure and performance tradition.

Drawing on hip-hop's characteristic intertextuality, Senegalese youth musically indigenize hip-hop in two ways that involve decentering musical elements of griot performance and recentering them in hip-hop. The first entails the sampling or incorporation of ethnically diverse music and instruments that are typically played by griots, such as the *kora*, the *balafon*, the *djembe*, and the *tama*, or pressure drum.[8] The emphasis placed on indigenous musical elements is contingent on the preferences of individual artists and therefore varies from one recording to the next. In some cases, local instruments and musical traditions constitute prominent stylistic elements, as is the case with internationally acclaimed rapper/producer DJ Awadi's song "J'accuse," whose musical track is built around a traditionally styled kora accompaniment. Similarly, Medina-based rap trio Zair ak Batine's song, "Doundou Ndakara" is based on traditional music, recreated through the combination of sampled djembes and traditional vocals with synthesized piano lines that imitate the melodic runs of the kora. Just as often, however, indigenous instruments are embedded in the multi-layered production of hip-hop beats in such a way that they may not be readily recognizable. For example, Medina hip-hop duo Sen Kumpë's song "Aythia gnu dem," is a fairly typical example of sampling indigenous music, as short, escalating bursts of tama drumming punctuate a beat that is otherwise indistinguishable from hip-hop produced in the United States. In other cases, indigenous instruments become a semi-prominent layer of a musical track, foregrounded during a musical break but mixed with synthesized Western instruments and drum machines.[9]

Senegalese rappers often use these instruments and music in a self-conscious effort to indigenize hip-hop, to mark their Africanness. As Mamadou, of the group 5kièm Underground, commented on the practice of sampling traditional instruments "rap comes from the United States, but to make a rap beat, we can make a sample that will describe the identity of that rapper (Diallo 2008)." The incorporation of local instruments is thus an explicitly indigenizing strategy that recognizes the diasporic nature of hip-hop while aurally marking the "Senegaleseness" of these particular recordings.

There is, however, another, more nuanced way in which rappers musically indigenize hip-hop through the repurposing of griot performance styles. Beyond sampling indigenous music, many rappers claim the griot verbal performance genre *taasu*, which consists of rhymed, rhythmic performance over drum accompaniment, as an aesthetic predecessor of contemporary rap music. In describing Senegalese traditional music, Los Angeles-based rap artist Sandstorm Ja commented, "It's like a lot of drums, you know what I mean, and a lot of something called taasu. It's just like, I won't say like hip-hop, but it just like, on that verbal, griots used to, you know, do that (Ndiaye 2006)." DJ Awadi of Positive Black Soul, often referred to as the founder of Senegalese hip-hop, sees this stylistic continuity between taasu and hip-hop as crucial to the development of Dakar's burgeoning hip-hop scene. When asked why hip-hop was so successful in Senegal, Awadi replied, "we have a traditional connection with hip-hop. If you ever come down to Senegal, you'll find traditional music called, Tasu or Kebetu very similar to hip-hop - you play the drum and talk on the beat. It's an old tradition so when hip-hop came, it was already in us (Blaze 2005)."[10]

Rapping not only constitutes a textual or linguistic element; it also functions as an important determinant of musical aesthetic. In U.S. hip-hop, this concept is encompassed in the term *flow*, which describes the rhythmic patterns and cadences of an individual rapper's lines as well as the intricate interweave of lyrical delivery and musical track. When considered in this light, the very act of rapping, conceived of as a modernized taasu performance, indicates performed intertextuality at the musical and speech genre levels. It also, however, creates an important link between the griot and the rapper as social figures, in which rappers are positioned as the contemporary counterparts of traditional griots. As Smoka Seezy, an immigrant rapper in Los Angeles described it, "people used to do rap, but it was more traditional, nobody ever took it like far as musically. So it was just something new." When asked if he meant that people used to rap in Senegal, he replied, "Yeah. It's called taasu. It's like a traditional thing; it's like from the ancient time. Like the griot used to tell you about your history, your grandfathers you know, like your great grandfathers, who they are, what they did, just like keep you with your history. And that's what rap used to be about. It was just traditional (Ndoye 2006)."

Beyond drawing a connection between taasu and hip-hop, many rappers also directly refer to themselves as griots, particularly when discussing the more overtly political manifestations of Senegalese hip-hop. The self-referential use of the word "griot" is in fact fairly commonplace, not only in specifically hip-hop-related contexts (such as interviews, concerts, and studios) but also as a general element of daily interactions. For example, I once overheard a rapper haggling with an actual griot over the price of a drum sternly tell that musician that "I'm a griot too; I know how much this should cost." Instances such as this highlight the fact that many rappers consider themselves to be griots not only in terms of performance style and delivery but also in terms of social function.

Griots in Senegal fill various social roles, including those of praise singers, genealogists, historians, and social commentators. Defined by family and professional caste, griots social roles are exclusive to members of particular lineages and are inseparable from griot performance practice, including taasu. While these roles have necessarily changed over time to accommodate social changes sparked by various factors such as French colonization and mass conversion to Islam, their general characteristics remain.[11] Like Smoka Seezy, however, many of these rappers refer to taasu as a thing of the past despite its continued practice, highlighting the fact that for urban Senegalese youth the griot is not always a socially relevant figure in his traditional context.

Although griots still exist in Senegal, the experiences of urban Senegalese youth seem to call for a new generation of griots, no longer defined genealogically but functionally. Conceived as indigenous performance practice, hip-hop becomes the vehicle through which young rappers assume the role of historians and social commentators. The aesthetic similarities between taasu and rap therefore enable an otherwise more tenuous social link between griots and rappers. In this process, the social role of the griot is transformed, as rappers draw on hip-hop's histories of resistance to frame their overtly political lyrics and activism as modernized griot practice. This manifests in political activism ranging from the international release of a video compilation drawing attention to the plight of orphans in West Africa[12] to the massive mobilization of youth to vote in Senegal's pivotal 2000 presidential elections.[13] When layered with Wolof-language lyrics that foreground local realities of urban postcolonial existence, the intertextuality that musically and discursively creates and sustains a connection between hip-hop and griot performance thus becomes an indigenizing force that grounds hip-hop performance practice in local culture.

transatlantic signifying

At three o'clock in the morning in Kaolack, a small city four hours outside Dakar, hip-hop label Jolof4Life finally kicks off its multi-artist performance to the delighted cheers of a young audience that has waited weeks for this show. Rap duo Sen Kumpë bounces on stage shouting "Medina in the house," in a formulaic yet enthusiastically received nod to their neighborhood, Dakar's "native quarter." As their music plays, the rappers quickly launch into energized verses in Wolof, Senegal's dominant indigenous language, until reaching the chorus: "hey la-di da-di relax your body, Senegal to New York." More than a catchy refrain, these lyrics draw on African American rap with a well known, oft-cited phrase from early U.S. hip-hop ("hey la-di-da-di,") while explicitly referencing hip-hop culture's transnational flows from "Senegal to New York" and back again. Through musical and lyrical intertextuality situated in performance, Sen Kumpë constructs a complex sense of place that is at once global and local.

Practices of musical, lyrical, and discursive intertextuality not only indigenize Senegalese hip-hop as local cultural production but also situate this music and the youth who produce it in a transnational network of hip-hop cultures. Through creating musical tracks that draw on the conventions of hip-hop production, incorporating African American Vernacular English (AAVE), and signifying on the lyrics of U.S. artists, Senegalese youth create a transatlantic dialogue with diasporic youth. When this intertextual relationship is layered with the indigenizing intertextuality described above, the result is a transnational music firmly grounded in local practice.

In Senegal, as in numerous hip-hop cultures throughout the globe, the shift from rapping in English to utilizing local languages is perhaps the primary way of localizing hip-hop.[14] But at the same time that linguistic choices function as a key indigenizing strategy, they are also central to the construction of Senegalese hip-hop as a transnational music. While many rappers make a point of rapping in Wolof, emphasizing the indigeneity of their music, as many perform (or express a desire to perform) in English so that their music might be more accessible to a transnational audience. As Ouakam-based rapper/singer Yourasta, of the group African Family, explained, "We prefer to sing in English, because when you sing in English, well, English is a language which, if you have it, then no matter what country you go to, there will be people that understand what you want to say (Ndiaye 2008)." Yourasta's sister, rapper Nene Touti, likewise expresses a desire to release an album in English. Similarly, Abdou of 5kièm Underground prefers to rap in Wolof but still sometimes uses English in order to reach a broader audience outside Senegal, stating, "We're working on our first album. In this first album, I did basically eighty five percent Wolof, fifteen percent English. I rhyme in English in there just so whoever might hear it might be like, 'oh, what are they talking about?' – [if] it's Wolof, you don't understand. But when you hear a little bit of English in there, you might have a little idea of what I'm talking about, of what I'm trying to rhyme on. And when you hear the English, you might be like, 'oh, the English rhymes are nice, so maybe he might be nice in his own language (Adiara 2008).'"

This isn't simply a question of English lyrics but of *which* English. Linguistic anthropologist H. Samy Alim describes the linguistic practices of U.S. hip-hop culture as both deriving from and expanding AAVE to create what he refers to as Hip-hop Nation Language (HHNL). Numerous hip-hop communities outside of the U.S., although often rapping in languages other than English, have adapted HHNL and incorporated it into their hip-hop practice (see Alim 2006; Mitchell 2001). The language and linguistic practices of U.S. hip-hop culture thus become a key medium through which a global or transnational community is imagined and sustained.

This is certainly the case in Dakar, where local variants of HHNL play an important role in marking people as hip-hop cultural practitioners. Beyond full verses or songs rapped in English, in their music and in daily interactions Senegalese rappers (as well as fans) pepper their speech with phrases of HHNL, creating a linguistic intertextuality that goes beyond musical performance to inform and shape daily interactions and sense of identification with a larger, transnational hip-hop community. This sense of belonging and community is bolstered by the fact that this type of vernacular speech is generally limited to those young people in Dakar who are in some way involved with hip-hop culture, whether as rappers, producers, or fans.

An important performative aspect of linguistic intertextuality is the practice of lyrical signifying that has almost always been central to hip-hop performance in the United States, as rappers respond to the words of other artists or repeat them, sometimes with a deliberately revised meaning. Signifying's generic significance is not lost on Senegalese rappers; Sen Kumpe's line "hey la-di-da-di" in the performance described above is just one of many instances of transatlantic signifying among Dakar artists. In repeating these lyrics, Sen Kumpë creates an intertextual relationship not just with old school U.S. rapper Slick Rick, whose 1985 single "La Di Da Di" originated the now ubiquitous hip-hop phrase, but also with the myriad rappers who have likewise used these lyrics, among them West Coast rapper Snoop Dogg, in his song, "Lodi Dodi," and female duo Salt 'n Pepa, in their song "The Showstopper." These particular lyrics have been sampled or signified on so frequently that they are certainly well known to most members of U.S. hip-hop culture, practitioners, and fans alike. In incorporating these lyrics into their own music, Sen Kumpë therefore constructs a musical and lyrical relationship both with U.S. rappers and with U.S. hip-hop culture more generally.

Alongside these instances of linguistic and lyrical intertextuality, the same musical intertextuality that indigenizes hip-hop also creates a transatlantic dialogue with the diaspora, as a connectivity with African American youth is musically constructed through an adherence to U.S. production techniques. As mentioned earlier, Senegalese hip-hop is not fundamentally different than U.S. hip-hop in its production style; instead, it works within the generic parameters of hip-hop to incorporate indigenizing elements. Dakar youth thus localize hip-hop in a manner consistent with U.S. hip-hop's longstanding history of aesthetically unique, locale-specific sub-styles.[15] Singer/rapper Yourasta described this localizing process of sampling indigenous instruments, "Usually if you want to make something that is original, you should take from other sources – your country's tradition. It's more original. You can mix hip-hop with your country's traditional music. . . You can add balafon, you can add kora, you can add djembe, you can add other things (Ndiaye 2008)." Similarly, rapper Abdoulaye of the group 5kième Underground describes the sampling of indigenous instruments as a substitution of African elements into a U.S. production style.

> Basically like, when you take guitar, you can replace it with some kora, I think . . . it depends on the song. If it is kind of emotional, kora is more touching the emotions better I think than guitar, and sometimes be more traditional and stuff, We put kora in it, sometimes we put balafon in the place of the piano, you know just to switch, to do some African stuff (Adiara 2008).

This substitution of indigenous instruments through sampling reinforces a foundational technique of hip-hop production, highlighting the fact that this is not a hybridizing process that results in something new. In the practice of sampling indigenous instruments, neither hip-hop nor indigenous music is fundamentally changed; instead, this can be viewed as an intertextual invocation of indigeneity within a diasporic genre. This most basic generic characteristic of hip-hop – sampling – becomes a vehicle of intertextuality through which rappers bring local performance into a transnational dialogue with the African diaspora.

If linguistic and musical intertextualities are instrumental in constructing a transnational relationship with the communities of the diaspora, the discourses surrounding hip-hop play an equally important part in this process even as they indigenize hip-hop as local cultural production. Despite the clear influences of a Senghorian negritude on perceptions of racial unity between Senegalese youth and members of the diaspora, more than race as an external identity marker or even a perceived internal essence is at stake here. Instead, Dakar youth discursively construct a relationship to African American youth through the spoken recognition of similar experiences of spatial and economic disenfranchisement motivated by imperialism and global capitalism.

In Dakar hip-hop, the colonized urban spaces of Senegal become analogous with the internal colonization of postindustrial U.S. urban centers. Nowhere is this as clear as in the racialized spatial organizations of cities; it seems almost inevitable that the present-day socio-economic context in which urban Senegalese youth exist would evoke comparisons with postindustrial urban U.S. centers. Most of the rappers cited here reside in Medina, the city's "native quarter," which formed in the early 20th century when an outbreak of bubonic plague spurred French colonists to create housing mandates which, masking racial motivations with concerns for public health, forced many of the city's African inhabitants out of their homes and into the poorly planned quarter. Decades later, the neighborhood is described as a "ghetto" by the rappers who live there, in an explicit reference to the same U.S. "ghettos" (such as the South Bronx) that gave rise to hip-hop music in the 1970s. The economic inequalities between the West and these Senegalese youth are thus seen to correspond to the poverty experienced among minority communities in U.S. urban centers, again exposed through early U.S. hip-hop lyrics and videos that violently thrust the harsh realities of life in the South Bronx, and soon South Central Los Angeles, into the security of suburban American living rooms and the volatile lives of Dakar youth. In a city where nearly fifty percent of the inhabitants are unemployed, hip-hop's visual and auditory testaments to black struggle in the so-called First World reaffirm a transatlantic connectivity grounded in commonalities of racialized socio-economic struggle.

conclusions

The complex intersections of music and discourse in Senegalese hip-hop culture can be read as instances of strategic and multi-layered intertextuality that blur the boundaries of indigenous and diasporic cultural production. Focusing on the imbrication of discourses, music, and texts allows a reading of the relationship between indigenous performance practice and hip-hop not as distinct, separate performance practices but rather as mutually constitutive of each other, in the sense that they are understood as and created through local, discursively constructed processes of identification with a African past and a diasporic present that are brought into dialogue through multi-layered practices of intertextuality.

While griots continue to follow traditional performance practices, Dakar's hip-hop scene has become a new context for the performance, interpretation, and mobilization of the griot, refigured functionally and musically to speak to the needs of urban Senegalese youth. Through hip-hop, Senegalese youth draw on both the social function and the performance style of the griot to create overlapping musical, social, and generic intertextualities. By discursively framing themselves as griots and their music as hip-hop, rappers draw on and transform the social potentialities of each genre. The traditionalizing trope of the griot is couched in hip-hop's history of resistance, pervasive lyrical and musical intertextuality, and emphasis on local place within transnational networks. Through emphasizing, rather than changing, the generic and aesthetic characteristics of hip-hop and griot performance, rappers are able to construct an otherwise unconvincing socio-historical continuity between themselves and griots. They therefore make hip-hop "African" not necessarily (or at least not exclusively) through altering its aesthetic characteristics but rather via the discourses of Africanity in and through which the music is created. At the same time, the very processes of intertextuality that indigenize Senegalese hip-hop as local cultural production also create an important connection with African American youth. This connection becomes one not based solely on a racial essence but also on understandings of shared histories of racially motivated socio-economic and spatial marginalization. Through discourse, performance practice, and production techniques, hip-hop practitioners in Senegal thus enact both local groundedness and a deep seated transatlantic connectivity with the North American communities of the African diaspora.

notes

1. For more on the globalization of hip-hop culture, see Basu and Lemelle 2006; Mitchell 2001; Spady et al. 2006.
2. Initially coined by colonizing Europeans in West Africa, the word *griot* is as invented as the tradition it came to signify. While many stratified West African societies include bardic figures/speech genres, the word "griot" lumped together disparate performance traditions that, while tied to similar social functions (such as praise singing, oral history, and relating genealogies), were/are aesthetically and culturally distinct from one local context to the next. Despite its problematic nature, however, I use the word throughout this chapter, mostly for lack of a better term. Although ethnically specific terms are certainly available (e. g. *jeli*, for the Mandinke groups in Senegal, *géwël* for the Wolof), to use an ethnically specific term in the context of an ethnically diverse environment would be to equally conflate diverse performance practices under a single name. In using the word griot, I therefore attempt to communicate the very inefficacy of an ethnically specific term to describe a diverse collection of performance practices. At the same time, however, I replicate the day-to-day language use of Senegalese hip-hop artists that communicate local perceptions,

influenced by colonial discourse, of griot performance as a unified, interethnic phenomenon.

3. The material in this chapter is drawn from ethnographic fieldwork I conducted with Senegalese rappers in the United States (from 2006 to 2007) and Dakar (in 2007 and 2008). My interpretations of Senegalese hip-hop culture are based on interviews, musical recordings and video clips, live performances, personal communications, and daily interactions with rappers and fans.

4. For distinctive approaches to hybridity in African popular music/ culture see, for example, Barber's 1987 volume on African popular culture; Erlmann's 1991 work on South African music; Turino's 2000 text on Zimbabwean music; and Waterman's 1990 work on Nigerian juju.

5. See *The Oxford English Dictionary*.

6. For quite some time, the griot has figured prominently in discourse surrounding African American music, particularly hip-hop. Hip-hop scholars and practitioners alike often position rappers as modern day griots, the contemporary manifestation of an authentic African past. While the relationship between African and African American music is a contested point in ethnomusicology and related fields, here I seek not to engage this particular debate but rather to elucidate the griot's unsolicited yet pervasive presence in my experiences of Senegalese hip-hop, as rappers both in Dakar and the United States consistently referenced what they perceive as stylistic and functional continuities between the griot and themselves.

7. A prime example of intertextuality in hip-hop is Public Enemy's "Fight the Power," which begins with an audio sample of Black Nationalist leader Malcolm X and layers ten different musical samples that include songs by funk icon James Brown and Afrika Bambaataa, the "godfather" of hip-hop.

8. These instruments are found among many of the Mande ethnic groups that live throughout West Africa. The kora, a harplute, has become emblematic of griot performance practice in the West, as has the balafon, or wooden xylophone with gourd resonators, although to a lesser extent. The djembe, a goblet drum with a goatskin head, enjoys immense popularity as a generic symbol

of "African" music throughout the world. The tama, however, although similar to other "talking" pressure drums in West Africa, is a Wolof rather than Mande instrument.

9. It seems likely that prominent sampling of local instruments is largely influenced by Positive Black Soul, Senegal's first nationally (and internationally) known hip-hop group and by far the most popular. PBS's 1996 album *Salaam* is marked by the incorporation of indigenous instruments and performance styles. The song "Ataya," even incorporates the sounds of the social gathering accompanying the making of tea, a central element of daily life in Senegal, as a musical element.

10. Interestingly, not only rappers make this connection; in a drum lesson with a Wolof *géwël*, or griot, in Los Angeles, the verbal element of the music (a sort of rhythmic chanting over the drummed beat) was described to me as being "like hip-hop, you know?"

11. For example, while the griot in pre-colonial Senegal was attached to indigenous political leaders, the colonial disruption of traditional power structures caused many griots to shift their allegiance to the *marabouts*, or Islamic leaders (see McLaughlin 1997).

12. *Orphelins du Monde* 2007.

13. See the 2009 documentary *Democracy in Dakar*.

14. See, for example, several of the chapters from the recently published *Global Linguistic Flows: Hip-hop Cultures, Youth Identities, and the Politics of language* (Alim et al. 2009), such as Allastair Pennycook and Tony Mitchell's discussion of the use of the Maori language in hip-hop in New Zealand, Jennifer Roth-Gordon's chapter on Brazilian hip-hop, and Angel Lin's exploration of the use of Cantonese in Hong Kong hip-hop.

15. From its inception, hip-hop has been infused with and defined by place, reflected and constructed through the combination of regionally accented styles of rapping with verbalized signifiers of place and locale-specific musical sub-styles. This marked localization of U.S. hip-hop is evidenced in sub-genres such as West Coast gangsta rap, "durty south" beats, and Oakland hyphy music, to name a few (see Forman 2002).

bibliography

Aidara, Abdou K. 2008. Personal interview with the author, July 23, Medina, Dakar, Senegal.

Alim, H. Samy. 2006. *Roc the Mic Right: The Language of Hip-hop Culture*. New York: Routledge.

Alim, H. Samy, Awad Ibrahim, and Alastair Pennycook, eds. 2008. *Global Linguistic Flows: Hip-hop Cultures, Youth Identities, and the Politics of Language*. New York: Routledge.

Barber, Karen. 1987. "Popular Arts in Africa." *African Studies Review* 30(3):1-78.

Basu, Dipannita and Sidney J. Lemelle, eds. 2006. *The Vinyl Ain't Final: Hip-hop and the Globalization of Black Popular Culture*. London: Pluto Press.

Bauman, Richard, and Charles L. Briggs. 1990. "Poetics and Performance as Critical Perspectives on Language and Social Life." *Annual Review of Anthropology* 19:59-88.

Blaze. 2005. "One on One with Awadi." *African Hip-hop.com: The Foundation of African Hip-hop Culture Online*. http://www.africanhiphop.com. Accessed June 4, 2008.

Briggs, Charles L., and Richard Bauman. 1992. "Genre, Intertextuality, and Social Power." *Journal of Linguistic Anthropology* 2(2):130-172.

Diallo, Mamadou B. 2008. Personal interview with the author, July 23, Medina, Dakar, Senegal.

Erlmann, Veit. 1991. *African Stars: Studies in Black South African Performance*. Chicago: University of Chicago Press.

Forman, Murray. 2002. *The 'Hood Comes First: Race, Space, and Place in Rap and Hip-Hop*. Middletown, CT: Weslyan University Press.

McLaughlin, Fiona. 1997. "Islam and Popular Music in Senegal: The Emergence of a 'New Tradition.'" *Africa: Journal of the International African Institute* 67(4):560-581.

Mitchell, Tony, ed. 2001. *Global Noise: Rap and Hip-Hop Outside the USA*. Middletown: Weslyan University Press.

Ndiaye, Cheikh. 2006. Personal interview with the author, June 4, Los Angeles, California.

Ndiaye, Nene Touti. 2008. Personal interview with the author, July 30, Ouakam, Dakar, Senegal.

Ndiaye, Youssou (Yourasta). 2008. Personal interview with the author, July 12, Ouakam, Dakar, Senegal.

Ndoye, Assane. 2006. Personal interview with the author, September 9, Los Angeles, California.

Spady, James G., et al., eds. 2006. *The Global Cipha: Hip-hop Culture and Consciousness.* Philadelphia: Black History Museum Press.

Turino, Thomas. 2000. *Nationalists, Cosmopolitans, and Popular Music in Zimbabwe.* Chicago: University of Chicago Press.

Waterman, Christopher Alan. 1990. *Juju: A Social History and Ethnography of an African Popular Music.* Chicago: University of Chicago Press.

discography

Daara J. 2003. *Boomerang.* London: Wrasse Records.

Positive Black Soul. 1996. *Salaam.* New York: Mango/Island Records.

Public Enemy. 1990. "Fight the Power." *Fear of a Black Planet.* New York: Def Jam Records.

Salt 'n Pepa. 1992 [1986]. "The Showstopper." *Hot Cool and Vicious.* London: London Records.

Sen Kumpë. 2008. "Aythia Gnu Dem;" "Job Lou Barri." *Freedom.* Dakar: Jolof for Life/99 Records.

Slick Rick. 1985. "La Di Da Di." *The Show & La Di Da Di* (single). New York: Def Jam Records.

Snoop Dogg. 1993. "Lodi Dodi." *Doggystyle.* Los Angeles: Priority Records.

Zair ak Batine. 2008. "Doundou Ndakara." *Xel Nangouwoul.* Dakar: Jolof for Life/99 Records.

filmography

Democracy in Dakar. DVD. Directed by Magee McIlvaine, Chris Moore, and Ben Herson. New York: Nomadic Wax and Sol Productions. 2009.

Orphelins du Monde. DVD. Paris: Senprod. 2007.

CHAPTER 2
rapping against the lack of change: rap music in mali and burkina faso

DANIEL KÜNZLER Tricia Rose, a prominent hip-hop scholar, states in her recent book that "commercially successful hip-hop has become increasingly saturated with caricatures of black gangstas, thugs, pimps, and 'hos (2008: back cover)." Many Europeans and/or North Americans spontaneously expect the same to be true for rap music in other regions throughout the world. However, throughout sub-Saharan Africa hip-hop is seldom about semi-naked women, expensive jewelry, and fast cars. Rather, it is often a tool by which African youth express oppositional viewpoints of the state, assert local identities, and voice societal and generational concerns (Künzler 2007). Can this be said to be true for hip-hop in Burkina Faso and Mali, two countries that have been neglected by hip-hop scholars?

Hip-hop herein is seen as a culture and form that includes musical elements based on rapping, deejaying, and beatboxing, graphical elements such as aerosol art, and elements based on motion known as breakdancing. The importance of these elements varies from place to place. Breakdancing in sub-Saharan Africa was often the first element to be appropriated; copied from North

American and/or French music videos. Nowadays, the musical element is the most common. This chapter focuses on rap music from Burkina Faso and Mali and neglects the other elements of hip-hop culture without insinuating that they are not present.

Within this chapter, I analyze nearly 30 rap albums from Mali and Burkina Faso, all of which were collected during initial trips to Mali and Burkina Faso in mid-2000s and later updated.[1] Focusing on rap albums has some implications, for not all rappers can afford to produce an album. It is reasonable to assume that it is easier for children from the (lower) middle class to accumulate the economic and cultural capital necessary to produce an album, while there are many more rappers from the lower class that rap and perform without ever releasing an album. My approach neglects their motivation and aspirations. Nonetheless, discussions with shop owners and street vendors confirmed that the albums analyzed cover the most publicly known artists in both countries. The public nature of their artistic expression lies not only in the airplay they enjoy on television and radio, but also in the public nature of music in urban Africa in general, as it is part of everyday life and played in public transport – an important place of communication – and in shops, stalls, bars, and other places.

Besides analyzing rap lyrics, secondary and tertiary material was consulted in order to help overcome, in some cases, the problem of limited understandability of lyrics in local languages. Among the rap albums analyzed, none tries to copy the aforementioned North American template, although some featured less political tomes. Most songs, as you will come to see, are political in nature.

a brief sketch of rap music in burkina faso and mali

Locally produced rap music can be found throughout sub-Saharan Africa.[2] Rather than merely appropriate the North American model, many African rappers produce, distribute, and promote their music within specific local, national, and regional socio-cultural contexts. Rap music is paradigmatic of local cultures meeting global cultures (Androutsopoulos 2003). The local adaptation of global culture is not a new phenomenon nor restricted to rap music. However, Western forms of popular music are taken up in sub-Saharan Africa. Heavy metal, rock, and punk music are marginal in most sub-Saharan African countries. Rap is an easily accessible oral form of expression. This is among the many reasons why hip-hop has been successful in sub-Saharan Africa.

In some sub-Saharan African countries, the local adaptation of rap music had already begun in the early 1980s, whereas in Mali and Burkina Faso hip-hop was appropriated much later (Künzler 2007). While it is not the purpose of this chapter to reconstruct the history of rap music in Burkina Faso and Mali, a rough sketch of the development of rap music since its emergence is important as contextual information. According to Mathcoolj (2005), rap groups were active in Burkina Faso's capital Ouagadougou in 1988. Among the early rappers was Smockey, who later temporarily stopped making music in order to work and further his education in France (SaintAnge 2009). However, it was not until 1997 that the first known rap album was produced by Basic Soul. The production of some compilations around 2000 and the establishment of Studio Abazon by rapper Smockey in 2001 boosted the production and performance of rap music in Burkina Faso. Subsequently, several albums were released. One of the first successful albums was "Juste 1 Peu 2 Lumière" released by Yeleen in 2001. Other important platforms in the early development of hip-hop in Burkina Faso included many small hip-hop contests and the annual Waga Hip-hop Festival, which today is known throughout the world.[3]

Early rap albums seldom featured scratching or sampling. If there was any sampling, it was mainly focused on the region's musical heritage. Tapping into the musical repertoire of the region, in turn, opened up rap music to other segments of the public. In the beginning, Smockey and his Studio Abazon in Ouagadougou were central to the production of rap music. However, the situation has changed. There are now more studios in Burkina

Faso and the network of artists is less centralized. Today, rappers use French, *Mooré*, and other local languages in their music. In the context of illiteracy and low education, rap music in local languages is especially comprehensible. Increasingly, rappers are also exploring other musical styles such as R&B, reggae, dancehall, *zouglou, coupé décalé*, and *tackborsé*. Furthermore, there are some rappers in the region doing slam poetry (cf. for example Fangafrika 2008).

As in Burkina Faso, the first rap album in Mali was produced rather late; to my knowledge the album was produced by Les Escrocs in 1998. After 2000, there was a certain boom in hip-hop production and several rap albums were released. Many early Malian rappers emerged out of the Invasion Family collective (e.g. Yeli Fuzzo, Ta-K-Mi, and SNK), while many artists produced their albums in the studio of the late musician Ali Farka Touré and released them under his Mali K7 S.A. label. In March 2005, this label was closed because it could no longer cope with media piracy. Nonetheless, rappers continued to release albums and many more studios where established in Bamako. Early in its development, respected musicians such as Salif Keïta, Ali Farka Touré, and Mory Kanté supported rap artists. As a result, rap music never became associated with youthful delinquency as was often the case in Burkina Faso. Rappers in Mali also use French and different local languages such as *Bambara* in their music.

On average, over the last ten years, there have been fewer festivals, concerts, and album releases in Mali than in Burkina Faso. However, in 2009 a new festival, known as the Bamako Rap Show, and the first Mali Hip-hop Awards were established. Time will tell if this is the beginning of a revival of hip-hop in Mali.

When I started to research African rap music, hardly any information was available from the Internet. Today, several rappers from both Mali and Burkina Faso use both myspace.com and youtube.com. Despite the use of computer technologies to increase exposure, ironically, rap is often sold in both countries on tape. To this end, distribution is problematic.

education, health care, poverty: a rapped critique of problems in the socio-economic sector

Both Mali (12.7 million inhabitants) and Burkina Faso (15.2 million inhabitants) are mid-sized sub-Saharan African countries (UNFPA 2008: 91f.). In both countries, urbanization is below the African average. For example, only 18.3 percent of Burkina Faso inhabitants live in urban areas (World Bank 2009: 335). Until recently, both Bamako and Ouagadougou were mainly experiencing population growth due to internal migration. Increasingly, more and more people are born in each of the capitals. In fact, Bamako still attracts inhabitants as it promises economic success and a different lifestyle. Yeli Fuzzo (2003) in "Ladji Kabako" tells the story of a failing migrant:

> Ladji Kabako (...) was the most respected man in the village, for his kindness and his courage. What was the destiny of Ladji Kabako? To go to the big city, the capital Bamako! He was going for the good of his community. (...) Ladji became the king of the big city; Ladji lost his sense of reality. He was the most respected man in the village. He forgot and repudiated his inheritance. The women took all his money. Ladji Kabako doesn't have any friends anymore. We are all Ladji Kabako. We are all blind and lost in Bamako. He went to the big city for his community. He came back to the village with nothing to give.[4]

Rappers from big cities such as Lagos, Nairobi, or Johannesburg often describe life in the shantytowns (Künzler 2007). However, in the context of Mali, rapping about "ghetto life" would be seen as a cheap imitation of North American gangsta rap. Bamako might have its dangers, but is still rather peaceful. As Rage (2002) states in "Interlude": "It is true that there is no township, no ghetto as in the United States. You don't get shot. There is no tribal war as in Rwanda...But corruption, fiddling, laxity, poverty are very well real, you see!" The situation in Ouagadougou is not very different from that in Bamako. Nonetheless, Smockey (2007) notes in "Ca craint!" that urban criminality is increasing in Ouagadougou.

The lack of urban dangers aside, hip-hop in both Burkina Faso and Mali is used to offer commentary on health issues and by extension health care. In both countries, less than two percent of the adult population (15-49 years) have contracted HIV/AIDS; the sub-Saharan average is five percent of the adult population (UNAIDS 2008: 215). Although clearly below the sub-Saharan average, the prevention of HIV/AIDS, as well as, the stigma that comes with living with the disease is nevertheless a topic in many rap songs. For example, "Le SIDA" by Les Escrocs (2001), "Le truc qui rend digne" by Smockey (2004), "Education" by O.B.C. (2004) and "Vision de vie" by Yeleen (2006) all take on the topic of HIV/AIDS. Other rap songs are about the lack of and expense of medical services. In "Pharma-scie" Smockey (2007) criticizes medical doctors for making profits by over-prescribing medication and requiring multiple consultations. Similarly, Yeleen (2006) deplores the fact that pharmacies are too expensive for the average citizen in "Vision de vie." Further in "Maxime," Yeleen (2001) describes the depressing conditions of the public health system in the Yalgado Hospital in Ouagadougou, where poverty leads to a lack of care:

> A phone call has informed him of his only child's accident. The only son he loved so much. The sirens of the fire brigade... Escorted like a president and then thrown in front of the emergency department like a beggar. That's how his father found him suffering the agony of death. The floor soaked with his blood. Maxime! (...) He was running around everywhere out of his mind. Nobody takes care as there is nothing in his pocket. He pays 2,500 F CFA [US$ 5.5] for a rotten mattress on a bed in bad repair.

He then calls his office and tries in vain to run into debt. Soon, the blaze of hope is gone. He still waits for the goodwill of a medical doctor. (...) Gazing at his son he sees him close to the abyss, unable to do anything. (...) A few minutes later, Maxime lost his bed to a patient richer than him. Once again his son lies on the floor. (...) A last sigh and the child is gone. Despite his ceaseless calls, he remains without life. That's how Maxime has left us very early, dead in the premises of Yalgado hospital.

Education is another important subject for Burkinabe and Malian rappers. Forty six percent of the population in Burkina Faso and 48 percent of the population in Mali is younger than 14 years old (World Bank 2009: 352). In both countries many youth do not finish primary school. In 2006, the primary education completion rate in Burkina Faso was 31 percent, while in Mail the primary education completion rate was 49 percent (World Bank 2009: 354). As a result, rappers like Les Escrocs (2001) are troubled in "Kalan" about the frequent educational strikes in Mali since 1991, which have led to the non-completion of school years from 1992 to 1994. Les Escrocs (2001) are further concerned for teachers in "Enseignant," deploring their low salaries and bad social status. Their compatriots from the group Rage (2000) also describe in "Acide constat" the deplorable situation of the educational system. Similar problems are condemned by SNK featuring Dodou Soul (2003) in "Je vois":

> Young people want to leave their countries. Why? Because nowadays, the level [of education] is low. (...) Sometimes I feel like being part of a sacrificed generation. I'm not saying government doesn't care about education. But stop neglecting it! It's the future of the entire country you endanger. Our students mostly haven't the level when they go abroad. When they stay home, it's always 'Strike! Strike!'

"In Faculté" Amkoullel (2002) criticizes students who blindly follow their selfish association leaders, while also blaming parents, teachers, and the national authorities for the educational crisis.[5] Members of the group Rage (2000) are rather pessimistic when they state in the "Interlude": "Schools are disconsolate! In seven years, young people won't go to school anymore. Who, who is going to govern the country in ten years? You see, this is worrying. I don't even know if there will be cadres." Even the lucky few finishing tertiary education do not have good job perspectives, mentions Baloukou (2008) from Burkina Faso in "Du rêve au cauchemar." Having a job helps one get married. It means recognition for young people by the older generation, as well as, more independence from family members.

Faso Kombat (2004) in "Diplomé Paumé" raps about the problems of university students in Burkina Faso, while Yeleen (2006) deplores the fact that students are prostituting themselves to get degrees. In "Juste 1 peu 2 lumière", they (2001) mention the violent clashes between protesting students and police forces: "Too many suffocated students. Too many students were falling, their hands and feet bound, beaten by policemen."

In June 2008, members of the presidential guard shot live ammunition when students protested at the university near the luxury mansion of "little president" François Compaoré, the president's brother. Smockey (2008) released a maxi with two songs about these events. "We are not dogs, after all," he complains in "A Balles réelles" and criticizes the temporary closure of the university, the eviction of students from housing facilities on the campus, and the withdrawal of scholarships and social benefits. Another song that deals with police brutality is "On est dans la rue" by Smockey featuring Sams'K le Jah. In this song they use a sample from the theme melody of Sergio Leone's 1968 film *Once upon a time in the West*. They rap about the "Wild West" methods the policemen used against people demonstrating rising food prices in Burkina Faso in 2008. The artists state that "social peace cannot be built on the terror of the people."

This song is a protest against the restriction of the freedom of expression and freedom of assembly that is covered up behind a democratic and constitutional façade. Similarly, hip-hop music was used as a kind of anthem during union manifestations in 2006 and 2007 against the high costs of living (See "Viima Ya Kanga" (Life is hard) by K-Ravane (2005)).

The majority of the population in both Mali and Burkina Faso has to live on less than two dollars a day: 77.1 percent in Mali and 81.2 percent in Burkina Faso (World Bank 2008: 19f.). "Looks like we're second last for the UNDP," states Smockey featuring Dicko Hamadou (2007) in "Relax, ici c'est le paradis." Indeed Burkina Faso is second to last on the *Human Development Index 2007-2008*, just three places behind Mali (UNDP 2007: 232). Burkina Faso and Mali are among the poorest countries in the world and as a result there are many social and economic problems. Both poverty and misery are popular subjects for rappers, particularly because they are seen as the source of violence and crime. See for instance "Pourqoui" by La Censure (2001), "Wari" by Fanga Fing (2000), "Mankene" by Yeli Fuzzo (2003) or "Je vois" by SNK featuring Dodou Soul (2003).

Other economic problems are popular subjects in the lyrics of Burkinabe and Malian hip-hop. In "Jamana Jo," Lassy King Massassy (2003) raps about the issue of imported products and their impact on domestic production in Mali. Mali's dependency on imports, according to Lassy King Massassy, has reduced Mali's farmers to mere consumers. In solidarity, Smockey (2004) states in "Ma diginité:" "Imported religion, imported policy, imported economy, conditioned by the WTO. I hope we'll not have to import our sperm in order to continue to live." The Malian government privatized many enterprises according to the policy principles of international organizations, an issue taken up by Tata Pound in various songs. For instance, see "Delivrance" featuring Tiken Jah Fakoly (2002), "Yelema" (2006), and "Mon pays S.A." (Fangafrika 2008).

In "Génération sacrifiée," Yeleen (2001) comments on the lack of economic progress, sentiment echoed by SNK featuring Dodou Soul (2003) in "Je vois":

> I see guys taking drugs, guys drinking alcohol, I see guys being fed up, abandoning school. (...) I see guys not respecting neither their fathers nor their mothers. I see guys that would kill their brothers for money. I see guys drudging. (...) I see despaired guys never becoming what their fathers hoped. (...) It is not a secret, since 1991 there has been no progress [in Mali].

Even when assessing the lack of progress, rappers do not ask for more development aid, to the contrary. Yeleen (2006) in "Vision de vie" critically asks who is profiting from the NGOs in the country. Pity is used in the name of development cooperation, states Smockey (2004) in "Ma dignité." And in "ONG" (2004), he bitterly describes the logic of humanitarian efforts:

> You have health problems? We are here. You want what? You want everything??? Ehm, we're not here anymore. If we give you everything, you don't need anything anymore, so you don't need us anymore. This is the social business.

"i rap, therefore i am": discussing the dream of migration and cultural questions of identity and tradition

Many young Africans dream of migrating to Europe and the U.S. But this dream may turn into a nightmare, according to Les Escrocs in "Tounga" (2001), for many migrants experience racism and hardship. In "A mon retour" Yeli Fuzzo (2003) tells us about the frosty social relations in the host country and depressed migrants. The disillusioning story of a migrant is also central to the song "Le chemin de l'exil" by Yeleen (2001):

> Shackled by the chains of exile you have to leave. It is dry here; you have to go in order to enrich yourself. It's better that people not say 'look, this is the son without future'! The morning will come when you pack your bags. (...) On the sill you will see the disapproving glance of your worried father, red of hate and thinking he's the reason for this pain. You will go with an almost empty bag (...) and the hope of returning one day. (...) Over there, it will be cold and there will be nobody anymore. Nobody, because over there it is everybody on their own (...). You are going to forget your parents and only keep your studies in mind. (...) You will write letters that never reach the postman. You will bring along nice pictures and say 'everything is perfect!' (...) You didn't want to return when your sick mother was suffering, you didn't want to respond when the village was writing, you will say you don't mind if your father is going to curse you. (...) But if you knew that your mother lost her life... If only you knew!

In "Zamana," Smockey featuring Sami Rama (2004) describes the case of a failed migrant:

> I go back to my place as I came. Ten years I've roamed in the corridors of Kennedy Airport hoping to see a damned visa. Here I am, forced to give up. Direction Ouagadougou, Burkina Faso. (...) I am afraid of not being accepted, of being regretted (...). To my big surprise, everybody turns out. A welcome committee waits for me with a smile. (...) What am I going to tell them? How am I going to explain my career as a gangster?

There is a differentiated approach towards African traditions. Several rappers affirm certain traditions as a form of respect towards parents and elders (Les Escrocs (2001): "Demissenw"; Yeleen (2001): "Génération sacrifiée"; Yeli Fuzzo (2003): "Mali Djaka"). Yet, many rappers are not willing to uncritically glorify certain cultural traditions and their contemporary manifestations. According to SNK featuring Ta-K-Mi & Mizé (2003) in "Fiers d'être malien" one should respect traditions and build on them, but also change them when necessary. Certain aspects of tradition are clearly criticized, for example forced marriages in "Pananki Pananzoï" by Faso Kombat (2004) and in "I-yamma" by Smockey featuring Biri Lingani (2007).

In the context of economic crisis, many young Africans have to struggle to get the economic means to marry. Premarital dating has become more common, especially in the urban areas, even if it is not yet openly accepted in society. Rappers explore gender roles and male and female relations. Ta-K-Mi (2003) sees some signs of change in "Mah kana kasi" as some women no longer allow themselves to be seen as objects of male domination. In "Le truc qui rend digne," Smockey (2004) denounces not only men exploiting young girls, but also female genital mutilation and the prohibition of abortions. Les Escrocs (2005) also discuss clandestine abortions in "Konotie Magni." Further, women are sometimes ostracized because they cannot give birth to children. This is deplored by Yeleen (2001) in "Le sentier de la tragédie" and linked to circumcision:

> A lonely woman, abandoned by everybody. (...) She accepts dying because of society's outrage. She accepts the reality that never, never is she going to have children. Never is she going to enjoy maternity. (...) I respect our African practices and concepts. I respect our ethics and its facets, certainly. I'm sure that God, our father never said that an intact woman was a bad mother. Why cutting? Why cutting? Why

think that a circumcised woman is an example of fidelity? African mentality, myth or reality. What I know is that a lot of women are in fact suffering. Don't touch my sister, don't touch her, my mother. I'm scared. It is time to open your eyes and consider the happiness of my sister. No to the laws of an ageing practice. (...) Educate... It is a question of mentalities. Everybody is talking about this, everybody is singing about it. But what is done to change it?

On the other hand, Yeleen (2001) criticizes women walking the streets semi-naked in "Génération sacrifiée." Young women only interested in material gain, working their way through lovers is also widely criticized, for "the quality of their feelings depends on the wallets," as Sofaa (2003) remarks in "Profile-bas." Les Escrocs (2001) talks about the dating behavior of public servants, while deploring the "little salary Malians" marrying several women and having many children without being able to take care of them financially.

Rap music assists many young people in contemporary Africa with constructing their identity. As Yeli Fuzzo (2003) states, "I rap, therefore I am." Among the most important identity markers used by rappers are age and social marginalization. As members of society born at approximately the same time and exposed to similar social problems, many rappers share a view of the world different from older generations. They see themselves as being part of the "sacrificed" or "lost generation" (Yeleen (2001): "Génération sacrifiée"; SNK featuring Dodou Soul (2003): "Je vois"; Sofaa (2003): "Le Beatraad"; Wed Hyack (2003): "Humanités troubles"). Rappers, because of their age and social position, declare themselves as marginalized citizens with limited access to political power and economic resources. They are marginalized, but not marginal, as important parts of the population are younger than 25 years old. Young people are normally not supposed to express their opinion in public. With rap music, however, they find their voice. As a result, Malian and Burkinabe rappers represent the different social groups they are part of, becoming by extension youthful spokespersons for said social groups (Wittmann 2004).

pan-africanist dreams, but lacking chance: rap and politics

Many rappers contribute to the reconstruction of African history, which can be seen as a form of historical reappropriation by Africans. Fanga Fing (2000) in "Masaya" and Yeleen (2006) in "Il suffit d'y croire" commemorate Sundiata Keita, the legendary king of the ancient kingdom of Mali. Wed Hyack (2003) raps in "History" about the slave trade, as do the members of Yeleen (2001) in "Génération sacrifiée." The latter also brand the collaboration of some Africans in the slave trade: "Black was the beast pursed in those black forests, sometimes delivered by his own black brothers, exchanged for a scrap of mirror." Both Yeleen (2006) and Smockey (2007) criticize the involvement of the Christian church in the slave trade. Colonial domination in western Africa was fiercely resisted by Samory Touré, who is recalled by Yeleen (2001) in "Génération sacrifiée" and by Sofaa (2003) in "Esprit de Sofaa."[6] On the eve of independence, African soldiers participated in World War II. They were not paid correctly and a protest movement in Dakar's suburb Thiaroye ended in a massacre by French Troops in 1944. This topic has been widely discussed in West Africa in recent years and is mentioned by several rappers (Faso Kombat featuring Yeleen (2004), "Pourqoui c'est comme ça"; Les Escrocs (2001), "Tounga"; Smockey (2004), "Ma dignité"; Sofaa (2003), "Tchéfari").

The military and revolutionary president of Burkina Faso, Thomas Sankara, is somewhat the Che Guevara of West Africa. He is rather uncritically revered by many rappers from Burkina Faso and other West African countries. Examples include Sofaa's (2003) "Tchéfari," Yeleen's (2006) "Il suffit d'y croire" and Smockey's (2004) "On est tous innocent." In fact, Smockey couldn't include his song "A qui profite le crime" on his 2007 album "Code Noir," as there were threats on his life (SaintAnge 2009; Sanon 2008). The song discussed the murder of Thomas Sankara in 1987, which is for many Burkinabe people linked to the acting president Blaise Compaoré who has lead the country autocratically since the murder of Sankara.

Among others, the first Prime Minister of the Congo, Patrice Lumumba and the Senegalese historian Cheikh Anta Diop are revered in "Il suffit d'y croire" by Yeleen (2006). To this end, rappers contribute to the reconstruction of a Pan-African identity on the continent. References to African unity and Pan-Africanism more specifically can be found in "Intégration Africaine" by Les Escrocs (2005), "Rêves brisés" by Koumankan featuring Faso Kombat (n.d.), "Afrika" by O.B.C. (2004) or in "Terre des ancêtres" and "Du rêve au cauchemar" by Baloukou (2008). In collaboration with the Malian Minister of African Integration, Yeli Fuzzo remixed a song for Africa Day with Ta-K-Mi, Don Mize, and Pamela (Traoré 2009). The mini-CD "Le jour de l'Afrique" was freely given away to people responding to questions on African integration on private radio stations in Bamako.

However, the reality on the continent looks different, for civil wars shatter the dream of unity. Civil wars and the fate of child soldiers attract the attention of La Censure (2001, "Pourqoui"), Lassy King Massassy (2003, "Fabara"), TA-K-MI (2003, "Enfants soldats") and Yeleen featuring Faso Kombat (2003, "Même combat"). Civil wars are often caused by the scramble for natural resources. Protagonists from Europe and Northern America fuel these fights, specifies Lassy King Massassy (2003) in "Fabara." One conflict that has attracted the attention of rappers is in the neighboring Ivory Coast. Immigrant workers from Burkina Faso contributed their manpower to the boom of cocoa and coffee plantations in the Ivory Coast and have now been displaced following the rebellion in 2002. Koumankan featuring Faso Kombat (n.d.) remind us of their fate in "Rêves brisés":

Incredible! Under the ardent sun in the cacao plantations our parents clenched their teeth to make you a
living from cacao. 'Biggest producer worldwide', but
thanks to whom? Be grateful and say at least thanks
to whom! (...) Incredible! They came to help you, you
deposed them, you killed them.

Samples of radio reports are used by Faso Kombat (2004) in
"Bayir Kamba" to recall the expulsion of farmers originating from
Burkina Faso by local communities in the Ivory Coast. Ivorian
farmers argue that "there is no room here" and that "it is for us
here" to explain the burning of villages and settlements. Together
with female Ivorian rapper Priss'K, Yeleen (2004) recorded a
song called "Parlons d'amour" which called for reconciliation
and peace. Sofaa (2003) denounce in "Ayo" the eviction of Africans by Africans but also the abuse of foreigners as scapegoats.
But there are also a lot of divisions in Burkina Faso, as Smockey
(2004) underlines in "Ma dignité" and in "On est tous innocent."
In "Ouaga c'est pas les States" he (2005) deplores the xenophobia
towards Lebanese living in Burkina Faso.

In Mali, many rappers grew up partly as children of democracy. The former military regime of General Moussa Traoré
was contested by public unrest in 1991. Traoré's security forces
killed over 100 demonstrators before he was overthrown by
General Amadou Toumani Touré. After democratic elections
in 1992 Touré handed power to Alpha Oumar Konaré and was
in May 2002 democratically elected president. Rage (2000) tried
to mobilize voters, especially young people for the elections of
1997 with their song "Votemania" without favoring any particular candidate. They state "vote, my buddy" and underline that it
is not difficult to register and participate in the voting process.
Despite their efforts, Rage (2000, "Interlude") are not happy with
the political system in Mali: "They try. They speak of democracy.
But in reality, for me, it is a graft that didn't take, because they
tried too much to copy the occident instead of finding a politi-

cal system that is adapted to our realities, you see?" Similarly, Tata Pound (2008, "Démocratie zéro") has also lost confidence in Malian democracy.

Violence during political rallies is known in many African countries. Yeleen (2003) tell their listeners in "Au nom de mon parti" about the death of a political activist during a rally because of panicking policemen. In "Vision de vie," they (2006) ask politicians to think of young people beyond elections. Election campaigns and shady politicians are caricatured by Smockey (2005) in "Votez pour moi!" which was released just before the presidential elections in Burkina Faso. He satirically proposes to act like a reverse Robin Hood, stealing from the poor to give to the rich. Smockey received the national music award (Kundé d'Or) in 2006, probably less due to the popularity of the song "Votez pour moi," but more as a sign of support by the artistic community. Ironically enough, the President's wife Chantal Compaoré was present at the ceremony and not happy with the decision (Saint Ange 2009).

Tata Pound (2002) mentions in "Politicien" the buying of votes and by extension the erosion of democracy. After elections, things do not always get better, as Rage (2000) assess in "Acide Constat." Tata Pound featuring Tiken Jah Fakoly (2002) talk in "Delivrance" about the absence of change: "We have protested, we have marched, nothing has changed. We have been optimistic, we have dreamt, we have hoped, nothing has changed." In "Cikan – le message", they (2002) directly address the president: "Tata Pound is speaking to the president who was coming for change. (...) This country belongs to us all without any exclusion, nobody is above the law, even those on the hill (where the presidential palace is in Bamako)." They also urge the new President Amadou Toumani Touré to fight corruption, injustice, and poverty. If the president is not able to govern, they want him to leave office. This message was kindly listened to by President Touré who invited Tata Pound into the presidential palace and referred to them in his address to the nation. They still are waiting to see things change.

These lyrics have a degree of outspokenness that is remarkable. However, the freedom of expression is in danger when voices get too critical. The members of Tata Pound (2006) received death threats in the run-up to the publication of their album "Yelema – La Révolution". They cut a part of the song "Yelema," which is still not played on state radio or television, as is the case with "Monsieur le maire." While "Yelema" deals critically with corruption, privatization, and the lack of changes in Mali, "Monsieur le maire" incriminates some mayors who were elected in 2004 but quickly forgot their electoral promises and even illegally sold estates. Cloonan and Drewett (2006) link censorship of popular music in Africa to questions of national unity or cultural values. This is however not the case with rap music in Mali.

Freedom of expression is also contested in Burkina Faso, as advocated by La Censure (2001) in "Séquestrés." One artist participating in the Zongo sampler, Sam's K le Jah, received death threats and his car was burnt. According to Smockey (2005) in "Ouaga c'est pas les States"), if "you're a journalist, artist – you're on the list." Smockey was also forced to censor a part of this song and, as mentioned above, has received death threats for his outspokenness. As is often the case, this kind of censorship boosts the popularity of artists and certain songs.

While not among the most autocratic states, there are obviously limitations to the freedom of the press in Burkina Faso. The most famous example kept alive by Smockey (2004) in "Lettre ouverte" is the killing of critical journalist Norbert Zongo in Burkina Faso on December 13, 1998. The rapper denounces the alleged innocence of the current government commonly linked to this murder in "On est tous innocent" (2004). He states: "We have unity. Wrong. We have progress. Wrong. Burkina Faso. Wrong." The latter statement is referring to the name of Burkina Faso, which translates as "Land of the honest people." A collective of artists, among them being Smockey, Faso Kombat, and Awadi from Senegal, recorded a song in 2008 about the fact that after ten years the authors of this crime have still not been punished ("10 ans d'impunité c'est trop").[7] They also compiled an album to commemorate the murder which is also remembered every year with concerts and thousands marching in the streets. It is however important to emphasize the impact of the liberalization of the media since 1991. As in Mali and other sub-Saharan African countries, private radio and television stations were extremely important for the growth of rap music in Burkina Faso.[8] In many ways, they offer a platform for expression by rappers and other members of civil society.

In "Dar es Salam," Yeleen (2006) write an open letter to President Blaise Compaoré and ask him to send the peace dove to Laurent Gbagbo, the former President of the Ivory Coast, and to the presidents of Senegal, Chad, the United States of America, the United Kingdom, Israel, and Palestine. I am not aware of any reaction by President Compaoré to this song, despite his reaction to other rap songs. Sanogo (2007) describes the rumor that President Blaise Compaoré himself, asked his ministers which young musicians made the popular song "Ici au Faso la vie est dure" (Here in Burkina Faso, life is hard). Apparently, only one minister was familiar with the name of the rap group the Wemteng Clan. According to Sanogo (2007), Compaoré allegedly also answered a journalists question about the living costs in Burkina Faso with a reference to a rap song: "Isn't it that you young people say 'viima ya kanga' (life is hard)?" I don't know whether these stories are true or not. However, these rumours are discourses that address the importance of rap music in Burkina Faso.

In 2007, President Blaise Compaoré attempted to pressure some rappers, including Yeleen, to perform at the festival celebrating the 20th anniversary of his seizure of power (Zougmoré 2009), which for many is equal to the 20th anniversary of the murder of Thomas Sankara. In "Mr. LeMaire" Yeelen present an indictment of Simon Compraoré's administration. There were rumors that Yeleen was paid ten million CFA franc (more than U.S. $21,600) by the president's brother François Compaoré to discredit his rival with this song. This rumor was vehemently denied by Yeleen, and controversially discussed in Burkina Faso (cf. the comments to Zougmoré 2009).

Generally, it is African leaders that are linked to this kind of rumor, not rappers. Indeed, corruption is the most widespread topic in African rap (Faso Kombat (2004), "Konscientization"; Rage (2000), "Interlude"; Tata Pound (2002), "Cikan – le message"; Tata Pound (2002), "Politiciens"; Tata Pound feat. Tiken Jah Fakoly (2002), "Delivrance"; Wed Hyack (2003), "Honte à Babylon"; Sofaa & Meltin (Various Artists 2007), "Au nom du peuple"). Sofaa (2003) criticize in "Tchéfari" African presidents who transfer stolen money to their famous Swiss bank accounts, a topic also mentioned by Smockey (2005) in "Votez pour moi!"

Indeed, relations in the international system are also discussed in rap music, especially the relation with the former colonial master France. While for Smockey ("Le Cycle," 2004) the Gallic cock has lost its cock-a-doodle-doo, independence is a myth for Rage ("Acide constat," 2000), Yeleen ("Génération sacrifiée," 2001) and Sofaa ("Tchéfari," 2003). According to Sofaa (2003) in "Tchéfari" it is quite clear where the controlling influences lie; not in West Africa, but in France. The term "Françafrique," coined by François-Xavier Verschave whose association Survie released the music sampler "Décolonisons!" (2007), is frequently used by rappers and others to describe neo-colonial relations between France and some of its former colonies. On this sampler there is the uncensored version of "Yelema" by Tata Pound (2006), which criticizes that the infrastructure of Mali which is only superficially improved when the French President arrives for the France-Africa Summit in 2005. Other rappers criticize French domestic policies (e.g. Faso Kombat (2004) and U.S. hegemony (e.g. Yeleen (2003)). Similarly, Faso Kombat (2007), in "Et ça continue" vehemently attacks the U.S. and its attempt to dominate the world as does Tata Pound (2008, "Démocratie zéro"). For Baloukou (2008, "Du rêve au cauchemar"), it is clear that "the African continent continues to contain all the shit of the occident."

conclusion

In the end, many rappers from Mali and Burkina Faso engage in critical discussions regarding political, social, and economic issues. As part of civil society, they contribute their critical voices to the creation of vibrant public spheres, which in years past were barely accessible to young people. Formerly voiceless, young people in both Burkina Faso and Mali have begun to articulate in their own language, their understanding of the world in which they live, their "meanings," in order to counter the "myth of consensus (Hebdige 1991: 18)." In their counter discourse, they criticize the social conditions of their respective countries, that is, the poverty, the lack of healthcare, the failing educational systems and more. In other words, this criticism is mainly about the lack of change for the majority of Burkinabe and Malian people, despite the formal establishment of democratic institutions in their respective countries. This is exactly what makes rap relevant to the society in which it is produced, for it allows oppositional interpretations of neglected and common social problems and phenomena.

Regardless of their criticism, rappers seldom offer solutions to societal problems, that is, rappers generally don't present concrete alternatives to the neo-patrimonial state.[9] As Yeleen (2006) state in "Vision de vie:" "I don't have a solution, I'm just sharing my worries." As Tricia Rose (2008: 268) cogently observed, rappers are far too focused on representing what is, than considering what actually should be. Nonetheless, some rappers have worked with various NGOs and development projects in an attempt to create a better future for themselves and their fellow citizens. For instance, Yeleen from Burkina Faso and others have supported the fair trade campaign "Big Noise" by Oxfam.[10] Rap music can thus give a voice to other social movements and help to mobilize support for them. Case in point, both Smockey and Tata Pound are part of a growing network of West African rappers interested in social change. One part of this growing network is AURA (United Artists for African Rap) (See chapter three of this volume). AURA developed out of an awareness concert and meetings organized by the NGO Plan in 2005. It includes rappers from Burkina Faso, Mali, Senegal, Mauritania, Togo, Niger, Gambia, Guinea, Benin, and the Ivory Coast who are interested in raising awareness about the rights of children and youth and their problems in the region. In an interview with the author, Togolese rapper Bobby from Djankatan expressed his optimism that the AURA network will continue beyond the NGOs support.[11] Time will only tell if the network can and will sustain itself. Regardless, many Burkinabe and Malian rappers see themselves as part of a growing and determined international movement for social change in Africa. As Malian rapper SNK (2003) articulates it: "Young people are uniting slowly, but surely."

notes

1. The author wishes to thank Simon Grab, Claudia Roth, Rebekka Gemperle, Daniela Walla and Silvia Volkart for providing information and music.
2. The region with the least locally produced rap music is probably the Horn of Africa, as my experience in Djibouti and Eritrea has showed.
3. These events have also boosted the growth of other hip-hop elements.
4. French lyrics were translated by the author. The idea behind the translation is to show the meaning and the style of the original lyrics.
5. The name Amkoullel is taken from the famous book "Amkoullel – L'Enfant Peul" by the West African author Amadou Hampâté Bâ.
6. The "Sofaa" were the combatants of Samory Touré.
7. Another example, although less well known, is the murder of journalist Michel Congo (Sanon 2008:7).
8. The role of radio animators in the development of rap music is clearly under analyzed.
9. Rap music is often disruptive to the existing social order and in this sense progressive. As some examples from Senegal show, it

can also be quite conservative and should thus not be seen with a sense social romanticism (Wittmann 2004).

10. The campaign focuses on agricultural subsidies making competition for African producers unfair. This aspect is also mentioned by *Smockey feat. Faso Kombat* (2007, "Et ça continue"). They charge the U.S. who talk of free markets, but subsidize their agriculture.

11. Interview ID 006TOLO, September 5, 2008.

bibliography

Androutsopoulos, Jannis. 2003. Einleitung [Introduction]. In *Hip-hop. Globale Kultur – lokale Praktiken* [Hip-hop: Global Culture – Local Practices], ed. Jannis Androutsopoulos, 9.23. Bielefeld: Transcript.

Cloonan, Martin and Michael Drewett. 2006. Concluding Comments on the Censorship of Popular Music in Africa. In *Popular Music Censorship in Africa*, eds. Michael Drewett and Martin Cloonan, 215-219. Aldershot/Burlington: Ashgate.

Fangafrika. 2008. *La Voix des Sans-voix. Rap made in West Africa* [The voice of the voiceless]. N.p.: Staycalm!/Mondomix. Booklet.

Hebdige, Dick. 1991. *Subculture. The Meaning of Style.* London/New York: Routledge. Reprint. Originally published London: Methuen, 1979.

Künzler, Daniel. 2007. The 'Lost Generation'. African Hip-hop Movements and the Protest of the Young (Male) Urban. In *Civil Society – Local and Regional Responses to Global Challenges,* ed. Mark Herkenrath, 89-127. Wien/Berlin: Lit Verlag.

Mathcoolj. 2005. L'Evolution du Hip-hop au Burkina Faso [The evolution of hip-hop in Burkina Faso]. *United Nations of Hip-hop,* article posted December 7, http://www.unitednationsofhiphop.com/African-Hip-Hop-News/African-Hip-Hop-News-Opinions-Articles-and-More/The-Evolution-Of-Hip-Hop-in-Burkina-Faso.html (accessed July 31, 2009).

Mikos, Lothar. 2003. 'Interpolation and sampling': Kulturelles Gedächtnis und Intertextualität im HipHop ['Interpolation and Sampling': Cultural Memory and Intertextuality in Hip-hop]. In *Hip-hop. Globale Kultur – lokale Praktiken* [Hip-hop. Global

Culture – Local Practices], ed. Jannis Androutsopoulos, 64-84. Bielefeld: Transcript.

Nazé, Hermann. 2009. Football et musique: Quand les Etalons deviennent des rappeurs [Soccer and Music: When Stallions start Rapping]. *Lefaso.net*, article posted July 15, http://www.lefaso.net/spip.php?article32412 (accessed July 31, 2009).

Rose, Tricia. 1994. *Black Noise. Rap Music and Black Culture in Contemporary America*. Hanover/London: Wesleyan University Press.

Rose, Tricia. 2008. *The Hip-hop Wars. What We Talk About When We Talk About Hip-hop – and Why It Matters*. New York: Basic Civitas Books.

Sanogo, Issa. 2007. Le RAP burkinabè serait-il sexiste? [Is Rap from Burkina Faso sexist?] *L'opinion 509*, July 11-17, http://zedcom.bf/actualite/op509/culture.htm (accessed July 31, 2009).

Saint Ange. 2009. Smockey: Je suis un politicien [Smockey: I am a politician]. *L'Eveil éducation*, article posted February 12, http://www.lefaso.net/spip.php?article30585 (accessed July 31, 2009).

Traoré, Kassim. 2008. Yeli Mady Konaté dit Yeli Fuzzo: Waraya dans les bacs en juillet [Yeli Mady Konaté a.k.a. Yeli Fuzzo: Waraya on sale in July]. *Bamako Hebdo*, article posted 28 June, http://www.malijet.com/index.php?news=3829 (accessed July 31, 2009).

Traoré, Kassim. 2009. Musique et Intégration: Yéli Fuzzo chante "le jour de l'Afrique" [Music and Integration: Yeli Fuzzo sings "Africa Day"] *Bamako Hebdo*, article posted May 23, http://www.maliweb.net/category.php?NID=44979&intr= (accessed July 31, 2009).

UNAIDS. 2008. *Report on the Global AIDS Epidemic 08*. Geneva: Joint United Nations Programme on HIV/AIDS (UNAIDS). http://www.unaids.org/en/KnowledgeCentre/HIVData/GlobalReport/2008/2008_Global_report.asp (accessed July 31, 2009).

UNDP. 2007. *Human Development Report 2007/2008. Fighting Climate Change: Human Solidarity in a Divided World*. New York: United Nations Development Programme. http://hdr.undp.org/en/reports/global/hdr2007-2008 (accessed July 31, 2009).

UNFPA. 2008. *State of the World Population 2008*. New York: UNFPA. http://www.unfpa.org/swp/ (accessed July 31, 2009).

Sanon, David. 2008. Smockey rebelle avec une cause [Smockey rebel with a cause]. *Waga Hip-hop 8*, Nr. 3, October 18. Ouagadougou:

Umané Culture/Planète Culture. www.wagahiphop.com/admin/ upload/file/wagahhmag3-bd.pdf (accessed July 31, 2009).

Wittmann, Frank. 2004. Sexismus, Islamismus und Ghettoromantik. Die Dakarer HipHop-Bewegung *Bul faale* im Kontext der globalen Postmoderne [Sexism, Islamism and Ghetto romanticism. The hip-hop movement *Bul faale* from Dakar in the context of global postmodernity]. In *Rap: More than Words*, ed. Eva Kimminich, 181-204. Frankfurt am Main: Peter Lang.

World Bank (2008): *World Development Indicators. Poverty Data. A supplement to World Development Indicators 2008.* Washington D.C.: The International Bank for Reconstruction and Development/The World Bank. http://siteresources.worldbank.org/DATA STATISTICS/Resources/WDI08supplement1216.pdf (accessed July 31, 2009).

World Bank. 2009. *World Development Report 2009. Reshaping Economic Geography.* Washington, DC: The International Bank for Reconstruction and Development/The World Bank. www.world-bank.org/wdr (accessed July 31, 2009).

Zougmoré, Merneptah Noufou. 2009. Musique: Yeleen et les millions de François Compaoré [Music: Yeleen and the François Compaoré millions]. *L'Evénement*, article posted June 20, http://www.lefaso.net/spip.php?article32135 (accessed July 31, 2009).

discography and videography

Amkoullel. 2002. *In Faculté* [Non Faculty]. Bamako: Mali K7 S.A.

Amkoullel. 2005. *Surafin* [Bribe]. Mali K7 S.A.

AURA (United Artists for African Rap). 2007. *Les Histoires extraordinaires des enfants du Poto-Poto* [The extraordinary stories of the Poto-Poto children]. N.p.

Baloukou. 2008. *Où va le monde?* [Where is the World going?] N.p.

Fanga Fing. 2000. *Fanga Follo*. Bamako: Invasion Records/Mali K7 S.A.

Fangafrika. 2008. *La Voix des Sans-voix. Rap made in West Africa* [The voice of the voiceless]. N.p.: Staycalm!/Mondomix.

Faso Kombat. 2004. *Parcours de Combattants* [The Path of the Fighters]. Ouagadougou: Studio Abazon.

Koumankan. N.d. *Oralité* [Orality]. Ouagadougou: Studio Abazon.

K-Ravane. 2005. *Viima Ya Kanga* [Life is hard]. Ouagadougou: Ex Sound Studio. Video, http://www.youtube.com/watch?v=8Srcv8JfDaY (accessed July 31, 2009).

La censure. 2001. *Séquestrés* [Seized]. Ouagadougou: 8ème Sens/Studio Abazon.

Lassy King Massassy. 2003. *Niokala So* [The Horse of Wood]. Bamako: Mali K7 S.A.

Les Escrocs. 2001. *Kalan* [School-Study]. Bamako: Mandika Kora Production.

Les Escrocs. 2005. *Mandinka Rap from Mali.* N.p.: Naxos World.

O.B.C. 2004. *Education.* Ouagadougou: Studio Abazon/8ème Sens.

Rage. 2000. *Cidew* [Messenger-Children]. N.p.: Le Maquis/Night & Day. Re-release. Original album 1998.

Ramses. 2009. *Malien* [Malian]. Bamako: Cabralbiz. Video, http://www.raphiphopmali.com/videos/ramses/2.php.

Smockey. 2004. *Zamana – Mon peuple* [My people]. Ouagadougou: Studio Abazon.

Smockey. 2005. *Votez pour moi!* [Vote for me!]. Maxi Ouagadougou: Studio Abazon.

Smockey. 2007. *Code Noir* [Code Black]. Ouagadougou: Studio Abazon.

Smockey. 2008. *A balles réelles* [With real bullets]. Maxi. Ouagadougou: Studio Abazon.

SNK. 2003. *Toujours underground* [Always underground]. Bamako: Invasion Records/Mali K7 S.A.

Sofaa. 2003. *Akili Kouman* [Word of Wisdom]. Ouagadougou: Studio Abazon.

Ta-K-Mi. 2003. *Wari* [Money]. Bamako: Mali K7 SA.

Tata Pound. 2002. *Cikan – le message* [The message]. Dakar: Studio Yes.

Tata Pound. 2006. *Yelema – la Révolution* [The Revolution]. Bamako: n.p.

Tata Pound. 2008. *Démocratie zero* [Zero Democracy]. Bamako: n.p. Video, http://www.youtube.com/watch?v=4a2K3W_JdZU.

Various Artists. 2007. *Décolonisons! Africa wants to be free 2* [Let's decolonize]. Paris: Survie.

Wed Hyack. 2003. *Wed est là* [Wed is here]. Ouagadougou: Studio Abazon.

Yeleen. 2001. *Juste 1 peu 2 Lumière* [Just a little light]. Ouagadougou: Studio Abazon.

Yeleen. 2003. *Dieu seul sait* [God only knows]. Ouagadougou: Studio Abazon.

Yeleen featuring Priss'K. 2004. *Parlons d'amour* [Let's talk about Love]. N.p.: Adonis Productions. Video, http://www.youtube.com/watch?v=VngmdunCCVE&feature=related.

Yeleen. 2006. *Dar Es Salam* [House of Peace]. Ouagadougou: Waga N'Djam.

Yeli Fuzzo. 2003. *Je rap donc je suis* [I rap, therefore I am]. Bamako: Invasion Records/Mali K7 S.A.

Yeli Fuzzo, Pamela, Buba, Habib Mar One, Aminata Laurence, Don Mizey, Master Soumi, Slash, Massara Kouyaté, Minata Kouyaté. 2008. *Allez les Aigles* [Go Eagles]. Bamako: Yéli Mady Music. Video, http://www.raphiphopmali.com/videos/yeli-fuzzo/3.php

CHAPTER 3
hip-hop political productions in west africa: aura[1] and its extraordinary stories of poto-poto children

JENNY F. MBAYE **introduction**

Marked by the oral character of its context, West African music can be assimilated to what Shusterman has called the "pragmatist aesthetics."[2] Indeed, this artistic expression insists on the profound link which unites art to life and through which art must serve as a means which structures ethics and individual lifestyle.[3] From this perspective, hip-hop music that has spread throughout West Africa has erased the borders separating art from life. Indeed, in West Africa, hip-hop music has become a concrete means for young people to affirm their rights to differential identities and alternative socialities. This musical genre has provided a form in which an alternative public space can be nurtured and a differential *praxis* of the city, in cultural and political terms, can be developed.

This chapter begins with the exploration of geographies of hip-hop musical actors in West Africa. Thus, allowing for a political, cultural, and economic contextualization of the youth and the "emergence" of its musical expression. Following this general incursion of the urban sociality of hip-hop actors, an aesthetic cartography is provided, revealing the *transcultural* as well as the *translocal* character of the "hip-hop experience" as a culture and as music. Indeed, hip-hop is nowadays a globalized urban phenomenon, which, in West Africa, recalls the translocal character of the condition of marginalization of the youngest generations throughout the region. In turn, this experience shared by West African urban youths participates in the elaboration of political productions that are specific to this musical genre. The *politics of difference* and *differential politics* will thus be introduced and illustrated through the actions of AURA members, a West African hip-hop collective. While AURA's *politics of difference* refers to the articulation of a transurban and pan-African identity beyond the cultural strangleholds of tradition, its *differential politics* stands as another political practice initiated on the margins of the institutional paths of democratic discourses. With respect, this chapter stresses that AURA's political productions are attentive to an alternative *praxis* that participates in the democratic inclusion of marginalized generations.

social geographies of west african urban youth

Through his concepts of *urban ethos* and its *limits of possibility,* Adam Krims argues that the paradox of contemporary urban change stands in "the simultaneous expansiveness and closure of the city."[4] In West Africa, this paradox invariably and specifically affects the youngest generations living in urban areas. The important gap persisting between youth expectations in terms of employment and the actual possibilities of the job market has serious social consequences; we indeed observe painful disillusions worsening a social demand already pretty high. Taking into consideration the paucity of information gathered by the Economic Community of West African States (ECOWAS) regarding this issue, I will refer to two distinctive metropolitan areas—namely Ouagadougou and Dakar – to illustrate the economic situation of West African youth.

In both Burkina Faso and Senegal, unemployment is higher in urban areas than it is in rural areas. In Ouagadougou unemployment is nearly 20 percent,[5] while in Dakar it is nearly 12 percent.[6] In Dakar, more than 50 percent of its population is under 20 years old;[7] similarly, Ouagadougou displays an average age estimated at 21.8 years old.[8] Unsurprisingly, unemployment especially affects the metropolitan youth and more particularly the most educated; unemployment rates increase with the level of education with around one fourth of those unemployed having reached the university level: 23.5 percent in Dakar's region[9] and 26 percent in Burkina Faso.[10]

Economic as well as political and cultural realities constitute significant burdens to young people's participation and full appreciation of civic life. As far as the official democratic system is concerned, we can notice the relatively weak implications of the youngest generations in traditional political processes that however affect them. This supplementary obstacle to the participative diversity of the political discourse is best exemplified by the average age of African political leaders. Although the global norm is 61 years old to which the African average approximately corresponds as it is of 62 years old,[11] this latter figure appears in stark contrast with the average age of the majority of its population. Finally, in cultural terms, the West African city appears to be subjected to a generational segregation where young people are victims of logics of exclusion based on the tradition of respect to the eldest. Indeed, this logic which implies obedience, reserve, and often silence, marginalizes them from the public and social sphere as well as from the private and familial sphere.[12] Therefore, these examples of Dakar and Ouagadougou suggest the translocal nature of youth economic, political, as well as, cultural experience in West Africa. Certainly, despite the national borders, the urban sociality faced by Dakar youth similarly resonates with what the youth of Ouagadougou actually live and experience.

aesthetic cartography of hip-hop music

> Aesthetics is more than a philosophy or theory of beauty; it is a way of inhabiting space, a particular location, a way of looking and becoming.[13]

First emerging in the Bronx (New York) in the 1970s, hip-hop and its musical expression are now part of the reality of multiple and diverse urban communities throughout the world. Hip-hop, both culturally and musically, as a culture and as music, is always embedded in the urban context from which it emerges. With respect, I argued elsewhere that hip-hop stands as a *transculture* in the sense that it surely exists by itself, but can only be articulated through other cultures.[14] From this perspective, hip-hop music is "transcultural" and can be apprehended as a *'form'* in the sense developed and applied by Barthes to a 'myth.' Rather than a concept or an object, hip-hop music stands as a system of communication, a type of speech which is *dissociable* from its content. In other words, it is a form which stands as a totality that is neither set nor stable.[15] Barthes stresses that a myth is 'a mode of signification, a form' and, as such, I understand that hip-hop music "can be a myth provided it is conveyed by a discourse."[16] Therefore, hip-hop music is vast and encompasses a multiplicity of discursive practices inscribed in various social, political, economic, geographical, or linguistic contexts. Put differently, hip-hop music is this *form* whose substance is open to any and every discursive orientation of a fantasist or real individuality. Consequently, as far as the myth or the music is concerned, "the form does not suppress the meaning, it only impoverishes it, it puts it at a distance, [and] it holds it at one's disposal."[17]

Besides, hip-hop music can be classified among what may be considered the oldest form of music, i.e. vocal music. The primacy of the human voice in hip-hop music is particularly relevant as the voice, "because of its physiological basis and its communicative functions, is a primary instrument for emotional expression."[18] Open onto an exterior towards which it aspires, through its very agency, the voice appears as a 'wish-to-speak (*vouloir-dire*) and a desire for existence.'[19] Therefore, making music and especially vocal music, can become a way of not only expressing ideas but also of genuinely living them.[20] With respect, "[...] Hip-hop is a mean for individuals to elaborate their own route"[21] and its musical expression has become this aesthetical emergence where everybody can project him/herself while having the opportunity to develop a critical judgement on his/her living conditions.

Throughout the world, various urban actors have disposed of hip-hop music as an expressive social commentary offering descriptions of existence and urbanity and/or interpretative as well as instructive messages to reshape urban reality. Indeed, since its origins, hip-hop music has been appropriated by various urban citizens, victims of the drawbacks of a global process of urbanization: Blacks and Latinos living in American ghettos, immigrant descendents stigmatized in French *banlieues*, autochthones people parked in Canadian reserves or young Africans marginalized in their urban spaces. These different urbanities have in common the fact that they experienced distinctive forms of social exclusion in the city and that they used this musical genre to deploy an alternative storytelling of the urban condition.

Therefore, hip-hop musical productions reveals the different cultural rationalities of the individual who grasps and invests in this medium. Auto-reflexivity is indeed salient at an individual as well as collective level, from an artistic as well as cultural perspective. For instance, sampling is a musical technique which implies the composition of an original instrumental *beat* through the appropriation of bits of musical events, i.e. through the selection and combination of parts of pre-recorded songs.[22] This very technique of hip-hop music creation – *sampling* – is always localized and embedded in the context of its emergence, and as such, it is constantly informed by the cultural affinities of the DJ.[23] To illustrate this point, I can refer to the United States where hip-hop artists from the West Coast sample tracks of local artists such as George Clinton while East Coast artists will rather tend to sample tracks of James Brown. Following the same logics, West African hip-hop artists, like the Senegalese Daddy Bibson who samples music from Oumar Pène, Baobab, Baaba Maal, or Salif Keita.

Besides, at a cultural and collective level, hip-hop music is used by West African actors in order to recognize and re-establish their real, true leaders who have often been disregarded by continental history. Among those characters, they notably refer in their *lyrics* to the Burkinabe revolutionary Thomas Sankara; the first president of Ghana, Kwamé Nkruma; the Mandingo hero who fiercely resisted French colonization, Samory Touré; the Senegalese academic and founder of the "African Renaissance," Cheikh Anta Diop; or Patrice Lumumba. Therefore, hip-hop musical production stands as a cultural product which is articulated, developed, and negotiated by multiple identities and their various collective and individual *praxes*. Hip-hop musical production is, in other words, the result of political sensibilities and cultural affinities which are structured around the production of an identity (*politics of difference*) and a specific and alternative discourse (*differential politics*).

aura and its hip-hop politics

AURA is a network of young West African hip-hop artists who have united together in order to deploy an ideological project based on a continental vision of the youngest generations and their future. AURA first emerged as a network following

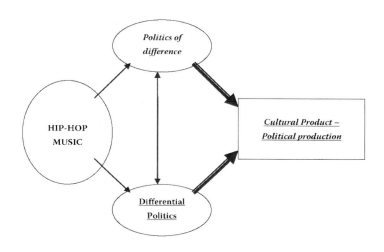

diagram 1: political cartography of hip-hop music[24]

a mega-concert organized in 2005 in Ouagadougou to encourage birth registrations among West African populations. This unique hip-hop collective includes the Senegaleses Didier Awadi and Numukunda (Radikal PBS), Xuman (Pee Froiss), Myriam (ALIF), Keyti (Rap'Adio) and Big D; the Mauritanian Big Power; the Togolese Bobby (Djanta Kan); the Nigeriens Pheno B (Kaidan Gaskia) and Safia; the Burkinabes Smarty (Yeleen) and Smockey; the Ivorian Priss'K; the Gambian Egalitarian; the Beninese Moona; the Guinean Moussa (Degg J Force 3); and the Malian Jo Dama (Tata Pound).

The seventeen members of AURA originating from ten different countries throughout West Africa (Benin, Burkina Faso, Gambia, Guinea, Ivory Coast, Niger, Mali, Mauritania, Senegal and Togo) have decided to engage with what it means nowadays to be part of the West African youth.[25] As such, AURA stands as a unique translocal collective dedicated to the reinvention of and the claim for a politics of identity for the West African youth. As one of its members put it, AURA politics involves *musical activism.*[26] Activism, in a general sense, can be described as an intentional action that aims to bring about social or political change.[27] Put differently, it stands as a claim for an alternative way of thinking and practicing democracy. From this perspective, music becomes a powerful vehicle for discursive productions that can be disruptive of the existing social order and thus liberating and progressive. Indeed, offering a perspective on the world that had been until then not voiced, music as the cognitive *praxis* of AURA becomes an impulse of change for social and political history.[28]

Moreover, *musical activism* includes not only a critical commentary of a lived reality but also a capacity to synthesize the political discourse and to vulgarize it in order to make it accessible to the entire population. It is a way of giving, to the people AURA stands for, the means to act upon and change their future in a way they decided. *Musical activism* is thus understood as an active force that fights for and encourages people to fight for the control of their historicity. Certainly, AURA members believe that, only in engaging Africa's currently largely marginalized youth population, it is possible to foster the continent's integrated development. Therefore, dedicated to West African young people, their musical expression becomes this space of negotiation and redefinition of their personal identity – who am I? – as well as of their generational sociality – what is my role and where is my place in that society? As such, AURA offers a politics of pride, a politics of possibilities, and political productions that redefine youth identity through the lenses of pan-africanism.

politics of difference

In 2006, AURA created the first West African hip-hop musical comedy "The Extraordinary Stories of the Poto-Poto Children," an awareness campaign focusing on children's rights and youth problems in West Africa.[29] The translocal character of the urban experience of youth throughout West Africa – and even from a continental perspective – thus stands as the fermenting ground on which this musical project is based. Indeed, through their musical comedy "The Extraordinary Stories of the Poto-Poto Children," AURA members inscribe at a regional level the struggles faced by many African youth. AURA's artistic depiction of youth experience recalls this collectively shared identity of West African youth and the pan-african nature of their daily lives. Indeed, "The Extraordinary Stories of the Poto-Poto Children" – where poto-poto means "mud," "ghetto," "misfortune," "hardship" – stands as a plea for the pan-african experience of West African youth.

Through their musical expression, those hip-hop actors participate in the recognition of the recurrent urbanities of the youngest generations, which are known throughout their respective countries. Using their own vernacular (French, English but also Hausa, Wolof, Bambara, etc.) in their musical expression, AURA members engage in this representation while each of them incarnates one of African youth's suffered realities. Indeed, the child-beggar (Moussa), the child-prostitute (Priss'K), the child-soldier (Awadi), the street fruits vendor (Moona) or the chronically ill child (Keyti) for instance, all constitute figures that are part of the urban cartography of West African population. Through their collective interpretation of a same reality, the AURA artists, while playing their musical show, inscribe a translocal identity of West African youth. In doing so, they engage in politics of recognition through which the "subjective voices of experience," "the voices from the borderlands who have been marginalised, displaced, oppressed or dominated"[30] are suddenly not only tolerated but valorized.

The urban individualities they represent through the characters they interpret in the musical comedy are given a role, a part to play in this fictional reality, which is the stage. Further than recognition then, and for an hour, agency is given to marginalized young urbanites: they act, they talk, they can express themselves, they ceased to be invisible in the city to become the main actors, the main agents, the visible agents of this musical comedy. The *politics of difference* articulated by AURA actors reaches then its full potential: those individualities usually marginalized and invisible in urban spaces are recognized and given credit on stage. Therefore, through their interpretation of those young characters in the musical comedy, hip-hop actors, articulate an alternative, a different politics and reality for marginalized youth than the one up-to-now imposed by the dominant cultural gerontocracy. In the "The Extraordinary Stories of the Poto-Poto Children," oppressed youth not only become visible and free citizens, but also translocal, regional actors united by a collective reality and a shared sociality. The politics of identity of West African youth who are no longer individually marginalized but here collectively recognized in their regional – if not continental – unity. And, while AURA inscribes itself in a transurban movement, it also outlines a new identity, another identity, a different identity calling for a differential political *praxis*.

differential politics

> "I wish to offer a plea for the importance of the local
> and particular – not least as a basis for democracy."[31]

After having explored how hip-hop music can articulate a *politics of difference* for West African youth, I want to rehabilitate the positioned politics of everyday life as historical forces of social change and foster an alternative scale of political practice. It has been asserted that the "most familiar response to deterritorialization [sic] is the desire to reterritorialize [sic]."[32] Therefore, young people in West Africa who feel 'out-of-place' in their own city, re-inscribe themselves in their 'local,' through "the situatedness of their knowledge."[33] Articulating their politics of alternative identity, their *politics of difference* through their aesthetics, AURA actors become acting social and political subjects: the private domain of identity construction and formation then constantly dialogues, interacts, interfaces with the public space of politics.

Bhabha understands modernity as being about "the historical construction of a specific position of historical enunciation and address"[34] and confronts it to the narratives of the borderline conditions, i.e. those articulating the experience of anxiety,[35] or whose identity is put at risk in the political process.[36] From this standpoint, AURA members, emerging from this borderline condition, develop discursive practices in order to contest the modern reality they face and which marginalize them. Put differently, in spaces of urban oppression, hip-hop music provides a speaking position from which 'out-of-place' people express their creativity, articulate their frustrations, assert their identity but also put forth a claim for entitlement.[37] Rapping then becomes a way of amplifying and dramatizing the message of marginalized individuals who choose to articulate their alternative urbanities through this specific vocal music.

Pro-establishment (national anthems) or anti-establishment (protest songs) music is not new. Drawing on the songs of contestation to articulate their *politics of difference*, AURA members then deploy a *differential politics*, another way of doing politics, integrating in their artistic practice a political, democracy-oriented discourse. With respect, in their individual musical productions, they address issues that are considered taboo in their respective countries: such as governmental corruption,[38] legalized injustices afflicting African women[39] (excision, rape, forced marriage, etc.), or excessive privatization of public services.[40]

Besides, such a *differential politics* is not only limited to a simple denunciation but also encourages young people to stand up for themselves, speak for themselves, and express their own opinions. Indeed, this alternative practice of political discourse recalls the primal role youth can play in contemporary politics as empowered citizens with the right to vote. Such a call for social change can be best illustrated by Didier Awadi's track, "Le cri du people," i.e. "People's Cry:"

Chaque fois que le peuple va aux urnes Man,
C'est parce qu'il espère un vrai changement.
Malheureusement j'entends encore toujours le même
cri [...]
Le président t'oublie, oublie le président [41]

Each time the people goes to the ballot box,
It is because it hopes for a real change.
Unfortunately, I still hear over and over the same cry
[...]
The president forgets about you, forget about the
president[42]

The *differential politics* developed by AURA members (but also by many other West African hip-hop artists) is therefore another space of politics, as an alternative to the traditional democratic system where an independent political voice can be nurtured and incensed. *Differential politics* is indeed of great importance as it fills a considerable gap existing between governmental officials and the people of the republic. The mobilization of AURA around the single "On ne signe pas" ("We don't sign") perfectly illustrates this point. In December 2007, Didier Awadi released a musical track denouncing the Economic Partnership Agreements.[43] A few days later, the other members of the network joined him in order to record a pan-african version of this track. The objective of this track, sung in English, French and in other languages represented by AURA artists, was to allow the population to understand what the EPA's were and what was implied by those agreements.[44]

> [...] he who talks does not talk about himself but about another, who is not one but Legion [...] s/he who talks does not have speech; s/he talks on others' behalf[45]

The example of AURA production of this musical track on EPA's recalls how hip-hop artists, through their musical performances, create this specific link between their individual lives and their community, their *emotional site* from and for which they speak. Their individual narratives erected as political actions hold as constant referent the community they represent. Bruno Latour defines politics, as a 'constituting enunciation' that aims to *put into existence* what would not exist without it. This definition is particularly relevant as it helps us to conceptualize the dialectics relating the individual hip-hop artists to their emotional site. West African populations boosted by their youth need to appropriate and make the political debate their own, and when fully understood, to be ready to take the consequent actions. With respect, AURA *differential politics* is dedicated to alert a united Africa, calling its citizens to become actively involved in initiating changes and in holding governments accountable for their actions.

conclusion

This chapter has demonstrated how West African cities are marked by a generational segregation that particularly affects the youth economically, politically, and culturally. Besides, a brief incursion into the aesthetic cartography of hip-hop music has allowed me to argue that this musical genre belongs to a transculture, namely hip-hop, that has been translated throughout the world in various contexts of urban oppression. As such, the emergence of this musical expression in West Africa recalls the translocal character of the urban experience for the youngest generations.

The political productions of hip-hop music – *politics of difference* and *differential politics* – were stressed and illustrated through the pan-africanist politics of the West African hip-hop collective, AURA. The musical project "The Extraordinary Stories of Poto-Poto Children" offered precious insights into the redefinition of youth identity engaged by AURA actors at a regional, if not continental level. This aspect of the political production of hip-hop music was referred to as a *politics of difference* reinvented through the rehabilitation of a collective reality and shared sociality of the invisible urban youth in West Africa. The exploration of the second musical mobilization initiated by AURA, namely the single "On ne signe pas!" acted as a reminder of the genealogy of protest songs inherent to West African hip-hop music. Indeed, this example illustrated the hip-hop *differential politics* whereby AURA members integrated a democracy-oriented discourse into their musical practices.

In conclusion, the objective was to demonstrate that aesthetics such as hip-hop music can be considered as a form of device enacting democratic principles as "it matters that democracy can be practiced [sic] in radically different, including unconventional, ways."[46] Indeed, the aim was to reveal how AURA members have managed to get together around common generational instances of urban difference, around shared values and solidarity (*politics of difference*) and while being engaged in democratic processes (*differential politics*) thought and fought across national borders. As such, AURA does offer a practical development and application of critical theories that are opposed to unequal and oppressive power relations as well as committed to social justice and transformative politics. Through its pan-africanist perspective and initiatives, AURA, has indeed risen as a translocal political force that aims to bring about social change of regional scale.

notes

1. AURA: Artistes Unis pour le Rap Africain / United Artists for African Rap.
2. R. Shusterman, "Art Infraction: Goodman, Rap, Pragmatism " *Australian Journal of Philosophy* 73, no. 2 (1995): 271.
3. D. Throsby, "The Music Industry in the New Millennium: Global and Local Perspectives" in *The Global Alliance for Cultural Diver-*

sity (Paris: Division of Arts and Cultural Enterprise, UNESCO, 2002), 117.

4   A. Krims, *Music and Urban Geography* (New York: Routledge, Taylor & Francis Group, 2007), xxxiii, 7-15.

5.   Institut National de la Statistique et de la Démographie (INSD), in *Analyse des résultats de l'enquête annuelle sur les conditions de vie des ménages et du suivi de la pauvreté en 2005* (Ouagadougou: Ministère de l'Économie et du Développement, Burkina Faso, Section Unité – Progrès – Justice, EA/QUIBB 2005), 5.

6.   Agence Nationale de Statistique et de la Démographie (ANSD), "Année 2006." in *Situation économique et sociale de la région de Dakar* (Dakar, Sénégal: Service Régional de la Statistique et Démographie (SRSD) de Dakar, 2007), 31.

7.   *Ibid.*, 49-50.

8.   INSD, *Analyse des résultats de l'enquête annuelle sur les conditions de vie des ménages et du suivi de la pauvreté en 2005*, 1.

9.   ANSD, *Situation économique et sociale de la région de Dakar*, 55.

10. Institut National de la Statistique et de la Démographie(INSD), *Tableau de bord social du Burkina Faso* (Ministère de l'Économie et du Développement: Burkina Faso, Secrétariat Général, 2005), 49.

11. S. Kodjo-Grandvaux, "Chefs D'état: Des Plus Vieux Aux Plus Jeunes " *Jeune Afrique*, March 11, 2007.

12. M. Diouf, "Urban Youth and Senegalese Politics: Dakar 1988-1994," in *Cities and Citizenship*, ed. J. Holston (Durham & London: Duke University Press, 1999), 42.

13. B. hooks cited in S.J. Smith, "Beyond Geography's Visible Worlds: A Cultural Politics of Music." *Progress in Human Geography* 21, no. 4 (1997): 503.

14. J.F. Mbaye, "A Hip-hop Space of Politics in France," in *Culture and the City*, ed. L. Nyströom and F. Eckardt (Berlin: Berliner Wissenschaftsverlag, 2009), 398.

15. P. Zumthor, "The Impossible Closure of the Oral Text," *Yale French Studies* 67 (1984): 15.

16. R. Barthes, *Mythologies* (London: Vintage, New Ed., 1993), 109.

17. *Ibid.*, 110.

18. K.R. Scherer, "Expression of Emotion in Voice and Music," *Journal of Voice* 9, no. 3 (1995): 246.

19. Zumthor, "The Impossible Closure of the Oral Text," 25.
20. Smith, "Beyond Geography's Visible Worlds," 522.
21. H. Bazin, "Hip-Hop: Le Besoin D'une Nouvelle Médiation Politique," *Mouvements* 11, no. La Découverte (2000): 44.
22. Shusterman, "Art Infraction," 273.
23. A further discussion on the roles of DJ and MC can be found in J.F. Mbaye, "A Hip-hop Space of Politics in France," 400
24. This is an original graphic model extracted from the theoretical framework developed by the author.
25. For more detailed information, please consult: http://www.aurahiphop.com/
26. This expression has been suggested by the Senegalese pioneer hip-hop artist, Didier Awadi, to describe his work.
27. See Wikipedia entry "activism," http://en.wikipedia.org/wiki/Activism
28. F. Howes, *Man, Mind and Music* (London: Seeker & Warburg, 1949), 169.
29. This campaign of awareness was initiated as well as supported by the NGO Plan International and structured around an album, a musical comedy and multiple concerts and workshops throughout the West African region
30. L. Sandercock, *Towards Cosmopolis: Planning for Multicultural Cities* (Chichester: John Wiley & Sons, 1998) 110.
31. C. Calhoun cited in D. Ley, "Transnational Spaces and Everyday Lives," *Transactions - Institute of British Geographers* 29 (2004): 162.
32. M. P. Smith, *Transnational Urbanism: Locating Globalization* (Oxford: Blackwell Publishing, 2003) 150-2.
33. *Ibid.*, 11
34. H.K. Bhabha, *The Location of Culture* (London & New-York: Routledge, 2004) 348.
35. *Ibid.*, 306
36. Smith, *Transnational Urbanism*, 135
37. *Ibid.*, 516
38. Listen to Smockey, " qui profite le crime" – song in one of his album that suffered from governmental censorship and thus was not released. But also Didier Awadi's songs "J'accuse" and "Stoppez-

les" in Staycalm! "Fangafrika: La Voix Des Sans Voix - Rap Made in West Africa." Paris: Harmonia Mundi, 2007, CD-DVD.

39. Listen to the Nigerien female rapper, Zarra Moussa known as ZM's last album, "Kirari"; and ALIF (Attaque Libératoire de l'Infanterie Féminine), Senegalese female hip-hop collective's song "Douta Mbaye" *Ibid.*

40. Listen to the Malian collective Tata Pound's track "Mon Pays S.A." *Ibid.*

41. D. Awadi, "Le Cri Du Peuple" in *Sunugaal* (CD): Radio France Internationale, 2007.

42. This translation is suggested by the author.

43. See the video of the song at http://www.awadimusic.com/

44. See the video of the song at http://blog.myspace.com/index.cfm? fuseaction=blog.view&friendID=172648791&blogID=344301313

45. B. Latour, "What If We Talked Politics a Little?" *Contemporary Political Theory*, no. 2 (2003): 145.

46. M. Saward, "Enacting Democracy" *Political Studies* 51 (2003): 174.

bibliography

Agence Nationale de Statistique et de la Démographie. "Année 2006." In *Situation économique et sociale de la région de Dakar*. Dakar, Sénégal: Service Régional de la Statistique et Démographie (SRSD) de Dakar, 2007.

Awadi, D. "Le Cri Du Peuple." In *Sunugaal*: Radio France Internationale, 2007.

Barthes, R. *Mythologies*. London: Vintage, New Ed., 1993.

Bazin, H. "Hip-Hop: Le Besoin D'une Nouvelle Médiation Politique." In *Mouvements* 11, no. La Découverte (2000): 39-45.

Bhabha, H. K. *The Location of Culture*. London & New-York: Routledge, 2004.

Diouf, M. "Urban Youth and Senegalese Politics: Dakar 1988-1994." In *Cities and Citizenship*, edited by J. Holston. Durham & London: Duke University Press, 1999.

Howes, F. *Man, Mind and Music*. London: Seeker & Warburg, 1949.

Institut National de la Statistique et de la Démographie. In *Tableau de bord social du Burkina Faso* Ministère de l'Économie et du Développement, Burkina Faso, Secrétariat Général, 2005.

——. In *Analyse des résultats de l'enquête annuelle sur les conditions de vie des ménages et du suivi de la pauvreté en 2005*. Ouagadougou: Ministère de l'Économie et du Développement, Burkina Faso, Section Unité – Progrès – Justice, EA/QUIBB 2005.

Kodjo-Grandvaux, S. "Chefs D'etat: Des Plus Vieux Aux Plus Jeunes," *Jeune Afrique*, 11 Mars 2007 2007.

Krims, A. *Music and Urban Geography*. New York: Routledge, Taylor & Francis Group, 2007.

Latour, B. "What If We Talked Politics a Little?," *Contemporary Political Theory*, no. 2 (2003): 143-64.

Ley, D. "Transnational Spaces and Everyday Lives," *Transactions - Institute of British Geographers* 29 (2004).

Mbaye, J. F. "A Hip-hop Space of Politics in France," in *Culture and the City*, edited by L. Nyströom and F. Eckardt, 395-416. Berlin Berliner Wissenschaftsverlag, 2009.

Sandercock, L. *Towards Cosmopolis: Planning for Multicultural Cities*. Chichester: John Wiley & Sons, 1998.

Saward, M. "Enacting Democracy," *Political Studies* 51 (2003): 161-79.

Scherer, K.R. "Expression of Emotion in Voice and Music," *Journal of Voice* 9, no. 3 (1995).

R. Shusterman, "Art Infraction: Goodman, Rap, Pragmatism," *Australian Journal of Philosophy* 73, no. 2 (1995): 269-79.

Smith, M.P. *Transnational Urbanism: Locating Globalization*. Oxford: Blackwell Publishing, 2003.

Smith, S.J. "Beyond Geography's Visible Worlds: A Cultural Politics of Music." *Progress in Human Geography* 21, no. 4 (1997): 502-29.

Staycalm! "Fangafrika: La Voix Des Sans Voix - Rap Made in West Africa." Paris: Harmonia Mundi, 2007.

Throsby, D. "The Music Industry in the New Millennium: Global and Local Perspectives." In *The Global Alliance for Cultural Diversity*. Paris: Division of Arts and Cultural Enterprise, UNESCO, 2002.

Zumthor, P. "The Impossible Closure of the Oral Text," *Yale French Studies* 67 (1984).

CHAPTER 4
jua cali-justice[1]: navigating the mainstream-under-ground dichotomy in kenyan hip-hop culture

CAROLINE MOSE **introduction**

Hip-hop culture is found virtually everywhere in various forms and adaptations. It is the commercialization of rap music as the culture developed into a multi-billion industry that first started the underground/mainstream dichotomy in hip-hop scholarship and discourse. In the 1980s, as the market potential of hip-hop was recognized due to its large following,[2] and as record labels in the U.S. started to cash in on the boldness and form of expression in hip-hop,[3] rap colonies in the East and West Coasts of America emerged, engaging in active competition that further fuelled album sales.

This American history is important to highlight, because many hip-hop scholars have, and continue to use it to analyze African hip-hop. African hip-hop, like North American hip-hop, is considered to have been established in the ghettos and slums of urban cities mainly to speak out against bad governance, police brutality, poverty, and crime. Over a period of time, African hip-hop is seen as having followed the commercialization route of its North American counterpart, resulting in and cementing the conscious/underground-mainstream/commercial dichotomy. A short discussion of these dichotomies is in order here.

Mainstream rap is said to be rap that is largely made for purely commercial purposes. This means that it is market-driven, made to suit a certain demographic within society (Ro 1996; Armstrong 2001). According to Philip Mwaniki, entertainment writer for a leading Kenyan daily newspaper, mainstream rap "gives the people what they want." Uganda-based Kenyan hip-hop producer Nik Punk is quick to note that 'what people want' is actually determined by media, namely, radio and television. Thus, creating a certain 'taste' in audiences. In many cases, it is usually North American popular music from MTV and other foreign music sources that determine one's aesthetic taste or disposition; music that is often littered with discourses of defiance, violence, and misogyny (Armstrong 2001: 1-5). For instance, Snoop Dogg's single "Sexual Eruption,"[4] a highly explicit song, was popular in Kenya.

In contrast, conscious/underground rap is said to be socially conscious. Keyes describes the underground as "[h]ip-hop music outside the general commercial canon...the term almost exclusively associated with independent artists, signed to small independent labels or no label at all... characterized by having more socially conscious, positive or anti-commercial lyrics than the mainstream (2004: 336)." In other words, many see underground hip-hop as not being beholden to the "sexist, misogynist, patriarchal ways of thinking...a reflection of the prevailing values in society...created and sustained by white supremacist capitalist patriarchy (hooks 1994: 116)." Its political and provoking content are mainly the reasons given for its lack of presence in the mainstream media.

It is evident that the definitions of underground and mainstream are made with specific reference to North American hip-hop. However, African hip-hop is increasingly being cast in a similar mould (Haupt 2003; Englert 2003; Kuenzler 2006; Casco 2006; Barkley 2007). For instance, Englert reports that in Tanzania, underground hip-hop artists sing a music with a "serious message (2003: 81)," while mainstream artists only sing about "the sunny side of life." Barkley (2007: 13-14) mistakenly equates American gangsta/mainstream rap to Kenya's *genge*,[5] setting her paper on a biased tangent that implies all non-underground hip-hop in Kenya is gangsta or *genge.* This commercialized/mainstream vs. conscious/underground dichotomy could be explained by the seemingly undeniable influence that North American hip-hop has on African hip-hop, the latter of which has many times been seen as inauthentic and merely copying the North American form due to the surface similarities between them. As a result, a North American analysis has been used, to a large extent, to analyze African hip-hop culture. Currently, the study of hip-hop culture in Africa is being approached from these two distinct perspectives, with the culture itself and its music, that of rap, being classified as either mainstream or underground.

My argument in this chapter is that the underground/mainstream dichotomy has, in many ways, robbed the analysis of African hip-hop culture of its broad nuances and complexities. While not denying that there is a difference between political rap and non-political rap in the classical sense, it is no longer tenable to simply approach African hip-hop in this manner while ignoring the several shades of grey in between. These shades of grey have been overlooked in the analysis of hip-hop culture even though they continue to shape the culture in both political and social ways. The mainstream/underground dichotomy has also boxed artists in categories that do not reflect the fluidity that is characteristic of African hip-hop cultures that are flourishing and still growing. Using specific examples from my current research on Kenyan hip-hop culture, I problematize and critique the blanket use of "mainstream" and "underground," first by approaching my analysis from two perspectives- the artist; and the message, or lyrical content of music. I then proceed to briefly discuss the "shades of grey" in Kenyan hip-hop culture, giving the example of religious hip-hop, and conclude by suggesting that the mainstream-underground classification be put aside for a more nuanced analysis of the culture that reflects its current reality.

artist and identity: fluidity and crossover

While hip-hop artists are generally identified as either mainstream or underground, a closer look at the culture in Africa reveals a high level of fluidity in both genre and artist. Thus, making it hard to pin them down as either/or. This fluidity raises three main questions.

First, the question becomes whether the dichotomy refers to hip-hop artists or hip-hop music- it is my observation that these are usually mutually exclusive categories. For example, the artist Jua Cali is considered a mainstream Kenyan hip-hop artist, but has done music that can be classified as both mainstream and/or underground in the classical sense.[6] Some of his music, however, cannot be classified as either/or. For instance, his song "Bidii Yangu" is about his personal effort over the years as a struggling musician and his rise to where he is now. In the second verse and the chorus he says:

Nimewacha sana watu wengi wakule, raundi ii niacheni pia mi ninone	*I have allowed other people to succeed, this time it's my turn to do so*
Safari yangu ingepeleka mbio lakini nimeamua kuenda polepole	*My journey would have been fast, but I have decided to take it slow*
Usifikirie nimechoka niko na nguvu ka zile ngombe nyi uona mtaani	*Don't think I am tired, I am as strong as the oxen you see in your neighbour-hood*

Stachoka kutafuta majani, stachoka kuendelea na safari	*I will never get tired of searching for greener pasture, I will never tire of this journey*
Wacha mguu zangu zitembee, wasanii wote wa nguvu wapepee	*Let me explore all I can, let all skilled artists succeed*
Kimaisha na kila kitu unafanya ni bidii na ukifika paali unataka	*In life, and in all you do, work hard and you will achieve all you desire*
Nataka tuu furaha yako	*I want you to be happy for me*
Nataka tuu heshima yako	*I want you to respect me*
Ndio ujue mahali bidii yangu imetoka	*So that you appreciate where all my hard work comes from*

But in "Kiasi,"[7] Jua Cali moves away from issues of personal identity and makes social commentary on a wide range of issues. For instance, in the second verse he speaks about a corrupt and brutal police force;

Watu jana walinishika ikabidi niwaachie yao (kiasi)	*Yesterday I was arrested by the police, and I had to bribe them*
Beste yangu akaanza kubishana nao akanyamazishwa na mambao (kiasi)	*My friend started to argue, and was slapped severally into silence*
Ei, chali yangu, ujaaiskia maneno ya hao watu hawana huruma hata (kiasi)	*Eh, my friend, haven't you heard, those police do not have even a little mercy*

While in the third and last verse, Jua Cali makes commentary about general issues;

Naskia raha sku hizi ngoma mbaya hazichezwi hata (kiasi)	*I am happy that these days, terrible music is not even played a little on radio*
Pia naskia raha unaeza chinjia manzi hata kaa ni mzee wako (kiasi)	*I am also happy that these days, one can woo a woman even if she is a little older*
Kabla niende kumwona lazma nipige nguo pasi na nijipake mafuta (kiasi)	*Before I go to see her, I have to iron my clothes and apply a little oil on my face*

"Kiasi" covers "serious" issues like police brutality and "lighter" subjects like a man wooing an older woman. It becomes difficult to pin down Jua Cali into a "mainstream" or "underground" category based on the content of his music. Jua Cali and his music are not the only examples to demonstrate this fluidity.

The song "Justice" by Mwafrika and Muki Garang, both considered underground artists, does the same. The first verse is introspective, urging listeners to look into themselves first before blaming anyone else for the challenges they face. But in the third verse, Mwafrika turns to a corrupt justice system, making reference to the 2005 Kenya referendum on the Constitution of Kenya. Moving from the introspective, the song takes a swipe at Amos Wako, Kenya's Attorney General. The presence of this top attorney in a corrupt system is problematized in the second verse and a reference to Lord Delamere is made[8] and with it, a highly political critique of the hierarchical system that Kenya is notorious for, where the wealthy are able buy justice, making it irrelevant and unfair to the poor. The references to the innocent languishing in jail awaiting trial is characteristic of the Kenyan justice system, where murder suspects can spend upwards of five years awaiting trial, while the case against Lord Delamere's grandson was quickly hurried through the courts.[9] Ndingi Mwana'anzeki is mentioned here as a cleric who, during his tenure, used his position as Archbishop in the Catholic Church to lambast corrupt leaders and governments. Before his retirement, Mwana'anzeki made inroads in the call for political reform and democracy in Kenya.

But, in the compilation "Mwafrika presents Muki Garang the Mixtape,"[10] Muki taunts certain artists;

> You thought you got it going on like Moktar Diop,
> But I stepped on the scene like the First Lady and
> made the party stop
> I leave you frustrated like a Kenyan cop
> If you test me thinking you got balls, I'm the dick on top

Moktar Diop was a former World Bank boss in Kenya, whose farewell party was stopped by the First Lady Lucy Kibaki, a neighbour of Diop, allegedly because there was too much noise being made at this party, depriving her of her peace and quiet.[11] Here, Muki equates himself to the powerful First Lady, and rival rap artists to Moktar Diop, warning them that he has enough clout to stop their "party" at will.

Strictly speaking, and in the classical sense, this is a *"dis"* track, where artists use songs in their albums to verbally attack other artists with whom they have real, imagined, or perceived differences. More robustly, this is an example of "hip-hop supremacy," where artists use arrogant tones to declare themselves superior to other artists using scatological language. This "hip-hop supremacy" is what Toop (2000: 29-34) and Githinji (2007: 89) call "the dozens," known as "sounding" or *mchongoano* in Sheng.[12] Kelley has suggested that the dozens are mainly intended to "get a laugh (2004: 128)," while Githinji argues that *mchongoano* is mainly used for socialization (2007: 93).

These arguments point to the "dis" as a practice within hip-hop as a tool of self-identity, competition, socialization, and comic relief. Ntarangwi (2000: 63) argues that the use of abusive language, what he terms as *"matukano,"* is a reference to masculine and social power displayed over competitors. Here, Muki uses a phallic reference, curiously portraying the "dick" as being superior to "balls." Ntarangwi (2000) argues that such phallic references aid in the construction of masculinity while, I would add, also demonstrates the tensions and anxieties that exist within that very masculine identity since Muki clearly directs his words at fellow male artists. These masculine-identity tensions constitute the superiority that artists seek to demonstrate over fellow artists.

Few scholars have outrightly classified the dozens as either a mainstream or underground practice, but it is accepted that they are a part of hip-hop culture worldwide. Nonetheless, the above lyrics here show the broad spectrum of issues that rap songs cover. Sometimes, one particular song may simultaneously cover subjects considered mainstream and underground. Similarly, an artist considered underground or mainstream may write and perform songs that are contrary to this labeling.

A second question concerning fluidity involves the economic and commercial aspects affecting artists. As mentioned, the commercialization of rap has been pointed out as the main distinguishing factor between the mainstream and underground. In the U.S., underground artists make modest sales of their albums to their respective niche markets. The underground artist Common for instance, sold 81,663 copies of his 2008 *Universal Mind Control* album in the first week of sales,[13] a modest figure compared to mainstream artist Kanye West's 957,000 first week sales (in the U.S. alone) of his 2007 *Graduation* album.[14] It is easy to see from these figures why the commercialization of rap and the gap between mainstream and underground continues to be a big deal, literally. Bottom line is that the nature of the industry in the U.S., together with its economy, makes it possible for hip-hop artists, whether mainstream or underground, to in the least earn an income from their art.

In Kenya, the story is different. Few artists live off their music. Many artists have day jobs that enable them to pay their bills. Fewer, like Jua Cali, are approached by corporations keen to use their popularity to sell products. Many more artists live austere lives in inner cities, the only places where they can afford the cost of living. This, according to Phillip Mwaniki, makes artists desperate to sing that one song that will get them notoriety so that they can escape poverty in these harsh economic times. Young upcoming artists look to Jua Cali's success and aim to replicate it, hoping to sign lucrative advertisement deals. Kuenzler (2006: 11-12) also points out that piracy in Africa continues to be a problem. Mwaniki asserts that pirates in Nairobi's River Road, a key business street, pocket millions of shillings every month from selling local music, hip-hop included. Pirated copies are usually lower quality, and much cheaper, meaning that legitimate copies of artist music remain unsold. On the one hand, Kuenzler confirms this when he says that "living from the sales of rap music is in Africa difficult...firstly the main public for this music, young people, hardly (have) any money to buy tapes or CDs. Secondly... cheap pirate copies can be found all over the continent (2006: 12)." Although made in 2006, this claim is still true today. On the other hand, Mwafrika points out that increasingly, artists in East Africa are making substantial money from live performances, both at home and on tours in the Diaspora. However, these are usually the more popular artists like Jua Cali, while younger, lesser-known artists still struggle to make ends meet.

These economic issues make it difficult to categorize artists within the established underground/mainstream dichotomy relevant to an established entertainment scene like that of the U.S. The need to survive and earn an income places Kenyan hip-hop artists in the cusp between "mainstream" and "underground," increasing the issues of fluidity. This means a larger number of artists are making catchy tunes that are easily played on the radio and in clubs. Hence, raising their profile and making them attractive to corporations willing to use them on television and billboard advertisements; or promoters willing to market them for live shows in the Diaspora. The mainstream/underground lines evidently become more difficult to draw in such circumstances, as musicians traverse different genres at different times to earn a living. An example here is Wenyeji's "Mizani," which begins

Ukoo Flani ndani ya lab na mizani, ukituona ndani ya club, samahani	*We, Ukoo Flani artists, go to the studio to create verses, but if later, you see us in the clubs, we apologize*

This is a telling start. Wenyeji are known as hardcore underground artists from the Ukoo Flani Mau Mau camp, with an unflinching political message. Indeed, "Mizani" itself is highly conscious;

Tupate kwa slums lazima tuwakilishe	When you find us in the slum, we represent
Jipate kwa show lazima ujulishwe ni Hip-hop, ni hii song haidistot hii single! (Ni nini?)	During our shows, we must tell you this is Hip-hop, it is this song, it does not distort its message (Then what is it?)
Ni legal, ni lethal ilivyo U.K-Double 'O', M.A.U Double	It is legal, it is lethal, it is Ukoo Flani Mau Mau

In the opening, Wenyeji acknowledge that they will have to create danceable tunes, something uncharacteristic of their reputation as hardcore-underground rappers. Indeed, "Mizani," Swahili for "verses," with its catchy tune and beats is considered "mainstream" due to its frequent airplay on mainstream radio and in clubs. However, an afternoon spent with Swaleh (Mwenyeji), one half of the duo, would reveal a deeply aware and socially conscious individual. This economic/artistic balance is usually not taken into account with a cut and dried mainstream/underground label.

The third question posed by this fluidity is best demonstrated by the "*collabo*." A *collabo* is a song done by more than one artist or group, usually as a collaboration. *Collabos* are increasingly common and are used mainly as a vehicle to break new artists into the market, or for an artist to reach an audience he most certainly would not be able to reach on his own. In many cases, *collabos* are done across musical genres. For instance, Kenyan pop and R&B artist Amani has done a *collabo* with the rapper Nyashinski of the group Kleptomaniax. The *collabo* allowed Amani access and acceptance amongst Kleptomaniax's fans and raised her profile substantially. It also raised Nyashinski's profile amongst Amani's pool of ardent fans. The artist Nameless, also a pop musician, did several *collabos* with the late E-Sir, one of Kenya's most gifted rappers. Newcomer Mejja has been made visible by featuring in Jua Cali's videos and songs, making him one of the most promising rap artists in the country today. These and many other kinds of *collabos*, some even done across national boundaries with artists performing traditional African forms of music like the coastal *taarab*, further blur the lines between the mainstream and underground, and continue to problematize both categories.

the message in the music

While the fundamental difference between underground and mainstream hip-hop artists is said to be ideological,[15] the most obvious difference, in general hip-hop discourse, is usually that of lyrical content, or the "message" in the music. Conscious hip-hop, also called "political rap" (Martinez 1997: 268-269) is said to have a serious message. This type of message is usually political, and in many cases, critical of structures of domination (Casco 2006; Kuenzler 2006; Haupt 2003). Kuenzler (See chapter two of this volume) documents the local adaptation of hip-hop culture in Mali and Burkina Faso and equates hip-hop movements in these countries to the development of civil society, defining civil society loosely as "the sphere between state and market, whereby state is founded on coercion, the market on competition and civil society on voluntary cooperation (2006: 3)." In this definition, Kuenzler places hip-hop culture in a decidedly political position where the culture, particularly its conscious rap, contributes to the formation of public opinion and serves to check the excesses of government and state. Conscious rap, he asserts, has lyrics that "reflect political and social problems (Kuenzler 2006: 5)."

Globally, conscious/message rap is usually associated with the early days of hip-hop culture. KRS One (2003: 193), together with Kool Herc, Afrika Bambaataa, and Grandmaster Flash (George 2004: 53-54) often speak of the "golden age of hip-hop," where much of the lyrical content of rap was socially conscious, that is, long before the commercialization of hip-hop produced "gangsta rap that only boasted about drugs, violence and sex (Kuenzler 2006: 5)." Kuenzler further stresses that gangsta rap "displays very little evidence of the hip-hop concept of knowledge of self and certainly makes no real attempt to engage critically with structures of domination (2006: 3)." The concept of self-knowledge for some artists is at the heart of hip-hop culture. For rap artist KRS One, knowledge of self is one of the pillars of hip-hop. Self-knowledge is the "idea that subjects need to achieve a significant level of self-awareness through a process of introspection so that they may engage critically with their reality (Haupt 2003: 2)." Gangsta rappers are said to lack self-awareness, a fact reflected in many of their lyrics.

Hip-hop cultures role of addressing societal challenges, while at the same time escaping the prevailing, hegemonic values and systems within that society, gives the culture a double-edged responsibility while placing upon it the burden of self awareness and self-knowledge without necessarily providing tools that aid artists towards that self-introspection. This, in my view, places undue pressure on artists indentified as "underground" to produce decidedly conscious music that engages with reality, where there is no clear expectation of what is "conscious." It also dismisses non-political artists to the periphery and classifies their music as irrelevant, unserious, and a product of mass culture. The result is an overly critical dismissal of so-called mainstream artists, and an equally non-critical acceptance of conscious/ underground artists.[16]

Consider Mashifta's "Majambazi," a song that directly attacks a corrupt political and social system in Kenya. Politicians, the police, and even religious leaders do not escape censure. The chorus is a summary of the song's point that;

Hii system ni ya majambazi, (magava, ma-minister, malawyer)	*This is a system of thugs (the police, cabinet ministers, lawyers)*
Na sisi vijana wa ghetto, majambazi	*And we, the young people in the ghetto, are thugs as well*
Askari wazazi	*And the police are our 'parents'(the source of corruption)*

These are obviously critical and politically conscious lyrics, typical of some underground artists like Girongi and MC Kah. Girongi's "Fyatua" shows a similar resentment for a corrupt Kenyan police. Girongi, who is considered a hardcore underground artist, starts the song by saying;

Hii ni dedication kwa msee yoyote anajua kutumia bunduki na hafanyi kazi kwa serikali...	*This song is a dedication to anyone who knows how to use a gun but does not work for any official government arm*

He then goes ahead to say,

Vidole trigger tunawawinda	*Finger on trigger, we hunt them*
Sisi ma-leader, sisi masoja nini wangoja?	*We, the leaders, we the soldiers, what are you waiting for?*
Chapa mafala, chomoka once	*Beat the idiots, take off quickly*
Hepa magava, dondoka mat	*Escape the police, jump off a moving matatu[17] if necessary*
Beba hiyo twanga akileta upuzi kanga huyo mbang'a...	*Carry that gun, and if that policeman brings nonsense, shoot him...*
Kila msee afyatue mbili kwa hewa	*Everyone, shoot twice in the air*
Fyatua, Fyatua, argh, argh, aaaargh!	*Shoot, Shoot, argh, argh, aaargh!*

It is said that during a performance of this song in Nairobi in February 2008, the crowd became so incensed the police had to be called to quell an impending riot. The concert was ended and the audience sent home.[18]

On the other hand, there is Flexx's "Nyundo," a song about sex. The song, featuring Jua Cali, begins with;

Nashindwa jo nizame wapi?	*I wonder, where am I going to enter?*
Nyundo yangu sasa itaua wapi?	*Where am I going to reach my sexual climax?*

Usiache ilale, we cheza nalo	*Do not let it sleep, you play with it*
Mpaka iseme jina zote zile unazo	*Until it cries out all your names*
Sijui nianze kusema vipi	*I really don't know where to start*
Wacha tu niseme uko fiti	*Let me just say, you are beautiful*
Kwanza venye umesimama mtoto	*In fact, the way you're looking beautiful, gal,*
Unafanya nashikwa na joto...	*You make me feel hot...*

Flexx uses the word "nyundo," which is Swahili for "hammer" as a metaphor for his manhood, ascribing to it the strength of the tool when put to work. He also uses the Swahili word "ua" which literally means to kill, but used here to mean "achieve a sexual climax." The very use of these euphemisms and metaphors in many ways makes the song implicit and "normal sounding," only allowing those who understand the colloquial manner of speech, plus the Sheng language, to understand exactly what he means. While some have argued that the song is obscene, it does not, for instance, have the same impact as Nonini's more explicit "Wee Kamu" which is a song that directly speaks about sex;

Leo niko kwa keja (kamu) stoki hapa	*Today, I am relaxing in my house (come), I am not going anywhere*
Kwa hivyo ukitakaa, wee kamu	*So, if you want some sex, just come over*

The aforementioned songs show the complexities of the "message" in both underground and mainstream hip-hop. Are Nonini and Flexx, both mainstream artists, merely misogynistic? Are Mashifta and Girongi, both affiliated with Ukoo Flani, a collection of underground hip-hop artists, merely critical of the status quo? Or do these songs illustrate a greater degree of nuance?

This becomes the first problem of the mainstream/underground dichotomy because it suggests that there are no other categories for hip-hop music. Even more problematic is that these labels rob the music of the benefit of a more critical analysis. For example, Nonini's "Wee Kamu" becomes analyzed from the point of view being "mainstream" and therefore, sexist, obscene, and gangsta. Approached from a more robust and critical point of view, "Wee Kamu" might be seen differently- as an attempt to bring the sensitive topic of sex into public discourse. As Nonini has repeatedly stated, people are having sex without necessarily being aware of the risks involved. Such risks, he maintains, include HIV infection, which continues to occur because the entire subject of sex is treated as taboo in Kenya.[19] Such a nuanced analysis has not been accorded "Wee Kamu" simply because the song has been relegated to the periphery of unserious, misogynistic, mainstream music. Even where critics of a song like "Wee Kamu" might disagree with its contents, nuanced critical debates over such kinds of lyrics do not follow simply because Nonini is tagged "mainstream" and thus dismissed. Interestingly, not many critics have lambasted "Nyundo," which is actually more sexually detailed than "Wee Kamu," demonstrating that the use of language in underground hip-hop has also been glossed over without deeper analysis.

Secondly, this dichotomy suggests that all underground music is political and that non-political music can only be mainstream and commercial; that any rap music with women as the core subject is decidedly misogynistic, sexist, and patriarchal. This is not necessarily the case. On the one hand, a non-political song like "Kiasi," which is considered mainstream, can be heard as providing insightful commentary about society. On the other hand, a politically-charged song can go overboard and erode its own usefulness in terms of its "message." Girongi's "Fyatua" for instance encourages the illegal use of firearms.[20] While it comments on the gross abuse of power and extra-judicial killings by the police in the inner city of Nairobi, it is nevertheless composed in the language of violence while still being considered underground and conscious. In the same vein, a song with a clear message can lose the "message" in its wording. Consider Circuit and Jo-el's song "Juala," a song intent on warning audiences about the dangers of unprotected sex;

eh! Naongea kuhusu manyake na sizile za butcha	*Eh, I am talking about 'meat', but not that sold at the butchery*
Manyake zikipita mtu anakula kucha	*When that 'meat' passes by, one bites his nails with longing*
si unajua zile zime fura?	*You know the plump ones I am talking about*
Kama zako hazijafura enda Father's ukule mutura	*If yours are not plump, go to Father's and eat some meat*
alafu ungojee pengine watu wataku-piga kura	*You are not my type but maybe someone else will fancy you*
manyake mtu ana'eza ziworship	*I tell you, those hips and buttocks can be worshipped*
Manyake all sizes, manyake kama prizes	*Hips and buttocks, all sizes, hips and buttocks like prizes*
Manyake kama balloon zina maji	*Hips and buttocks like balloons full of water*
Juala ndio wahitaji	*You must use a condom*

By equating women's hips and bottoms to "meat," the song "Juala," Sheng for "polythene bag" or condom, loses its meaning, and even becomes offensive.[21] Despite being a song with a message, that is, warning audiences about unsafe sex, it ends up being misogynistic due to its constant references to women as objects that are fought over and used, albeit with a condom. It even goes as far as telling women who are not well-endowed to go and eat so that they get some curves that will make them popular. This song reflects a male reality in conversation. While showing a societal reality of Kenya, the song also reveals the highly phallocratic and sexist manner in which men view women and their bodies.

The third issue with the dichotomy concerns the "message" and what it means. Does it mean something positive? If so, what determines it? Does analysis of the message only apply to the content of the song or does it also apply to the artist? At the heart of hip-hop culture is the hip-hop artist who does not exist in a vacuum, but within a society that directly influences his/her processes of thought. As pointed out, most artists live in the inner city of Nairobi, where crime, violence, and poverty are a reality. The question then extends to whether the argument that this violence and crime is justified in being articulated in hip-hop music as it is the "reality" or the "real" in hip-hop music; and whether that articulation is mainstream or underground.

"Keeping it real" is an occurring theme in hip-hop music, and has been used invariably to mean staying true to yourself and speaking the truth. It has also been used as a yardstick with which mainstream music is dismissed as not engaging critically with society's structures of domination. While a discussion of societal structures of domination and hegemony are not the subjects of this chapter, my argument here is that the overall assumption that "the real" in hip-hop includes messages alluding to hardship, poverty, and crime is erroneous. Kelley problematizes the representation and construction of the inner city as a "reservoir of pathologies and bad cultural values (2004: 120)." This construction, he argues, is the reason why urban cultures like hip-hop are reduced to being "expressions of pathology, compensatory behavior, or creative "coping mechanisms" to deal with racism and poverty (Kelley 2004: 120)." Staples (1995) makes a similar argument when he states "the most dangerous myth...is that... only poverty and suffering, and the rage that attends them, are real (78), rubbishing the 'magical nobility somehow conferred on the dispossessed (79)." This has been a prevalent notion in African hip-hop scholarship. The idea is that authentic hip-hop or one that "keeps it real," is one that speaks as a "voice of the people (Casco 2006: 1)," and against societal ills (Haupt 2003: 2-3). This implies that true hip-hop artists and true hip-hop music must out of necessity be poor and ghetto. As a result, denying African societies of the nuances of class and culture by implying that Africans exist in two main classes that are in constant battle, that is, the rich/powerful and the poor/marginalized. Further, classifying hip-hop artists within these two parameters that are similar to the mainstream/underground dichotomy means that artist upward mobility economically automatically robs them of authenticity as it catapults them from the poor to the rich, an assumption that is erroneous as it is incredible.

Kelley reminds us that urban cultures do not have one singular identity, and practitioners of these cultures are not "cardboard typologies (2004: 120)," but demonstrate varying levels of complexities and hybridities. He further states that urban cultures are also expressions of pleasure.

Hip-hop culture was birthed during block parties where members of respective neighborhoods would converge to drink, dance, and have fun (Chang 2006: 67-68). The main aim of these parties, many times held outdoors in parks during the summer, was simply for people to have fun, interact, dress up, and show off. George (2004: 51) explains that rappers felt the need to dress up because their audiences were paying up to ten dollars to enter these parties to watch them perform. These accounts, given by the founding fathers of hip-hop,[22] mean that at its foundation, hip-hop culture was not necessarily a "message culture," but one in which its practitioners found some source of relief and suspension from the harshness of everyday reality where violent gangs controlled the inner city of New York. Without suggesting that hip-hop culture was merely an adaptive culture used only as a means of escape from harsh ghetto life, it is obvious that the assumption that "real hip-hop," or hip-hop that "keeps it real" is the kind that only articulates these harsh realities; while delegating all other forms of hip-hop into a "mainstream" is erroneous.

Obviously, the development of hip-hop culture and its establishment in the inner cities places it in a space where it articulates the realities of life- including that of violence and crime- but must also be allowed to articulate pleasure and joy. The latter spheres especially must not be overlooked. Mashifta's "Majambazi," Girongi's "Fyatua," Mwafrika and Muki's "Justice" and Jua Cali's "Kiasi" all articulate these realities, albeit in different ways. The tone in each song vary from the political to the playful. As Light (2004: 144) argues, hip-hop music is, by definition, political, whether explicitly or implicitly, as it gives voice to under-represented and many times silent communities. Equally, Mwafrika points out that "Hip-hop is hip-hop simply because it is provocative, controversial and non-conformist."

All of the aforementioned songs demonstrate these qualities, and qualify, simply as hip-hop music. This is not to suggest that hip-hop is monolithic, but then neither is it dichotomous. Hip-hop music is varied both in style, content, and purpose. Below, I discuss at least two different styles of hip-hop music in Kenya that demonstrates the irrelevance of the mainstream/ underground dicotomy in hip-hop culture by revealing "shades of grey" between them.

shades of grey: alternative hip-hop styles and nuanced classifications

Hip-hop's founding fathers- DJ Kool Herc, Afrika Bambaataa and Grandmaster Flash- have called the mainstream-unserious/ underground-real classifications of hip-hop "ignorant (George 2004: 50)." According to DJ Kool Herc, hip-hop has different forms and feels- some soft, some hard, insisting that it is about "experimenting and being open (George 2004: 5)." While lamenting the shift in focus within hip-hop cultures from community to the self (George 2004: 54), they nevertheless agree that hip-hop culture has a variety of forms that cannot be confined to the mainstream/underground dichotomy. North American hip-hop artist Mos Def, considered a "conscious" rapper, is also on record as having said of the mainstream/underground dichotomy;

They've got their little categories, like 'conscious' and 'gangsta'...that's just some more white folks trying to think that all niggas are alike...it used to be one type of nigga; now its two. There is much more dimension to who we are...the real joy is when you can kick it with everyone. That's what hip-hop is all about...[23]

            – Mos Def (2003)

Speaking as hip-hop artists, they introduce an argument that has largely been ignored by many hip-hop researchers and scholars-one that critiques this dichotomy, and even calls for it to be set aside altogether. Kenyan hip-hop artists Mwafrika and Jua Cali[24] have expressed similar sentiments. Jua Cali insists that he has never called himself "underground" or "mainstream," but has been tagged "mainstream" by writers and other artists. Mwafrika maintains that this dichotomy has long been the invention of radio presenters who have used the name "underground" to mean "music they do not personally enjoy," meaning that "mainstream music," played on radio, meant music acceptable to presenters' tastes. He further says that the term "underground" has also been used by media and radio audiences to mean "people that don't like other forms of popular music in Kenya like *genge* or *kapuka*.[25]

The mention of *genge* and *kapuka* begins a discussion into how popular music, including hip-hop, is classified. Names like these continue to be used and misused in describing Kenyan and African music. For instance, some artists and audiences have argued that Jua Cali himself is not a hip-hop artist, but a *genge* musician. On pressing some to say what they mean by this, they loosely claim that "*genge* is not hip-hop." However, Jua Cali and other artists who identify themselves as *genge* artists claim that the name "genge," which translates into "music for the masses," was created in order to give Kenyan hip-hop music a distinct identity, much the way *kwaito* conjures up a South African identity (Mose 2009: 4). This illustrates the many layers of complexity in the various types of hip-hop sounds that DJ Kool Herc speaks about. When those sounds are translocated from the U.S. and assimilated into various African cultures and contexts (Wa Mungai 2008: 282), the result is a myriad of different forms that make up hip-hop culture, which normally get lost between the mainstream and underground.

Jua Cali suggests that in Kenya, hip-hop music can loosely be classified as "political," "social," and "something in between." Social hip-hop speaks on more general societal issues, while political hip-hop speaks from a space of a more hard-line political standpoint. Kalamashaka's "Angalia Saa" for instance has a singular stance that critiques the seeming marginalization of freedom fighters and political heroes, most of whom die in abject poverty;

Damu, jasho, machozi,	*Blood, sweat and tears*
Mau Mau wakashinda war, mashedi wakaenda na trophy,	*The Mau Mau won the nation's independence but homeguards and collaborators were rewarded for it*
Mtu anatusi matiti ya mother alinyo-nya, alafu anapigiwa makofi za kilo?	*How can a man despise his mother's breast where he suckled, and then get applause?*
Wa-shoot, Muthoni...the same root wa-rape mama yetu Njeeri, hii sini betrayal ya ma-hero?	*They shot Muthoni...and raped Njeeri our mother- isn't that a betrayal of our heroes?*

The lyrics, beginning with saying that the Mau Mau freedom fighters achieved independence but were relegated to the margins of power sets the stage for a stinging critique of governance in the country. They go as far as rebuking the attackers of writer Ngugi wa Thiong'o's[26] wife Njeeri, expressing their outrage and using the incident as an example of the blatant disdain of heroes in Kenya.

On the other hand, Mashifta's "Majambazi" and Mwafrika and Muki's "Justice" straddles both the political and the social, as does Jua Cali's "Kiasi" and "Bidii Yangu." What Jua Cali suggests here is not the application of rigid dichotomies, but on a more general, case-by-case analysis of content that falls under the umbrella of hip-hop. He further acknowledges, as I have argued, that many hip-hop songs cover many topics at once, and that many artists produce different content over time. Using himself as an example, Jua Cali says that an artist cannot, for instance, paint the same picture repeatedly, but will paint "a lion today, a building tomorrow, and a woman the next."

The artist Madd Traxx, for instance, does social commentary in a musical style akin to that of *crunk*, a hip-hop style that has emerged from the southern U.S. that is characterized by a rapping technique that is much slower than that of classic rap.[27] One of Madd Traxx's popular songs gives commentary about a group of young people who have "borrowed" a parent's car in order to go out on the town. These young people drink away all their money and leave only a little to fuel the car for a ride home. On the way back, a policeman stops them and asks for the driver's license. The driver, Madd Traxx, has none, and is compelled to surrender his fuel money as a bribe to the policeman to prevent himself from being arrested, leaving the entire bunch stranded in the middle of nowhere. Madd Traxx, recounting this dilemma, proceeds to ask in typical hip-hop call-and-response pattern "*utado war*" ("what can one do in such a situation"), whereupon his audience responds "*utaride bodaboda*" (one can only afford to take a bodaboda[28]). The song is a funny rendition of the use of the bodaboda form of transportation in Kenya, but ends up making commentary about corrupt police and the folly of young people bent on driving a car without a license. This *crunk* style of rapping is gaining popularity among artists and audiences in Kenya, together with independent rap (indie rap) that does not necessarily follow the rules of classic rap. For instance, rapping speeds are reduced; artists might do poetic narrations accompanied by background beats; or artists might actually mix singing with rapping. These are all independent forms of hip-hop music that are not being considered in classic hip-hop scholarship that is cast within a mainstream/underground framework.

Another form of hip-hop that has been ignored is religious or gospel hip-hop. In Kenya, gospel rap is now very popular. Artists like Juliani, Hey-Z, Astar, and Michelle continue to make albums that are well received. Juliani, a former member of Ukoo Flani Mau Mau, now a Christian, states "gospel is not my genre, gospel is the message, my genre is hip-hop." He says that through hip-hop culture and music, he is able to pass on a certain message to his audience which consists mainly of young people. He insists that what he practices is hip-hop, only that his message is different in the sense that it is religious. However, he is quick to say that he is not a preacher, but a hip-hop artist with a unique message bent on provoking thought. Hip-hop, he says, is about rapping styles, music production, mixing of beats and performance, attributes he shares with fellow hip-hop artists. A closer look at his music reveals a high level of vocal prowess. His song "Hela" for instance is quite thought provoking;

Wanaweka trust kwa hela Chumvi kwa chai sukari kwa chakula	*Those that place their trust in money Are like them that add salt to tea and sugar to stew*
Mse msoto analia njaa sonko ana complain obesity	*A poor man complains of hunger, while a rich man worries about being obese*
Okay uko sensitive kila picha una negative	*So sensitive, like developing a negative copy of a picture*
Shida huezi hata hata uwe actor wa matrix	*You won't escape problems, even if you were an actor in the movie 'The Matrix'*
Circumstances nje ya circumference ya God	*Living a life outside God's special boundaries*
Sambamba naku vaa vest kwa ma Eskimo	*Is like an Eskimo walking around the Pole wearing nothing but a vest*

Obviously, Juliani here makes a statement about people who are wealthy without having a spiritual anchor. He equates them to fools using clever word play and metaphor. His message is clearly religious- that those who are rich and have placed their trust in their wealth are only lying to themselves. However, he also uses popular culture signifiers like many hip-hop artists- in this case, the movie "The Matrix" in which main character Neo develops special abilities, which allow him to perform incredulous acts. Juliani states that even a superhero like Neo cannot avoid problems in real life, regardless of how wealthy he is. While Juliani and other upcoming hip-hop artists have been looked down on by the traditional church, new churches like Mavuno Dome, a Nairobi church patronized by the youth, continue to support these artists. For example, Juliani launched his album *Mtaa Mentality*[29] at the Mavuno Dome[30], with support from hip-hop artists like Wenyeji, who have also done a collabo with Juliani called "Something More." This means that hip-hop can have a religious message that has been ignored by many researchers because it does not fit within the underground/mainstream classification. Further, the issues raised in this chapter also apply to religious hip-hop, including the issue of artist cross-over and *collabos*. Juliani has done *collabos* with Wenyeji, a non-religious "underground" hip-hop group, with support from Ukoo Flani Mau Mau and Jua Cali, who are both considered "mainstream." Here, the lines between underground, mainstream and other hip-hop forms merge and disappear into what Mwafrika simply calls, hip-hop. In Tate's words (1995: 19), "there is no such thing as good hip-hop or bad hip-hop, progressive hip-hop or reactionary hip-hop, politically incorrect hip-hop or hip-hop with a message. It's either hip-hop or it ain't. Shit."

conclusion

Kenyan hip-hop has come a long way since the culture was established in the country in the early to mid-1990s. To date, Kenyan hip-hop can boast its own authentic identity, and equally boast a history of growth and development that is unique to Kenya. Currently, there are many hip-hop artists and crews across the country, and across genres.

In this chapter, I have argued that the mainstream/underground dichotomy, which is widely popular in hip-hop studies, is problematic particularly in the Kenyan context for a number of reasons, including the fluidity of artist and content across genres; economic tensions of artists; the *collabo*; and the problematic of the "message." I have also briefly discussed the non-specificity of the terms "underground" and "mainstream," showing that they may mean different things in different contexts, and as such, become unreliable in understanding hip-hop culture and its music. I then alluded to the "shades of grey" that lie between the underground and mainstream, paying particular attention to alternative hip-hop musical genres like gospel hip-hop.

I conclude by reiterating that African hip-hop and specifically Kenyan hip-hop can no longer be broadly classified in terms of mainstream or underground. A more nuanced and robust analysis of the culture and its music is required, including a keen interest in emerging, alternative forms of hip-hop music, such as gospel and alternative rap. In the end, transcending these traditional classifications will offer a more balanced analysis and more in-depth and nuanced understanding of hip-hop culture which, with its socio-political reach is arguably, the largest of urban cultures in Africa and indeed, worldwide.

notes

1. *Jua Cali* is the name of a popular hip-hop artist. His name is a euphemism for a Swahili word for 'hot sun', which denotes the Kenyan informal business sector populated mainly by medium to low-income earners. *Justice* is the name of a rap song by hip-hop artists Mwafrika and Muki Garang. This title is an interplay between the underground-mainstream dichotomy, the subject of

this chapter, as Jua Cali is considered "mainstream," and the latter "underground." A big "thank you" to Mwafrika for his invaluable assistance in rendering the song lyrics correctly.

2. By this time, hip-hop had spread outside the U.S., with emerging audiences in Africa and Europe.

3. Hip-hop's "boldness" came from its frank and often explicit lyrics in all its subject matter.

4. Played on the radio as "Sexual Seduction" from the Snoop Dogg album *Ego Trippin.*

5. Genge has mistakenly been defined as Kenyan commercial rap, or Kenya's gangsta alternative. Genge is the Swahili word for "a group of people." The name was coined by the producer Clemo of Calif Records in Nairobi, together with the artist Jua Cali. Jua Cali explains that Clemo and he coined the word in order to give Kenyan hip-hop a unique and distinctive identity. The name "hip-hop," he says, conjures up an image of North American gangsta music, something he sought to distance Kenyan hip-hop from by giving it a local name and a local identity.

6. Here I mean that mainstream hip-hop is characterized by non-political, sexist, and even misogynistic themes, while underground hip-hop is characterized by political, socially conscious, counter-hegemonic themes.

7. "Kiasi" is a song that has the Swahili word "kiasi," meaning "a little bit" as the *kiitikio*, or rejoinder, where the singer's (or in this case, rapper's) every line is answered by the word "kiasi." Jua Cali makes statements in each line that are answered by the word 'kiasi' in a poem-format.

8. The Lord Delamere's Grandson Tom Cholmondeley who owns vast tracts of land in Kenya's Rift Valley has been to court twice for allegedly killing two black Kenyans- the first victim's case, a Kenya Wildlife Service guard, did not make trial due to what Amos Wako called a lack of evidence. It is this case that Mwafrika refers to here, echoing public sentiment that the Delamere kin got off simply because he is a wealthy man.

9. See Vasager, Jeevan 'Gun Killing that divides the Rift Valley' in The Observer, Sunday May 8th 2005.

10. See a review of the Mixtape on the Greamhouze blog, July 23rd 2006 entry here http://greamhouze.blogspot.com/2006/07/mwaf-rika-presents-muki-garang-mixtape.html accessed 29th August 2009

11. See Kenya's First Lady at it Again, Afrol News, 13th December 2007 at http://www.afrol.com/articles/27519 Accessed on 29th August 2009

12. Sheng is the name, derived from "Swahili-English," of the slang tongue spoken in the urban areas of Kenya. It is said to have originated in the inner cities of Nairobi, and it continues to be the lingua franca of urban youth and of hip-hop culture in Kenya. See Githiora (2002), Githinji (2006, 2007, 2008) and Samper (2002, 2004) for their interesting analyses of the origin, types and uses of Sheng in Nairobi. Samper's writing especially, gives interest-ing analysis of how hip-hop artists, using Sheng, become cultural brokers of society.

13. See http://www.hip-hopindex.com/index/news/id.8366/title.hip-hop-album-sales-the-week-ending-1-4-09 accessed 23rd August 2009.

14. Christman, Ed (11th September 2009). "Early Sales Projections Put Kanye Ahead Of 50, Chesney". *Billboard*. Nielsen Business Media, Inc. http://www.billboardmagazine.com/bbcom/esearch/article_display.jsp?vnu_content_id=1003642725. Accessed 27th August 2009.

15. Underground hip-hop is said to be based in the ideology of knowledge of self (Haupt 2003; KRS One 2003) which alludes to self-awareness achieved through a process of introspection that enables an artist to engage critically with his/her reality by addressing the challenges of society through his/her work. This is the fundamental difference between underground and main-stream, where mainstream artists are said to have no conscious-ness of their self or their reality, and thus bow to what hooks calls "white supremacist capitalist patriarchy (1994:116)" by producing essentially meaningless lyrics.

16. Many critics of mainstream/gangsta hip-hop have been caught flat-footed when they confessed at having not bothered to listen to the music they have lambasted wholesale; and many propo-

nents of underground hip-hop have accepted music they have not bothered to listen to (Kitwana 1994; Rose 1994a; Williams 1992; Armstrong 2001). This becomes counter-productive in analysis of hip-hop as is demonstrated here.

17. A *matatu* is a 14-seater or 28-seater vehicle used as public service vehicles in all major cities and towns in Kenya. Many do not necessarily follow traffic rules, and an adventurous passenger can jump off a slow-to-moderately-moving matatu at any point on one's journey, provided the police do not see one.

18. This is an unconfirmed report from several respondents and acquaintances that were in attendance at this particular performance. There are no official reports documenting this incident either with reporters or with bloggers. I include it here to demonstrate the extent to which these lyrics, in perception at least, appear to be incendiary and inciting.

19. See Nyaga, Caroline 'The Genge Revolution' in The Standard Newspaper, 13th March 2009 at http://www.standardmedia.co.ke/InsidePage.php?id=1144008724&cid=123& accessed on 21st August 2009.

20. The law in Kenya explicitly allows the police, army personnel and politicians' bodyguards to carry licensed firearms. Ordinary citizens are very rarely allowed licensed firearms. Normally, those who carry firearms outside these privileged groups acquire and use them illegally, and according to police statistics, use them mainly to carry out violent crimes, many carrying the death penalty upon conviction in a court of law.

21. See http://www.eastandard.net/mag/InsidePage.php?id=1144008724&cid=123&, where Kenya's First Lady lambasted Circuit and Jo-el for the song Juala for being obscene and offensive. Retrieved 25th August 2009.

22. The founding fathers of modern hip-hop culture are said to be DJ Kool Herc, Afrika Bambaataa, and Grandmaster Flash. These three are said to have been the DJs who started to experiment with various sounds during block parties in the inner city of New York in the early 1970s, creating venues that birthed hip-hop culture.

23. See http://misnomer.dru.ca/2003/12/conscious_hip_hop_vs_gangsta_rap.html accessed 28th August 2009.

24. Both artists have been quoted here owing to their being the de-facto representatives of the "mainstream" and the "underground." Jua Cali is seen as the "King of Genge," while Mwafrika has been dubbed the "King of the Underground."
25. *Kapuka* is the name given to general popular (pop) music in Kenya. The word has its origins in the song "Kapuka this" that was performed by the hip-hop group K-South in 2001. The beat of that song, replicated in subsequent pop songs, saw the rise of a pop genre called "kapuka."
26. Writer Ngugi wa Thing'o is known as a highly political writer, whose anti-establishment writings landed him in detention during the Kenyatta and Moi regimes where he was tortured. In the early 1980s, Ngugi went into exile in the U.S., only returning after the Moi regime finally fell in 2002. This first visit home after so long was marred after his wife who was accompanying him, was brutally raped in an attack that Ngugi attributed to his unchanged political stance. He is included in this song because he is seen as a freedom hero, akin to the Mau Mau.
27. Matt, Miller. "Dirty Decade: Rap Music and the US South, 1997-2007," *Southern Spaces*, 10 June 2008. http://www.southernspaces.org/contents/2008/miller/8b.htm
28. A *bodaboda* is a manned bicycle that is used as short-distance public transportation in Kenya. For a small fee, a passenger jumps on the back seat of a bicycle and is given a ride to his destination.
29. Sheng for *Street Mentality*. In this album, Juliani attempts to bridge the gap between the church and the street. Casco (2006) documents that in its early stages, hip-hop was perceived as "muziki wa wahuni"- music for criminals and delinquents, owing to its ghettoization as I have discussed above.
30. See Juliani album launch http://www.kenyangospel.com/news/juliani-album-launch-recap.php. Accessed 29th August 2009.

references

Agawu, Kofi. 1992. "Representing African Music" in *Critical Inquiry*, Vol. 18(2): 245-266.

Alridge, Derrick P. and James B. Stewart. 2005. "Introduction: Hip Hop in History: Past, Present, and Future." in *The Journal of African American History*, 90(3): 190-195.

Armstrong Edward G. 2001. "Gangsta misogyny: a content analysis of the portrayals of violence against women in rap music 1987-1993." in *Journal of Criminal Justice and Popular Culture*, 8(2): 96-126.

Askew, Kelly. 2003. *Performing the Nation- Swahili Music and Cultural Politics in Tanzania*. Chicago: University of Chicago Press.

Barber, Karin. 2007. *The Anthropology of texts, persons and publics: oral and written culture in Africa and beyond Cambridge*. New York: Cambridge University Press.

Barkley, Divinity L. 2007. "*Kaya* Hip-Hop in Coastal Kenya: The Urban Poetry of Ukoo Flani." ISP: University of Southern California.

Bosire, Mokaya. 2006. "Hybrid Languages: The Case of Sheng." in *Selected Proceedings of the 36th Annual Conference on African Linguists*, ed. Olaoba F. Arasanyin and Michael A. Pemberton, 185-193. Somerville, MA: Cascadilla Proceedings Project.

Bourdieu, Pierre. 1991. *Language and Symbolic Power*. Oxford: Blackwell.

Bourdieu, Pierre. 1993. *The Field of Cultural Production*. Cambridge: Polity Press.

Casco, JAS. 2006. "The Language of the Young People: Rap, Urban Culture and Protest in Tanzania." in *Journal of Asian and African Studies*, Vol. 41, pp 229-248.

Cassidy, Francis. 1991. "Young people, Culture and Popular Music." in *Youth Studies* 10(2): 34-45.

Celious, Aaron K. 2002. "How "bitch" became a good thing – or, at least not that bad." in *African American Research Perspectives* 8(2): 90-96.

Chang, Jeff. 2007. *Can't Stop, Won't Stop: A History of the Hip-Hop Generation*. New York: Ebury Publishing.

Cohen, Abner. 1993. *Masquerade Politics: Explorations in the Structure of Urban Cultural Movements*. Berkeley and Los Angeles: University of California Press.

Decker, J.Louis. 1993. "The State of Rap: Time and Place in Hip Hop Nationalism." in *Social Text*, 34: 53-84.

Drewal, Margaret T. 1991. "The State of Research on Performance in Africa." in *African Studies Review*, 34(3):1-64.

Dyson, Michael Eric. 2004. "The Culture of Hip-Hop." In *That's the Joint! The Hip-Hop Studies Reader*, edited by Murray Forman and Mark A. Neal, New York & London: Routledge.

Englert, Birgit. 2003. "Bongo Flava (Still) Hidden "Underground"- Rap from Morogoro, Tanzania." *Vienna Journal of African Studies* 5(3): 73-93.

Englert, Birgit. 2004. "Africa Raps Back: Reflections on Hip-Hop from Tanzania and South Africa." in *Crossing Borders: Interdisciplinary Approaches to Africa*, edited by Schörder, Anne. Berlin Lit Verlag, PP. 77-97.

Fernando, S H. 1994. *The New Beats: Exploring the Music, Culture and Attitudes of Hip hop*. New York: Doubleday.

Flexx, 2005. *Nyundo*. Clemo: Calif Records.

Forman M and Mark Anthony N. (eds). 2004. *That's the Joint! The Hip-Hop Studies Reader*, New York& London: Routledge

George, Nelson. 2004. "Hip-Hop's Founding Fathers Speak the Truth." In *That's the Joint! The Hip-Hop Studies Reader*, edited by Murray Forman and Mark A. Neal, New York & London: Routledge.

Githinji, Peter. 2006. "Bazes and Their Shibboleths: Lexical Variation and Sheng Speakers' Identity in Nairobi." in *Nordic Journal of African Studies* 15(4): 443–472.

Githinji, Peter. 2007. "*Mchongoano* Verbal Duels: Risky Discourse and Sociocultural Commentary." in *Art, Culture and Society Vol. 1- Cultural Production and Social Change in Kenya: Building Bridges*, edited by K. Njogu and G. Oluoch-Olunya, pp. 89-109.

Githiora, Chege. 2002. "Sheng: Peer Language, Swahili Dialect or Emerging Creole?" in *Journal of African Cultural Studies*, 15(2):159-181.

Hager, Steven. 1984. *Hip Hop: The Illustrated History of Break Dancing, Rap Music, and Graffiti*. New York: St Martin's Press.

Haupt, Adam. 2003. "Hip-Hop in the Age of Empire: Cape Flats Style." in *Dark Roast Occasional Papers Series* No. 9. Cape Town, Isandla Institute.

Hebdige, Dick. 2004. "Rap and Hip-Hop: The New York Connection." In *That's the Joint! The Hip-Hop Studies Reader*, edited by Murray Forman and Mark A. Neal, New York & London: Routledge.

Henderson, Errol. A.1996. "Black Nationalism and Rap Music." in *Journal of Black Studies*, 26 (3): 308-339.

hooks, bell. 1994. "Gangsta Culture - Sexism and Misogyny: Who will take the rap?" in *Outlaw Culture: Resisting Representations*. New York: Routledge.

Jua Cali, 2006. *Jua Cali Sekta*, Clemo: Calif Records.

Kearse, 'Mo Deezy' Randy. 2005. *Street Talk: Da Official Guide to Hip-Hop and Urban Language*. Indiana: AuthorHouse.

Kelley, Robin DG. 1994. *Race Rebels: Culture, Politics and the Black Working Class*. New York: Free Press.

Kelley, Robin DG. 2004. "Looking for the "Real" Nigga: Social Scientists Construct the Ghetto." In *That's the Joint! The Hip-Hop Studies Reader*, edited by Murray Forman and Mark A. Neal, New York & London: Routledge.

Keyes, C. L. 1991. "Rapping to the Beat: Rap music as Street Culture Among African-Americans," PhD dissertation, Ann Arbor, Michigan: University of Michigan.

Keyes, C. L 1996. "At the Crossroads: Rap Music and Its African Nexus." in *Ethnomusicology*, 40(2):223-248.

KRS-One. 2003. *Ruminations*. New York: Welcome Rain Publishers.

Kunzler, Daniel. 2006. "The 'Lost Generation': African Hip Hop Movements and the Protest of the Young (male) Urban," *World Society Focus Paper Series*, Zurich.

Light, Alan. 2004. "About a Salary or Reality? – Rap's Recurrent Conflict." In *That's the Joint! The Hip-Hop Studies Reader*, edited by Murray Forman and Mark A. Neal, New York & London: Routledge.

Lipsitz, George. 1994. *Dangerous Crossroads: Popular Music, Postmodernism and the Poetics of the Place*. London and New York: Verso.

Martinez, T.A. 1997. "Popular Culture as Oppositional Culture: Rap as Resistance" in *Social Perspectives* 40(2):265-286.

Mashifta, 2006. *Majambazi* (single). Ukoo Flani Mau Mau.

Miller, Matt "Dirty Decade: Rap Music and the US South, 1997-2007," *Southern Spaces*, 10 June 2008. http://www.southernspaces.org/contents/2008/miller/8b.htm

Mitchell, Tony, (ed). 2001. *Global Noise: Rap and Hip- hop Outside the USA*. Connecticut: Wesleyan University Press.

Moore, A.F (ed). 2003. *Analyzing popular music*. Cambridge: Cambridge University Press.

Mose, Caroline. 2008. *"Skuodi Ya Watu Kumi na Mbili:* The Discourses, Negotiation and Art In Underground Hip-hop in Nairobi, Kenya," Masters Thesis, University of Oxford.

Mose, Caroline. 2009. *Ngeli Ya Genge*: "'Glocal' Hip-hop Culture and the quest for Self-Identity in East Africa." Paper presented during the *Eastern African Literary and Intellectual Landscapes* at the University of the Witwatersrand, Johannesburg, 23rd – 24th October.

Mwafrika and Muki Garang, 2006. "Justice," (single) (independently produced).

Nilan, Pam and Feixa, Carles. 2006. *Global Youth? Hybrid Identities, Plural Worlds*. Oxford: Routledge

Njogu, Kimani, and Maupeu, Herve (eds). 2007. *Songs and Politics in Eastern Africa*. Dar es Salaam: Nyota Publishers.

Ntarangwi, Mwenda. 2000. "Malumbano or Matukano:Competition, Confrontation, and (De) Construction of Masculinity in theTaarab of Maulidi and Bhalo" in . *Mashindano! Competitive Music Performance in East Africa*, edited by Gunderson, F. and Gregory Barz. Dar Es Salaam: Mkuki na Nyota Press.

Ntarangwi, Mwenda. 2003. *Gender, Identity and Performance: Understanding Swahili Cultural Realities through Song*. Trenton, New Jersey: Africa World Press.

Ntarangwi, Mwenda. 2007. "Hip-Hop, Westernization and Gender in East Africa' in *Songs and Politics in East Africa*, edited by Kimani N and Herve Maupeu. Dar Es Salaam: Mkuki na Nyota Press, pp. 273-302.

Ntarangwi, Mwenda. 2007. "Music, Identity and Swahili Networks of Knowledge." in *Cultural Production and Social Change in Kenya-*

Building Bridges, Vol. One, edited by K. Njogu and G. Oluoch-Olunya. Nairobi: Twaweza Publications.

Ntarangwi, Mwenda. 2009. *East African Hip Hop- Youth Culture and Globalization.* Urbana and Chicago: University of Illinois Press.

N.W.A. 1988. *Straight Outta Compton.* Ruthless/Priority Records.

Nyairo, J. 2005. "'Modify': Jua Kali as a Metaphor for Africa's Urban Ethnicities and Cultures," Mary Kingsley Zochonis Lecture, Royal African Society.

Nyairo, J. & J. Ogude. 2003. "Popular Music and the Negotiation of Contemporary Kenyan Identity: The Example of Nairobi City Ensemble" in *Social Identities* 9(3):383-400.

Nyairo, J. & J. Ogude. 2005. "Popular Music, Popular Politics: Unbwogable and the Idioms of Freedom in Kenyan Popular Music" in *African Affairs* 104(415):225-249.

Nyairo, J. & J. Ogude (eds). 2007. *Urban Legends, Colonial Myths: Popular Culture and Literature in East Africa.* New Jersey: Africa World Press Inc.

Perry, Imani. 2004. *Prophets of the Hood: Politics and Poetics in Hip-hop.* Durham: Duke University Press.

Pihel, Erik. 1996. "A Furified Freestyle: Homer and Hip Hop" in *Oral Tradition* 11(2):249-269.

Rebensdorf, Alicia. 1997. "'Representing the real' Exploring Appropriations of Hip-Hop Culture in the Internet and Nairobi." from http://lclark.edu/~soan/alicia/ rebensdorf. 101.html

Ro, Ronin. 1996. *Gangsta: Merchandizing the Rhymes of Violence.* New York: St. Martins.

Rose, Tricia. 1994. *Black noise: Rap music and black culture.* Hanover: New England University Press.

Samper, David A. 2002. "Talking Sheng: The Role of A Hybrid Language in the Construction of Identity and Youth Culture in Nairobi, Kenya." PhD dissertation, University of Pennsylvania.

Samper, David A. 2004. "'Africa is still our mama": Kenyan Rappers, Youth Identity, and the Revitalization of Traditional Values' in *African Identities,* 2(1): 37-51.

Scott, Derek B. 2000. *Music, Culture and Society.* Oxford: Oxford University Press.

Servant, Jean-Christophe. 2000. "Rap: Africa Talks Back" in *Le Monde Diplomatique*, December 15 (6323):17.

Sexton, Adam (ed). 1995. *Rap on Rap: Straight-up Talk on Hip-Hop Culture*. New York: Dell Publishing.

Shuker, Roy. 2001. *Understanding Popular Music*. United Kingdom: Routledge.

Shusterman, Richard. 1991. "The Fine Art of Rap" in *New Literary History* 22: 613-32.

Smitherman, Geneva. 1997. ""The Chain Remain the Same": Communicative Practices in the Hip Hop Nation" in *Journal of Black Studies* 28(1):3-25.

Smith, Christopher Holmes. 1997. "Method in the Madness: Exploring the Boundaries of Identity in Hip-Hop Performativity" in *Social Identities*, 3(3):345-374.

Spears, Richard A. 2006. *American Slang Dictionary: The Ultimate Reference to Nonstandard Usage, Colloquialism, Popular Jargon and Vulgarisms*, 4ᵗʰ Ed. New York: McGraw-Hill.

Staples, Brent. 1995. "The Politics of Gangster Rap." In *Rap on Rap: Straight-up Talk on Hip-Hop Culture*, edited by Adam Sexton .New York: Dell Publishing, pp78-80.

Street, John. 1997. *Politics and Popular Culture*. Philadelphia: Temple University Press.

Tate, Greg. 1995. "What is Hip-Hop?" In *Rap on Rap: Straight-up Talk on Hip-Hop Culture*, edited by Adam Sexton .New York: Dell Publishing, pp. 17-21

Toop, David. 2000. *Rap Attack 3: African Rap to Global Hip Hop*, 3ʳᵈ Edition. London: Serpent's Tail.

Wahl, Greg. 1999. ""I Fought the Law (And I Cold Won!):" Hip-Hop in the Mainstream" in *Cultural Violence* 26(1): 98-112.

Wa-Mungai, Mbugua. 2007. "'Is Marwa!' It's Ours": Popular Music and Identity Politics in Kenyan Youth Culture." (2007) in *Art, Culture and Society Vol. 1- Cultural Production and Social Change in Kenya: Building Bridges*, edited by K. Njogu and G. Oluoch-Olunya, pp. 47-59.

Wa-Mungai, Mbugua. 2008. "Made in Riverwood: (dis)locating Identities and Power through Kenyan Pop Music" in *Journal of African Cultural Studies* 20(1): 57-70.

Wa-Mutonya, Maina. 2007. "Joseph Kamaru: Contending Narrations of Kenya's Politics Through Music" in *Art, Culture and Society Vol. 1- Cultural Production and Social Change in Kenya: Building Bridges*, edited by K. Njogu and G. Oluoch-Olunya, pp 27-46.

Wenyeji. 2007. *Siku Njema 'Vichwa Ziface Juu*. Ukoo Flani Mau Mau.

CHAPTER 5
colouring the cape problem space: a hip-hop identity of passions

REMI WARNER

It is not culture which binds the people who are of partially African origin now scattered throughout the world, but an identity of passions. We share a hatred for the alienation forced upon us by Europeans during the process of colonization and empire and we are bound by our common suffering more than by our pigmentation.

– Ralph Ellison (1953)

We [Cape Flats youth] could identify with the things that people were saying in the rap songs more than anywhere else [in South Africa] because that was the Bronx of South Africa at the time, I reckon...The identity was bigger...so that's why they could identify with it. Their struggles were the same.

– Sky 189 (2002)

The thing is, is that there's a connection man. You know what I'm saying. There's a connection. There's an identity that we're feeling.

– DJ Rozzano (2002)

introduction

Hip-hop history in South Africa begins in Cape Town, its first major cultural base being amongst those youth inhabitants forcibly relocated to the 'Cape Flats' region on the sandy outskirts of Cape Town, whom apartheid legislators officially classified, under the 1950 Population Registration Act, as 'Coloured': a complex, heterogeneous and residual category for 'mixed race' populations deemed neither fully 'native' ('African', 'Black' and/ or 'Bantu') nor quite 'White'.[1] This chapter examines the reasons why hip-hop first took root where and when it did, amongst 'Cape Coloured'[2] youth in the 1980s, drawing on archival research and one year of anthropological fieldwork in one of Africa's oldest hip-hop scenes (Cape Town, South Africa). Two primary lines of explication are pursued in this effort: the first focusing on issues of *access* to global media and hip-hop cultural flows, foregrounding the means and channels of hip-hop's early cultural diffusion to Cape Town and the role of global and late apartheid political and economic transformations as these impacted the organization and regulation of media and entertainment; the second, focusing on the resonant histories and problem spaces[3] of Cape Coloured and Black and Latino American youth, which I argue, together, fostered a trans-Atlantic 'identity of passions'[4] among Cape Town hip-hoppers.

accessing an identity of passions

Among the most widely invoked markers of hip-hop's emergence in Cape Town is the South African reception, in 1982, of the American hip-hop movie, *Wild Style*,[5] produced that same year, and widely celebrated as the first of its kind to feature *all* of hip-hop's elements (breaking, DJing, emceeing, graffiti) in their authentic street form.[6] Other audio-visual media are accorded an equally instrumental role in diffusing hip-hop to Cape Town, in old school Cape Town hip-hop accounts, in particular break-dance featuring movies the likes of *Flashdance* (1983), *Beat Street* (1984), *Body Rock* (1984), and *Breakin 1 and 2* (1984), and music videos such as Michael Jackson's *Thriller* (1982), Malcolm McLaren's *Buffalo Girls* (1982), and the Rock Steady Crew's *Hey You*. While some of these blockbuster movies aired in Cape Flats township cinemas in the 1980s – a decade also witnessing the first airings of music videos on South African TV – various Cape Town-Europe 'bootleg networks' were a mainstay of hip-hop's dissemination in Cape Town.

In a rehearsal I would hear time and time again, original school Cape Town 'b-boy' (breakdancer), Gordon, fondly recollected, from his home in the (formerly Coloured-only) Cape Flats township of Bonteheuwel, how after watching *Beat Street* in a local, Bonteheuwel cinema he immediately rushed home to practice memorized and subsequently memorialized break-dance moves. Gordon's own reputed early Cape Town b-boy crew – the *Cape Town City Breakers* – bore the traces of such movie-going influence in their very name, which itself signified upon the legendary *New York City Breakers* crew famously featured in the (1984) *Beat Street* movie.[7] "We realized, when *Beat Street* and those movies came out that what was tied to this was an entire culture," another old school b-boy and hip-hop founder of the South African chapter of the Universal Zulu Nation, King Jamo, explained in our discussion at his home in Tafelsig, Mitchell's Plain. "It was break dancing, it was spray-can art, it was djing, it was emceeing and we realized that we could actually pull all of those together you know and make it one big thing."

The zeal with which the few videos trickling through South African television airwaves were vigilantly and diligently consumed by South African *headz* was conveyed by one of South Africa's first hip-hop DJ's, 'Rozzano X', from his home in Lintegeur, Mitchell's Plain. "Let me tell you something" he exclaimed, with a glimmer of nostalgia in his eye that immediately brought to mind my own video-induced, hip-hop birthing rites of b-boy mimesis as a youth in Hamilton, Ontario, Canada: "If one hip-hop video came on TV, the WHOLE of the hip-hop community would talk. They will mention the time, the date, everybody will be so excited. WHAA – there was a hip-hop song on TV!" That almost identical hip-hop genesis tales have been recounted from Los Angeles to Cape Town to Canada – all referencing the same 1980s b-boy movies and videos as catalysts for the development of local hip-hop scenes – illustrates the unprecedented scope and penetration of the global entertainment industries as these evolved over the course of the 1980s. Hip-hop may indeed be the first American popular musical-cultural form to have gone national (from New York to the west coast) *and* global (from New York to the world) simultaneously,[8] in ways clearly challenging geographically-delimited and exclusivist notions of hip-hop authenticity premised on spatial proximity to hip-hop's earliest centers of cultural production.

transformations in local and global media and entertainment

The very fact that hip-hop videos and movies were able to reach South Africans over the airwaves and in movie theaters during the politically tumultuous 1980s is reflective of key transformations in the regulation and organization of domestic and global media and entertainment during this era. Among the developments within the international music and entertainment industries helping to bring hip-hop to Cape Town's shores in audio-visual forms in the 1980s was: (1) the increasing global reach of the music industries over this period,[9] facilitated by the deregulation of communications and media in the U.S. (and increasingly, under the latter's influence, internationally) and the oligopolistic growth of cross-media invested, multinational, communications/ electronics/entertainment firms with the power to deliver globally;[10] (2) the emergence of a new, post-Fordist production regime within the music industry characterized by increasing (albeit asymmetric) symbiosis between 'major' record companies and 'minors', which enabled formerly marginal, niche-marketed music, such as rap, to enter into the global mainstream;[11] and (3) the advent and development of music-television along with VCR, cable, and satellite transmission technologies over this period, which increased the import, scale, and role of cross-media investments, as evidenced in the key role of movies in hip-hop's diffusion to Cape Town in the early 1980s.

Coinciding with the growing global scale and scope of the international music and entertainment industry over the course of the 1980s was a gradual loosening of the apartheid state's censorial grip over media and broadcasting, in the context of P.W. Botha's 1978 rise to power, and his hegemonic 'Total Strategy.' The fact that Cape Town rap pioneer, Shaheen, of Cape Town's legendary rap group, *Prophets of da City*, heard his first rap song on a rural, 'homeland' (formerly 'Radio Bop') radio station, whilst traveling with his jazz musician father throughout the homelands, is indicative of the kinds of pragmatic concessions and hegemonic accommodations increasingly afforded by the apartheid regime, as the seventies and eighties progressed, in their attempt to hold on to power and secure ideological consent.

During the preceding 'Grand Apartheid' era, under the political leadership of Dr. Hendrik Verwoerd (1958-1966), the same Bantu Radio services, serving as "*the* principal media wing of the Bantustan system,"[12] were charged with the goal of fostering 'national consciousness' amongst South African 'tribes', through the appropriate selection of music and cultural programming in accord with 'the nature, needs and character' of the homeland ethno-linguistic group served (Hamm 1988:24; also see Tomaselli et al. 2001:60). By the 1980s, the stringency of such programming criteria had been significantly relaxed, as hybrid, popular,

English-language genres increasingly made their way to the airwaves, for several reasons, to do with: (1) Radio Bantu's pragmatic response to the threat of a dwindling black audience, beginning in the late 1960s, as traditional musical programming became increasingly spurned by black audiences due to its associations with NP 'separate development' policies and ideology, forcing a reconsideration of Radio Bantu priorities; and (2) the evolution of independent radio services in the homelands (declared 'national states' by the NP in the 1970s and 1980s) as part of the NP effort to sustain the mirage of national ('tribal') autonomy, the strategic calculations of which enabled the less administratively constrained and directly censored homeland radio services to drift further and further away from the original Radio Bantu mandate and mission of reproducing ethno-linguistic difference and authentic tribal custom (see Hamm 1991). "By the 1980s," Hamm thus observes of the hegemonic detente in broadcasting, "Top 10 countdowns mixing international hits with pieces by the best South African pop performers had become standard on all 'homeland' services (1991:170)," including evidently, the Sugar Hill Gang's *Rapper's Delight*.

The gradual opening up of the media and broadcasting environment in the 1980s (until the 1985 State of Emergency) is evidenced in the recollections of old school Cape Town hip-hoppers, 'Hamma' and 'Trash.' Original school b-boy, and contemporary emcee and DJ with the celebrated Cape Town hip-hop crew, *Brasse Vannie Kaap* ('Brothers from the Cape'), Hamma provides one of the more detailed and evocative accounts of the media environment at the time of hip-hop's emergence in the Cape in the 1980s:

> There was a lot of stuff going on at that time, um, with apartheid, so a lot of things were like – we were cut off from experiencing anything else but what the system wanted us to experience. And at that exact same time America was blowing up, in the sense of like it was

crossing over all countries' borders. It was just invading the airwaves, what we see on tv, what we read in magazines and everything. So while the system was trying to prevent us from getting to certain points of our being or hearing certain information, other things were just filtering through, like the American, the westernized, the western world was just filtering through...Songs like Malcolm McLaren's *Buffalo Girls*, *Rock the Box*, those music that blew up in the States at that time, all those type of music came out. Movies like *Break Dance 1* and *Beat Street* and um, yeah, basically through the media like that...The little bit of information that was there basically circulated around the neighbourhoods and especially in the townships...So like the exact same means that they used to restrict us from proper information also brought us hip-hop.

The increasing visibility of Black American characters and programs on South African TV in the 1980s is further conveyed by early Bontiheuwal b-boy and 'freestyle dance' pioneer, 'Trash', who jokingly recollected:

Black and white TV – during apartheid! Funny hey! What!...I would go nowhere on a Thursday and on Sundays just because I wanted to watch TV, cuz, that guy [Fred Astaire] was like floating on water, you know. The way he moved. And THEN, *the* man came along! Michael Jackson, you know! If they can even, if they even know Michael Jackson, it's amazing!... *Flashdance* was also like an inspiration to us. I can remember, *Flashdance* on TV. It was a movie, and it came out with that other Aquarius movie [*Footloose*]. And *Fame*, of course!

In addition to the above factors already mentioned, part of the reason for the infusion of American TV programming in the

1980s stemmed from the lack of alternative sources of programming as a result of the British Equity boycott of South Africa in the 1980s, during which time a growing number of UK companies refused to sell TV programs to South Africa,[13] leaving America as one of the few remaining major world television content providers.

The fact that television featured at all in such accounts of early 1980s Cape Town hip-hop (never mind shows, such as *Fame*, featuring 'modern', 'urban' Black characters and multi-racial casts) is indicative of significant transformations, in policy and outlook, within South African ruling political circles. Up until 1976, TV had been banned altogether from South Africa, out of fears of the medium's subversive potential as an 'agent of American cultural imperialism' and 'miscegenation' (the main threat being cast as American liberal-humanism and 'melting pot' ideology). The somewhat reluctant introduction of TV in 1976 in many ways marked the beginnings of a shift in power within the governing apartheid National Party ruling base, from the petty-bourgeois aligned *verkramptes* (conservatives), with their ardent Christian-nationalist *kuluurpolitiek* (cultural politics) and *volkskapitalisme*, towards the increasingly British and big-capital aligned *verligte* ('enlightened') wing of Afrikanerdom, headed by P.W. Botha. Botha's introduction of TV, and endorsement of black television programming specifically directed at urban black audiences, reflected the new 'total strategy' of the apartheid government. Responding to growing economic crisis, black resistance, and its radicalization, Botha's infamous 'Total Strategy' had the avowed aim of "guarantee[ing]...the system of free enterprise" by incorporating and assuaging the increasingly volatile *and* anti-capitalist forces of black resistance through the creation of a privileged black class stratum (see Saul and Gelb 1986).

The growing number of modern, urban (and transnational) black characters appearing on South African TV after 1979 also reflected the growing acceptance, even encouragement, by ruling segments within the Afrikaner capitalist class, of the

native tongues: an african hip-hop reader

development of a permanently-settled, urban skilled black labor force *within* the officially white republic, as this was deemed increasingly essential to the fulfillment of the economy's growing demand for consumers and skilled labor over this period (particularly service sector vocations, such as nurses, teachers, bureaucrats, and administrators) (see Tomaselli et al., 2001:156). The creation of two TV channels the very same year as hip-hop's take-off in South Africa (1982) were in fact 'tailor-made' to reach urban black middle class audiences, as part of such 'Total Strategy' goals. The latter were reflected in the programming content of these telecasts which, being almost exclusively English-language-based, showcased well-to-do black lifestyles and examples of black middle class mobility, not infrequently using African-American programming to this end (one of the most popular shows throughout the 1980s broadcast in South Africa being *The Cosby Show*).[14]

The calculated *perestroika* within the realm of public media and broadcasting clearly had unanticipated effects and consequences for the ruling party, as manifested in the new self-assertiveness and black consciousness of Cape Town hip-hoppers over the course of the 1980s, thanks to media disseminated forms of hip-hop. That "certain points of [Hamma's] being" were "reached" through the "the exact same means that [the apartheid state] used to restrict [township youth] from proper information" illustrates the unpredictability, in popular reception, of hegemonic strategies and representations, particularly when pitched on the densely-coded, oft opaque terrain of popular culture. As Tomaselli et al. (2001) argue of the limits of formal cultural analyses of South African (total strategy steeped) television broadcasting aimed at black audiences:

> Scholars who believe in the monolithic nature of TV 2/3 as a means of manufacturing a mass culture are clearly unaware of the contradictions operating within the medium and of the fact that even the

people involved in the 'manufacturing' are themselves, at times, undermining the process of negotiating consent because of a lack of knowledge about
the textual codifications that govern the medium
(Tomaselli, Tomaselli & Muller 2001:175).

Tomaselli et al. (2001) nevertheless caution against over-estimat-
ing the subversiveness of black and multiracial TV programming
in the 1980s, due to the amenability and assimilation of a great
deal of such televisual content – including hip-hop representations, even of a black cultural nationalist variation (as explored
elsewhere; see Warner 2007) – to the goals of the NP's evolving
'Total Strategy', particularly through the diffusion of a black capitalist ethos.

Lest such transformations in the regulation and content of
South African media be overstated as a force for hip-hop's transmission to Cape Town in the 1980s, it should nevertheless be
noted that contending authoritative accounts reveal that most
Cape Town hip-hoppers continued to experience a restricted
flow of, and access to, hip-hop during this early period. The
main avenues of hip-hop dissemination, contrasting with today's
situation, were rather interpersonal ('underground'), hand-to-
hand, tape-to-tape, audio, and video bootleg networks, hip-hop
having had rare national media exposure, for reasons recalled by
Shaheen of Prophets of the City:

> Due to economic sanctions and political pressure
> from overseas, music and information were very dif-
> ficult to get hold of. It usually came from pen pals,
> family and friends in exile or the occasional imported
> record or magazine. Cassette copying and passing it
> along to friends and family was the main vehicle for
> the dissemination of earlier hip-hop music (2004).

Such audio and video tape networks were often traceable back
to more privileged white South African hip-hop fans with the

means and mobility to obtain highly sought after hip-hop material from abroad. As former POC member and world renowned DJ, Ready D, recalled: "a lot of white people would travel and bring music back."[15] "Radio wasn't playing it," he further relates, as was similarly recollected by original school DJ Rozzano:

> The radio just, they weren't catering for our needs...
> Nobody was, absolutely nobody was catering for us,
> so we [DJ's Rozzano, Ready D and later Shamiel] had
> to dig for this music, but we worked hard and we
> found it...

Costly import record purchases from *Rag Time Records* in central Cape Town (whose name is revealing of a much longer history of Cape Town contact with Black American music and expressive culture) were one of the more costly means of rap music acquisition, for Cape Town's few hip-hop DJ's in the early 1980s (primarily just Rozzano and Ready D at this time), as Rozzano related of the gems he unearthed while 'digging in the crates':

> Hip-hop records, classic hip-hop singles that are
> worth loads of dollars now, we used to pick up on
> sale here in Cape Town...at *Rag Time Records*. They
> were bringing in the stuff, and they couldn't believe
> that we were buying this music.

Access to formal and informal media and commercial networks, extending beyond the over-policed denizens of the townships, was thus a crucial determinant of hip-hop cultural participation in the 1980s. The fact that the government-constructed 'Coloured' townships generally had electricity, with many Coloured households, moreover, owning a TV and VCR, unlike many of the rural Bantustans and urban black township residences, also partially explains why hip-hop may have first spread among the 'Coloured' youth of the Cape Flats region, particularly given hip-hop's initial dependence on audio and video tape recordings as a chief means of dissemination (as Klopper has suggested elsewhere; see 2000:183). Such race and class disparities in media access continue to shape hip-hop's dissemination and reception in South Africa to this day.

the tavern of the seas

In addition to such political, social, and economic determinants of access to hip-hop and global media, Cape Town's geographical positioning, as a historically pivotal "port city" at the intersections of East and West, also favored Cape Town as South Africa's first hip-hop destination, as argued by Shaheen of Prophets of the City, among others:

> If you look at where Cape Town is situated, right, it's a port, and part of the reason why a lot of stuff came in [including hip-hop] was also because of sailors and people that were traveling and stuff like that.

Cape Town has long been a central hub of international traffic in commodities, peoples and cultures – known historically as the 'Tavern of the Seas' – its peoples, expressive cultures and famous neighborhoods (District Six for example)[16] being distinctly imprinted with and by a cosmopolitan sensibility, as aurally and visually on display each year at the 'Coon Carnival'.[17] Cape Town's continuing importance, as a transnational hub and entry point for cross-cultural currents, is evidenced in South African hip-hop pioneer, DJ Blaze's, account of hip-hop's origins in Cape Town:

> I think that there was a few DJ's at the time coming from overseas, you know, who were staying in Cape Town and brought music through. And music was a problem, especially during the apartheid era when everything was so controlled you know and black music wasn't really getting that much play, especially on radio so you know...people didn't have access

...So a lot of music just came, just shored on Cape
Town through networking and through connections.
And that's where it started popping. People started
making home tapes and recordings and circulating,
that's how it got so big out there so quick you know...
because of the connections.

Such extra-local connections continue to define contemporary
hip-hop identities in Cape Town, which have a long history preceding and supporting them. As one former District Six inhabit-
ant evocatively relates of the global reach of his 'Cape Atlantico'
cultural identity:

I'm a product of a port city, Cape Town, New Orleans,
Rio, Barbados, New York. We have much in common
with each other because we are bound by the Atlantic and all that happened on that ocean whether it
was slave-trade or commerce or whatever and our
rhythms and our language and our so-called culture
is more outward looking (cited in Soudien 2001:124).

colouring the cape problem space

Whilst geography combined with political and economic
developments in media and governance provided the necessary
'hardware' conditions for hip-hop's emergence and growth in
Cape Town in the 1980s, less tangible ('software') factors, lodged
within the historical memory and contemporary imaginaries
of Cape Town youth, were equally responsible for anchoring
hip-hop in the Cape, as Cape Flats youth residents increasingly
came to see their own histories and problem spaces reflected in
those of their Black Atlantic hip-hop peers. "We adopted [hip-
hop] cuz it was the only time when we ever experienced people
of colour doing exactly what we're doing, or feeling exactly what
we've been through" Hamma explained in one of our interviews.
Such senses of affinity – or 'identity of passions' – and resonant

problem spaces underlying Cape Town youth identifications with hip-hop are the subjects of the remainder of this chapter.

Constituting a majority of the population in the Cape, and yet just ten percent of the population nationally, one of the more notable and distinguishing features of Cape Town's Cape Coloured community is their sharing with the populations of the African Diaspora a history of slavery and cultural dispossession, the majority of Cape Town's Coloured population being the mixed descendants of enslaved peoples brought from various regions along the Dutch Indies trade routes between the 17th and 19th centuries to toil on the expanding farms, vineyards, and towns of the bourgeoning Cape Colony (slavery lasting from 1658 to 1834).[18] The divide and rule aims informing the redefinition of the category 'Coloured' at the turn of the 20th century – from a category formerly referencing all non-white populations indiscriminately in the Cape, to only those deemed of 'mixed stock', as defined for the first time in the 1904 census – is pointedly conveyed in the words of South African High Commissioner, Lord William Palmer, who advised ruling South African authorities as early as 1905:

> Our objective should be to teach the Coloured people to give their loyalty to the White population. It seems to me sheer folly to classify them with the Natives, and by treating them as Natives to force them away from their natural allegiance to the Whites and making common cause with the Natives (cited in Goldin 1987:164).

The apartheid government would come to entrench and institutionalize this divide and rule strategy ever more firmly upon coming to power in the 1950s,[19] most divisively through the promulgation and implementation of the Group Areas Act (1950) and Coloured Labour Preference Policy (1955). Whereas the former uprooted and relocated Blacks and Coloureds from mixed urban neighborhoods into separate townships on the less desirable and more removed Cape Flats, the latter legally institutionalizing the preferential hiring of Coloured laborers over Black laborers throughout the Western Cape (even if enforcement of this policy was more often than not driven by economic exigencies).

With the life-world of 'apartheid subjects' being so comprehensively governed by the racial semiotics and institutions of the apartheid state, those distinguished as 'Coloured' over the course of the 20th century acquired differing degrees of self-consciousness as a 'group' with a unique history and collective experience of its own.[20] It is in no small part the historical imbrication of 'Coloured' identity in colonial and apartheid discourses and strategies of divide and rule that made hip-hop such a resonant resource for the making and remaking of Coloured youth identities and identifications in the Cape beyond the strictures and ascriptions of the apartheid state (see Warner 2007 for instance for more on hip-hop's formative role in inculcating Black Consciousness among Cape 'eX-Coloured' youth). The question of individual and collective self-identification, in this historical context, is one that has assumed paramountcy within the late and post-apartheid 'Cape Coloured problem space.'

'cornered communities' and conceptual complicities

> The paradox of cultural heterogeneity, or cross-cultural capacity, lies in the evolutionary thrust it restores to orders of the imagination, the ceaseless dialogue it inserts between hardened conventions and eclipsed or half-eclipsed otherness, within an intuitive self that moves endlessly into flexible patterns, arcs or bridges of community.
> —Wilson Harris, 1983[21]

It has been said so often that the Negro is lacking in originality, that it has almost become a gospel... the Negro is a very original human being. While he lives and moves in the midst of a white civilization, everything that he touches is re-interpreted for his own use.

–Zora Neale Hurston, 1934[22]

While there are important and significant differences between Cape Coloured and African American social and political histories and problem spaces deriving from differing U.S.-South African delineations of the color line (or lines in the South African context) – Cape Town being racially ordered by a tripartite racial schema versus the U.S. binary one drop rule – both populations nevertheless can be seen to share a historical fate of those Eduouard Glissant describes as 'cornered communities (1989:14-15),' in his effort to distinguish the unique historical and existential predicaments of uprooted, transplanted and formerly enslaved populations.[23] A distinguishing feature of the creole communities and expressive cultural forms produced out of such trans-Atlantic historical encounters and situations is the clear visibility of their *constructedness* "out of fragmented cultural materials," which have been made "available in the contexts of slavery, colonialism, and cultural dispossession (Erasmus 2001:23)." 'Composite peoples,' as Glissant names them, cannot easily hide or deny their trans-local and composite constitution. It is precisely the visibility of the seams of encounter/relation, within such communities, that forces them to have to continually contend with claims, in no small part anthropologically constituted, that they are a people without culture or history. "That's one thing that us as a coloured community has been totally stripped of," a WildLife Society crew member in Beacon Valley, Mitchell's Plain for instance related to me on one occasion, evidencing the widespread internalization of this view. "You know, our language, our nationality, our history. We don't have even history here. Coloured people in the whole Cape Flats area don't have history." Further compounding the question and problematic of Coloured identity, undergirding the Cape Coloured problem space, is the necessary negotiation, by members of this community, of a category hegemonically framed and cast, in the context of colonial and apartheid rule, as a sign of racial impurity and pollution.[24]

Old school Cape Town hip-hoppers were highly conscious of trans-Atlantic convergences in histories of slavery and displacement. "Back in the days, you had to listen to NWA, Public Enemy, Run DMC and all that people right...They were rapping and spreading the message about slavery and way back stuff. They took it way back to the time when they used to ship Africans to America and all that stuff," Steady D for instance explained, of the engagement with such histories in the rap songs making their way across the Atlantic in the late 1980s. A younger Cape Town hip-hopper, Zinaida, attributed hip-hop's ('so-called') Coloured origins in South Africa to such notable ('cornered community') historical affinities. As she argued:

> In the Cape Flats where hip-hop was originated, in Cape Town, there's a larger grouping of like, mixed race people, so-called Coloured people and um, so-called Coloured people in South Africa identify very strongly with American culture, because...in America, they were also called Coloured and they are non-white people who kind of speak English and no other language...They're [both] social hybrids. So it has a far bigger and much more foundational following there initially than it would have in Johannesburg because there's that connection, you know.

DJ Rozzano likewise asserted the importance of language as a factor in hip-hop's origins in the Cape, mapped onto a more immediate visceral connection: "Why Cape Coloured folk hooked on to black music coming out of the States was that it was English and they could understand it, and subliminally they were proud that they could see THEIR type of people on a record." Such socio-historical affinities between Cape Coloured and Black Diasporic communities partially accounts for the reason why Cape Coloured communities have historically been at the forefront of introducing Black American musical-cultural styles and forms into the South African musical-cultural formation (see Coplan 1985; Hamm 1988).

The explanation of hip-hop's cultural appeal in Cape Town in terms of Cape Coloureds alleged *lack* of an existing culture to draw upon is an all too commonplace assertion apparent not only in the discourses of Cape Coloured youth (albeit for understandable historical-ideological reasons), but also in the little social scientific literature to date on hip-hop in South Africa, much of which has reproduced the narrative of Coloureds as a 'people without culture or history.' In his otherwise informative (2001) article, `*Simunye, we are not one': ethnicity, difference and the hip-hoppers of Cape Town*, Lee Watkins, for instance, hypothesizes that "[f]or hip-hoppers who identify themselves as coloured, hip-hop is a culture that fills the void left by the absence of a 'culture' (2001:35)"[25] – a purported absence that, in effect, reproduces the very discourse of cultural paucity/poverty justifying colonial/apartheid rule.

Exemplifying the ongoing impact and internalization of such discourses in popular and academic circles, notions of Coloureds as a people bereft of an authentic culture of their own were expressed on numerous occasions by old school Cape Coloured hip-hoppers:

> Look the Coloureds are impersonative, you know. Like they are copy-cats man....Coloureds can be very quickly influenced [snaps finger, as if to say 'just like that'] and they can change [snaps finger again] there on the minute. You understand? They can change there on a minute. Where[as] the Blacks have their

tradition, and their principles, and their way of living, right [and] the whites, right, are more flexible, by running with the trend of the environment around them, you understand (Interview with Cape Town old school b-boy Bernard).

In his explanation of hip-hop's origins and popularity in the Cape, DJ Hamma gave voice to a similar notion of Coloureds as lacking in identity and culture, in contradistinction to resistive Blacks, and innovative Whites. As he explained:

White people were always in the process of achieving, looking within themselves and then achieving more. And Black people were always in the process of just freeing themselves. So Coloured people had more time on their hands, that's why we got hold of this shit first. Just because that time the system made us to be like people that's not really that busy. So we were never really in the process of creating or becoming ourselves. We were always in the process of adopting something that we picked up from tv, or adopting something that we picked up from radio. That's why if you go to Coloured townships you will always see something that you've seen on TV, playing off in them. You'll be like, shit, ok, the vatos locos. Now there's a vatos locos gang in the township. Junior Mafia, now there's a Junior Mafia gang and like west side, east side, in the coloured communities, that was like hardcore. People were killing each other over bullshit like that [Biggie vs. Tupac affiliated gangs].

It is not difficult to see how a political economy structurally reinforcing white agency and hampering black and brown, could give rise to such a view of whites as "always in the process of looking within themselves and then achieving more" (versus resistive blacks, thrust into oppositional mode, by white hegemony, and 'passive' coloureds, cast in a liminal space of unbecoming). Though drawing on dominant apartheid-media-reproduced racial stereotypes,[26] Hamma nevertheless begins here to articulate the specificity of the predicament and experience of cornered communities alienated from traditional or conventional "methods of existence and survival, both material and spiritual (Erasmus 2001:22, citing Glissant 1989:103)."

The notion alluded to above by Hamma that Coloureds are 'idlers' and 'lackeys' of the system, though not entirely without historical referent,[27] is nevertheless contradicted by the historical record and active role of Coloured youth in precipitating a rising tide of resistance in the 1980s (see Karis & Gerhart 1997). Indeed, a significant (though not always explicit) part of hip-hop's resonance for Cape Coloured youth over this period was its communication of a sense of Black agency and oppositionality in general, and, translated into the South African context, against the prevailing apartheid order in specific. As Ray of the pioneering Cape Town hip-hop crew, *Black Noise*, related in this respect, at once referencing and contesting dominant narratives:

> whenever people have got no past, and schools and the white structures keep on telling these people that they're creation is slavery, and they got no past but one of slavery, um, kids like, they try and fight against the status quo and hip-hop is, initially it's completely chaotic, you know. It's a lot of colours, it's a lot of brights, bright colours, a lot of sound which at first sounds like a whole lot of noise and people being very very controversial. I think a lot of the youth were attracted to that: going against the grain of what society is all about. So a lot of kids were like 'irie cool' when you do this. I mean, it's a new culture, no one can tell us what to do...Then you see this entire culture emerging from the Cape Flats.

His description of hip-hop's functioning at the time as 'noise', in disruption of the apartheid obsession with 'order', is apt, illustrating as it does both the counter-hegemonic 'colours' and 'noise' attracting headz to this 'new culture', and the pull of its democratic ethos and aesthetic sensibility ('no one can tell us what to do'), in the context of an authoritarian, racially and culturally prescriptive apartheid state.

Demonstrating the ambivalence often surrounding Coloured identities and identifications in South Africa, Hamma offers a more positive reading of Cape Coloured culture in another interview where he embraces and affirms the creative and life enriching creolité of places like Mitchell's Plains:

> Mitchell's Plain is the best place in the world...You can feel the soul man, you feel energy, you feel creativity there man, you feel it. Everybody's always up to something, you know. Uh...you walk in Mitchell's Plain, you see things and you're like, 'Ja man, wat vang die bastards nou weer aan?' [What're these bastards up to now?]. It's like, jissus, how they come up with all these things just like...the way they talk, dress, shit they like, how they go into stuff and what they get out of it, only they know man. It's the best place (cited in Lombard 2001:18).

Hamma here begins to articulate an alternative "language for comprehending mixture outside of jeopardy and catastrophe (Gilroy 2000:217)," one more consistent with the etymological roots of the term creole – which derives from the Latin *creare*, meaning *"to create."* While a distinguishing feature of creole cultural formations may well be their formation under unequal conditions out of cultural fabrics not originally of their own making, we as cultural analysts would do well to highlight the great ingenuity, skill, and agency exercised in bringing something culturally new into the world from the space of the consummate cultural tactician.[28] This refined ability to "convey in a language that is not one's own the spirit that is one's own" (Ashcroft et al. 1989:38, citing Rao) is poignantly alluded to by original school Cape Town hip-hopper, Shaheen, formerly of Prophets of the City:

> Hip-hop came to a people who had their histories stripped, their voices stripped, ill issues around self-worth and all of that and provided them with [a voice] like hey, look, whoah, you know, shit the only avenue was through *there* but it's still *ours*, you know what I mean!

Further contributing to hip-hop's special appeal and resonance in the Cape is hip-hop's 'cut'n'mix' aesthetic and break-beat musical-cultural form, which bears resemblance to other creole musical-cultural traditions in the Cape, from the popular musical adaptations annually trumpeted out by marching bands in the Coon Carnival processions (see Martin 1998) to the long tradition of Cape Town jazz, and before that, minstrelsy, all of which similarly foreground improvisation, innovation, and re-mix savvy. "It was easy to latch onto something that felt familiar," Shaheen tellingly related of his gravitation towards hip-hop in this respect, implicitly articulating a sense of familiarity born, arguably, in part from his own familial upbringing and exposure to South African jazz by way of his jazz musician father; hip-hop aesthetic practices, like jazz, being extremely adaptable, and uniquely suitable, to the creative reconstruction of fractured and displaced histories and (diasporic) subjectivities (see Rose 1994; Walser 1995; Watkins 2001 for analogous arguments to this effect). Indeed, it is precisely the honing of such creole cultural-artistic skills by 'cornered communities' the world over, that assists and enables them to continually resist and endure ongoing histories of displacement, as argued by Hamma, in his revaluation of the creole Coloured predicament:

Adapting is like an easy thing for our people man. Like, they know how to adapt – they're used to getting all fucked up and getting back on their feet. They down, but never down-and-out you know...So new communities were formed [on the Cape Flats] (cited in Lombard 2001:18).

Cultural imperialism aside, it is the very adaptability of the cultural forms borne of such situations, in and by communities of creolité that helps to explain their worldwide popularity and ease of diffusion.

'urban renewal': from america to south africa

In looking at the historical contexts more immediately conditioning hip-hop's development in 1970s New York and 1980s Cape Town, numerous and quite striking parallels come into view, which have undoubtedly indirectly contributed to the stirring of a hip-hop identity of passions in the Cape. Particularly notable, in this regard, is the experiential sharing of a brutal process of communal destruction and relocation, in the aftermath of government-sponsored and executed 'urban renewal' projects. The overlapping policy rationales of such projects on both sides of the Atlantic (engaged below) are in many ways illustrative of the relative non-exceptionalism of racialized urban development policies in South Africa, as compared to other (post)industrialized urban metropolises.

group areas act

Among the policies having the greatest impact upon Coloured communities in the Cape under apartheid rule was the Group Areas Act. Legislated into existence in 1950, in conjunction with the Population Registration Act, and enforced with rigor in the late 1950s and 1960s with the coming to power of

'Grand Apartheid' architect, Henrick Verwoerd, the Group Areas Act was part and parcel of National Party efforts to create a white-only South Africa, surrounded by satellites of 'tribal homelands' ('bantustans'). Where the latter proved impractical, owing to economic exigencies and the difficulties posed to apartheid ethnology by 'composite' and 'trans-local' peoples with questionable relationships to 'native soil', racially delimited and circumscribed neighborhood enclaves on the outskirts of major urban centers functioned in there steed. Being unable to invent a separate homeland for 'Coloureds' and 'Indians' *outside* of the declared white republic of South Africa, Coloureds and Indians became the principal targets of the Group Areas Act, representing, by 1975, 63 percent and 35 percent of all those resettled under this legislation (Pickel 1997:30). By 1970 a total of 208 new towns had been created for Coloureds, as part of a concomitant effort to monopolize residential and commercial urban space for white residents and businesses (Pinnock 1984:48).[29]

The official ideological justification for this massive project of racial-spatial engineering was known as 'racial friction theory' (Western 1996:85), which purported that contact between the races would always and inevitably produce 'friction'. Residential segregation, it was argued, would help eliminate such friction, whilst promoting healthy 'national' cultural 'pride' (as 'nation' increasingly came to replace 'race' as the favored NP discourse of difference, in an attempt to gain international legitimacy). Unstated in such rationales were the heavily weighted concerns with 'national' – i.e. 'white' – security, as articulated in the *Outline of (the Foreshore) Scheme for Cape Town*. Initially proposed by the Cape Town City Council in 1935 as part of a project to reclaim urban city space for railway development, *Outline of (the Foreshore) Scheme for Cape Town* would later go on to form the blueprint for the Group Areas Act. The 1935 Outline stated:

> Having fixed the position of the town from the geo-
> graphical and economic points of view, its defense

is now the important matter for consideration. Its protection against external and internal attack must be planned for (E.E. Beaudouin, *Outline of Scheme [Foreshore] for Cape Town*, Cape Town, 1940:24, cited in Pinnock 1984:44).

The main consultant contracted by Cape Town City Council to draft and implement this scheme – Chief French government architect, Eugene Beaudouin – based his *Foreshore Outline* on the ideas of Swiss urban planner Le Corbusier. Heralded as a pioneer of modern functionalist architecture (in particular the concept of a house as a 'machine for living'), Le Corbusier, founder of the Congress Internationaux d'Architecture Moderne (C.I.A.M.), has also been accredited with the design of "bombable blocks of flats, the minimum living cell for workers (14 sq.m), the Volkswagen Beetle...and *grands ensembles* of 'graph-paper' flats (Pinnock 1984:43)." Many of the security concerns that would later materialize in the Group Areas design of the Cape Flats were in fact first articulated by such mainstream, 'modern' urban/architectural planners as Le Corbusier, who argued in depth about the need to establish 'protective zones' between the city centre and surrounding housing areas in such treatises as *The City of Tomorrow and Its Planning* (1929), where he advised:

> Surgery must be applied to the city's centre. Physics must be used elsewhere. We must use the knife...Our first requirement will be an organ which is compact, rapid, lively and concentrated: this is the city with its well-organised centre. Our second requirement will be another organ, supple, extensive and elastic: this is the Garden City on the periphery. Lying between these two organs, we must *require* the legal establishment of that absolute necessity, a protective zone... (p.166, cited in Pinnock 1984:44, 47).

Another 'template' for the new racially-segregated Cape Flats ghettos was provided by Ebenezer Howard's (1898) *Garden Cities for Tomorrow, A Peaceful Path to Reform*, which would later inform the modern suburb concept in urban planning. The book calls for the establishment of "a 'ring of satellite towns served by a rapid transport network," in order to "canalize [sic] the flow of population...from the existing centre to new centers...surrounded by a belt of green vegetation (38)." Howard's concept of 'green vegetation belts' between cities and towns – the designs of which, Pinnock argues, were in no small part a "response to the rapid growth of an urban proletariat in the London inner-city of the late-19th century" (1984:45) – would later become translated by South African Group Area Act planners into 'machine gun belts' and 'buffer zones.'

u.s. slum clearance program

When we compare developments under the Group Areas Act in Cape Town with those carried out under the auspices of New York's Slum Clearance Programs, numerous intersections are apparent, lending further credence to Pinnock's parallel-making between the functions and goals of apartheid urban planning, and urban capitalist planning more generally in the modern era. The very South Bronx housing projects from which hip-hop's first generation of cultural producers emerged after having been relocated there following the building of the Cross Bronx Expressway and completion of the Federal 'Urban Renewal'/'Slum Clearance Program' were likewise modeled after the designs of the Swiss modern functionalist architect, Le Corbusier. The public housing 'superblocks' built throughout New York City and urban centers across the United States– intentionally designed, following Le Corbusier, in such a way as to create a physical gulf between the city grid and the new 'ex-slum' residents (much as in Cape Town, undoubtedly in part for unstated security reasons) – achieved, in effect, what apartheid planners achieved by decree: the concentration and containment of poor Black and Latino communities

in condensed and containable 'living spaces of poverty.'[30] Justifi-
cations for such measures, moreover, took on similar ideological
overtones in both places: the Group Areas Act and Slum Clearance Programs both being avowedly pursued for 'community
development' ('urban renewal') purposes, designed to pre-empt
the further breeding of crime, 'disease', 'moral pollution', and
'disorder' in 'blighted areas' (citing the words of P.W. Botha in
Pinnock 1984:30). The key lesson to be gleaned from this brief
history of coincidences in international urban planning designs
and networks is, again, in many ways the non-exceptionalism of
the South African case: "post-war urban replanning [being] not
merely the product of apartheid or Afrikaner racism" but also a
very basic and widespread "spatial response to the development
of monopoly capital on a world scale" (Pinnock 1984:45).

rebuilding: a hip-hop identity of passions

In accord with the opening quote by Ralph Ellison, the
hip-hop 'identity of passions' cultivated in the Cape derives in
no small part from such analogous socio-historical experiences
and resulting cultural affinities. Among the many disheveling
impacts of the Group Areas removals, for the communities
moved into the new low-rise 'apartheid dumping grounds' (as
they became known) on the Cape Flats region, was a shattering of
long-established kinship and neighborhood networks, together
with the social and economic supports that these provided. Such
dislocations had the effect, in the new locations, of augmenting
fear, isolation, marginalization, substance abuse, and criminal
gang activity, as strangers became thrown together in new hostile
environments, distant from each other and the city, in environments lacking recreational facilities and resources, economic
opportunities, and a sense of community cohesion (see Pinnock
1984). As original school Cape Flats DJ, Ready D, vividly recol-
lects of the impact of his relocation from inner-city Cape Town's
District Six to the more remote Cape Flats:

[I remember] ja, like it was yesterday...I was eleven years old...We were more happier that side of the mountain [District Six], even though people were living all on top of one another, but there was really a strong sense of community and people you could depend on. You knew exactly what was going on, so you have to – how could a person say? – you have to readapt, you have to find new ways of surviving because there were no neighbors [sic] you could run to. You didn't know the people who were next to you. And I think that also contributed to a lot of the gang problems on the Cape Flats, especially Mitchell's Plain, because people from so many different backgrounds and different areas...and ganglands were all just thrown in....And that contributed to setting fuel to the flames as well, just apart from everyday trying to survive, you know... (cited in Lombard 2001:4).

Dr. Oscar Wolheim of the Cape Flats Distress Association cogently summarizes the impact of the Group Areas removals as being "like a man with a stick breaking spider-webs in a forest. The spider may survive the fall, but he can't survive without his web. When he comes to build it again he finds the anchors are gone, the people are all over, and the fabric of generations is lost" (cited in Pinnock 1984:56). The resonance of this depiction of the impact of the Group Areas Act with Tricia Rose's description of the dishevelling social and economic impact of the building of the Cross-Bronx Expressway, and implementation of Title I Slum Clearance program, affecting hip-hop's founding Bronx, New York communities, is considerable. As Tricia Rose concludes, in her assessment of the impact of such policies and programs in the American hip-hop context:

> Subsequent ethnic and racial transition in the South Bronx was not a gradual process that might have allowed already taxed social and cultural institutions

to respond self-protectively; instead, it was a brutal process of community destruction [that]...devastated kin networks and neighborhood [sic] services (1994:30).

The rapid growth of an illicit economy and proliferation of gangs and territorial wars, in response to this dearth of social and economic institutions and opportunities, was among the more pronounced outcomes of such policies of urban renewal in New York City and Cape Town; New York City, at hip-hop's (1973) birth, having some 315 gangs with 19,000 members,[31] and the Cape Flats, with the highest murder and incarceration rate in South Africa, and one of the highest in the world, having an estimated 280 self-identified gangs with some 280,000 members at the time of hip-hop's appearance in 1982.[32]

It is in this context – among communities "whose older local support institutions had been all but demolished along with large sectors of [their] built environment (Rose 1994:34)" – that hip-hop arose as a creative force, reconstructing value, community and identity for (breakin' yet not broken) youth in settings systematically depleted of social and economic resources, as conveyed in the following juxtaposed trans-Atlantic testimonies, evidencing a translocal hip-hop identity of passions:

> **Kool DJ AJ[33] (New York)**: See, in the South Bronx we really had nothing to do. There wasn't no movie theatres – everything we did was like something just to make a little bit of excitement in the area...And then when people seen Kool DJ Herc, it was like some excitement, and it drew a crowd. I just took notice, and it was interesting.

> **Trash (Cape Town)**: We live in a ghetto. This is a ghetto...It's bad in the backstreets, you know... During apartheid we never had any recreation facilities, up to today... We had to create something for

ourselves, because why, the groups you know, they came from the ghetto...

Afrika Bambaataa (U.S.): When we made Hip Hop, we made it hoping it would be about peace, love, unity and having fun so that people could get away from the negativity that was plaguing our streets (gang violence, drug abuse, self hate, violence among those of African and Latino descent). Even though this negativity still happens here and there, as the culture progresses, we [continue to] play a big role in conflict resolution and enforcing positivity.[34]

Gambit of Native Sons (SA): See, hip hop is a way out of the ghetto. Not just the physical ghetto, that's obvious. It's really a way out of the ghetto of the mind. And that's the hardest part to escape. The poverty, the alcoholism, the drug abuse – hip hop is a way of dealing with the way these things have affected our minds (cited in Harris 2004).[35]

notes

1. The opening section of the 1950 Population Registration Act, so crucial to the administration of apartheid, offers relational definitions of racial subjects, as described by Reddy:

    A 'coloured person', [this 1950 Act] says, 'means a person who is not a white person or a native' (Statutes, 277). A 'native' 'means a person who in fact is or is generally accepted as a member of any aboriginal race or tribe of Africa'. And a 'white person means a person who in appearance obviously is, or who is generally accepted as, a white person, but does not include a person who, although in appearance obviously a white person, is generally accepted as a coloured person' (Statutes 277; cited in Reddy 2001: 74-5).

The apartheid state's reliance on 'general acceptance' as a measure of race, as opposed to physical features exclusively, evidences not only the socially constructed (ideological) nature of such categories, but also the impossibility of unambiguous racial classification, using strict phenotypic criteria (in contradistinction, as Reddy points out, to the alleged 'obviousness of race' proclaimed by the apartheid state).

2. Quotation marks surround the term 'Coloured' here to signify the contested nature of this historically multivalent, ideologically vested racialized category of identification among those so labeled in twentieth century South Africa. I will not be employing quotation marks henceforth in this chapter, having flagged this issue here.

3. Drawing on the work of David Scott, the notion of the problem space, as I use and develop it, essentially refers to the socio-historically conditioned 'space of questions' – and contending answers – navigated and negotiated by social actors in a particular historical moment, in and through social and cultural practice (see Warner 2007). In my 2007 thesis, I argue that it is primarily through the prism of generically organized discourse and practice – or what I call 'genre rules (drawing methodologically on the work of Simon Frith) – that such 'problem spaces', and positionings within them, are negotiated and contested in the world of popular music.

4. Part of what distinguishes Ellison's formulation of the basis of trans-Atlantic Black solidarity is his attention to 'ties that bind' beyond race and culture – commonly assumed, unproblematically, to underlie Black Atlantic cultural exchange and affinity, as exemplified in and through African hip-hop. Ellison's invocation of an identity of passions moreover draws attention to the shifting, sometimes inchoate, polymorphous nature of such identifications, borne of common suffering and alienation from Euro-modernity, owing to their passional origins and lodging beneath the surface of explicit consciousness (in Gramscian terms). Extending Ellison's insights, I elsewhere develop the notion of Black Globality -conceived of as a distinctive contemporary black vernacular form of cosmopolitanism – as a conceptual framework for thinking about

the multiple and varied kinds of identifications and affiliations forged by and between hip-hoppers globally (see Warner 2007).

5. Recently inducted into the Rock and Roll Hall of Fame as one of the ten best rock'n' roll movies of all time, *Wild Style* is widely championed for its holistic and authentic documentation of the early days of hip-hop in New York, largely due to its combination of cast and producers (Charlie Ahearn and Fab Five Freddy), most of whom are drawn directly from the early hip-hop community.

6. See Richochet Skillz One on hip-hop's 1982 diffusion to South Africa via the movie Wildstyle (http://www.zulunation.com/hip_hop_history_2.htm).

7. Beat Street features a legendary battle between the Rock Steady Crew and the New York City Breakers.

8. While hip-hop remained primarily confined to the Northeastern states of America between 1978 and 1982 (Forman 1997: 166), hip-hop would soon feature in major blockbuster movies such as *Flashdance* which spread the form to the west coast of America and, simultaneously, to the rest of the world (See famed L.A b-boys, Skeeta Rabbit and Baby Huey on the key role of *Flashdance* in hip-hop's spread to the west coast in Israel's *The Freshest Kids: a history of the b-boy*, 2002; Also see Cross 1993 for similar account dating 1982-83 as a pivotal year in hip-hop's diffusion to L.A).

9. Key to the global reorganization of the music industry was the huge success of Michael Jackson's 1982 hit album, *Thriller*, which became the biggest-selling record in history, largely thanks to international record sales, which exceeded domestic sales. Such international success set a precedent for other major recording companies to follow, as they "increasingly looked outwards internationally for new markets" in the 80s (Burnett 1996: 47-8).

10. See Gronow & Sauinio (1998: 188) and Burnett (1996: 51) for a description of the 1980s 'merger mania' in the music recording industry.

11. See Burnett 1996; Hesmondhalgh 1996:144; Garafalo 1999: 342; Straw 1993.

12. Radio became '*the* principal media wing of the Bantustan system' following Afrikaner Broederbond SABC appointments, mainly

for reasons of accessibility and (il)literacy among the intended African audiences (Nixon 1994: 65; emphasis mine).

13. Following the worldwide coverage of the Soweto uprising and its bloody aftermath, the British actors' union Equity initiated a boycott of program sales to South Africa that would last until the end of apartheid, which in broadcasting terms meant that most acquired programming came from the United States.

14. TV 2, created in 1982 for black audiences, split into two separate channels in 1983 (TV 2/3), with "TV4 operating off the TV2/3 frequencies after those stations closed down at 9:30pm, and for an hour between 6pm and 7pm (Tomaselli et al., 2001: 110)." For discussion of the place of Black American programming such as *The Cosby Show* in South Africa, see Ron Krabill's 2002 Ph.D. "Starring Mandela and Cosby: Television, Identity, and the End of Apartheid." See also Tomaselli et al. (2001: 156,163,166).

15. Ready D Interview by McCloy, 'Are You Ready?', *Rage* [ezine], Issue 12, cited at http://www.rage.co.za/sess_id=d13eced261a4a4dbbb3 44d1f05387084/ragemore2.php3?pre_sess_url=/ragemore2.php3 &moreid=ready&moreissue=12&template=frags/rage-arc.htmlt.

16. See Soudien (2001: 118) on the history of District Six and the great diversity of peoples historically populating it.

17. See Martin 1998: 529 and Martin 1999.

18. Most slaves worked in the Cape Colony on farms and vineyards, with roughly one third working as craftsmen, domestic servants and salesmen in the bourgeoning Town (Martin 1998:525; see Worden and Crais 1994). Altogether, at least some 60,000 slaves were imported to the Cape between 1658 and 1807, with an estimated 36.40 percent coming from India, 31.47percent from the East Indies, and 26.65 percent from Africa (more than half of whom came from Madagascar) (Martin 1998: 525). Western describes "[t]he main ingredients in the 'mix' that is the Coloured people today" as "Madagscan, East African, Ceylonese, Bengali, and Malayo-Indonesian slaves (1996: 12)."

19. South African governmental policy and discourse would alternate over the course the 20th century between efforts to 'append' Coloureds, as lesser partners to white ruling populations (as 'brown Afrikaners'), and efforts to socially engineer a distinctive and sep-

arate Coloured 'nation', equidistant from both Blacks and Whites, as was the favoured strategy by the *verkramptes* (conservative) wing of Afrikanerdom which came into power in 1948, ushering in 46 years of apartheid.

20. Rather than being merely imposed and prescribed from above by apartheid decree, 'Coloured' identities as such were "made and re-made by coloured people themselves" over the twentieth century (Erasmus 2001: 16; see also Martin 1998).

21. Wilson Harris. *The Womb of Space: The Cross-Cultural Imagination.* Westport: Greenwood, 1983, p. xvii.

22. Hurston, Zora Neale. "Characteristics of Negro Expression." *Zora Neale Hurston: Folklore, Memoirs and Other Writings.* Ed. Cheryl Wall. New York: Library of America, 1995. pp. 830-46.

23. See Frederickson (1981: 255-6) for more detailed elucidation of the differences and parallels between South African Coloured and African American communities in this respect.

24. Particularly because social structure and identity formation in South Africa has been so staunchly and starkly ordered and configured by absolute boundaries between black and white, cemented in large measure by discourses of racial 'authenticity' and 'purity', 'coloured' has long signified a "debased in-betweener [and] perceived product of the transgression of a sacrosanct boundary (Lewis 1987:133)." Such depictions of Coloureds are powerfully conveyed in the words of celebrated South African writer and feminist, Olive Schreiner, who wrote of Cape Coloured's debased nature and predicament, only sixty years after emancipation:

> The Half-caste of all created things is at war with his own individuality....Without nationality, tradition, or racial ideals...robbed of racial self-respect...The English-man will swear to you on the word of an Englishman, and the Bantu on the word of the Bantu, but no Half-caste ever yet swore on the honour of a Half-caste. The world would break into cackling laughter did he do so: 'The *honour* of a *Half-caste!'* (Schreiner 1923[1890]: 126-127, *Thoughts on South Africa,* cited in Western 1996: 15).

native tongues: an african hip-hop reader

Though represented as inferior to whites yet superior to blacks in the tripartite racial hierarchy of the Cape, "a tension [has nevertheless] always existed between the proclaimed superiority which the taint of white blood conferred on 'mixed' descent peoples versus the 'purity' of descent/blood ascribed to Africans," observes Hendricks (2001: 43).

25. In the same quote Watkins (2001) describes "rap music [as] a metaphor for displaced people, for people without culture and roots," in the process reifying 'culture' as a thing to be had, found or lost.

26. In their (2001) study of 1980s SABC television programming for nonwhite audiences, Tomaselli et al. for instance observe, in regards to the stereotype of whites as cultural creatives, that "the motor for class aspiration" in such shows "appears to be hinged on the way whites are presented (or intrude): *skilled, educated, innovative, creative,* fashionable, a sort of 'You too, can be like me' (p. 165; italics mine)."

27. Hamma's depiction of coloureds as politically passive and/or apolitical is not without some historical credence, as Karis & Gerhart contend of the Coloured youth joining and spearheading the resistance movement in the 1980s:

> Most Coloured students came from apolitical homes where economically aspiring parents put emphasis on academic success [rather than political commitment]. Others had been exposed to the dominant political tradition among Coloureds in the western Cape, the principled but essentially passive, rejectionist tradition of the Non-European Unity movement [which] prescribed noncollaboration with all racially discriminatory institutions, but offered no solution to the reality that only one university – a racially segregated one – was open to Coloureds (1997:138).

28. De Certeau distinguishes between the cultural space of production defined by the tactic – shaped by the *absence* of power (conse-

quently requiring 'poetic ways of making do' within the dominant cultural order) – and that of strategy, which is conversely "organized by the postulation of power (De Certeau 1984: 38)."

29. As part of this Act, one in every six Coloured persons was removed and relocated into a Coloured township (totaling 306,000 people), with one in four Indians experiencing a similar fate, as compared to 1 in 666 Whites (Western 1996:73). When the sum of both those removed and those waiting to be removed are expressed as a percentage of the total population in each racial group, the proportions are 16.2 percent of Coloureds, 25.6 percent of Indians, and 0.15 percent of Whites (Western 1996: 72).

30. Such growing segregation, reinforced by white/middle class flight to the suburbs (itself partially facilitated by the building of the Cross Bronx Expressway) is evidenced in the fact that while in 1970, 20.2 percent of the South Bronx population was white, 33.9 percent Black and 35.1 percent Hispanic, by 1980, 91 percent of the population had become Black and Hispanic, a full 87 percent of the white population having by then moved out (Rodriguez 1991:109 cited in Rivera 2000:49; see Rose 1994 for a more detailed account of the consequences of urban renewal, including the building of the Cross Bronx Expressway and New York's Title I Slum Clearance Program).

31. Statistics cited in Keyes 2002, p. 46.

32. Statistics cited in Pinnock 1984: 4. Also see South African Survey statistics to this effect (1999: 62). Much as in the U.S. case among Blacks and Latinos, such social dislocation and marginalization registers itself in the disproportionately high rate of prison rates for those categorized as 'coloured' in South Africa – among the highest in the world (66 percent higher than the national average) as revealed in prison population statistics for the period from June 1979 to 1980:

Coloureds:	729 per 100 000 of the coloured population;
Africans:	362 per 100 000 of the African population;
Whites:	81 per 100 000 of the white population;
Asians:	57 per 100 000 of the Asian population

(Argus 14.10.1980, based on calculations by M. Slabbert; cited in Pinnock 1984: 75).

33. Kool DJ AJ was an early, widely respected, hip-hop DJ and promoter. This quote is taken from Fricke & Ahearn (2002: 35).
34. "ZULU ANNIVERSARY", http://www.jayquan.com/zulunews.htm.
35. Cited in Iain Harris' "Guerrilla hop – explorations in Cape Town's musical underground. Native Sons – Two turntables and a microphone, one laptop many voices", http://home.worldonline.co.za/~afribeat/beatroutes_nativesons.html. Downloaded 10/12/04.

bibliography

Ariefdien, Shaheen. 2004. Personal correspondence.Nov. 23, 2004.

Ashcroft B, Griffiths G, and Tiffin, H. 1989. *The empire writes back: theory and practice in post-colonial literatures*. London: Routledge.

Bambaataa, Afrika. 'Zulu Anniversary', <http://www.jayquan.com/zulunews.htm>.

Barnett, Clive. 1999. The limits of media democratization in South Africa: politics, privatization and regulation. *Media, Culture & Society* 21 (5): 649-671.

Burnett, Robert. 1996. *The Global Jukebox: The International Music Industry*. London:
Routledge.

Coplan, David. 1985. *In Township Tonight: South Africa's Black City Music and Theatre*. London, New York: Longman.

De Certeau, M. 1984. *The practice of everyday life*. Berkeley: University of California Press.

Drachler, J. 1975. *Black homeland/Black diaspora: cross-currents of the African relationship*. Port Washington, N. Y.: Kennikat Press.

Ellison, Ralph. 1953. Some Questions and Some Answers. *Shadow and Act*. New York: Random House.

Erasmus, Zimitri. 2001. Introduction: Re-Imagining Coloured Identities in Post-Apartheid South Africa. In *Coloured by History, Shaped by Place: New Perspectives on Coloured Identities in Cape Town*. Ed. Z. Erasmus. Cape Town: Kwela Books: 13-28.

Forman, M. 1997. "The 'Hood Comes First': Race, Space, and Place in Rap Music and Hip Hop, 1978-1996." Ph.D. Dissertation. McGill University.

Fredrickson, G.M. 1981. *White supremacy: a comparative study in American and South African history.* New York: Oxford University Press.

Fricke, J, Ahearn C, and Experience MP. 2002. *Yes yes y'all: the Experience Music Project oral history of hip-hop's first decade.* Cambridge, MA: Da Capo Press.

Garofalo, R. 1999. From music publishing to MP3: Music and industry in the 20th Century. *American Music.* 17: 318-353.

George, Nelson. 1998. *Hip hop America.* New York: Viking.

Gilroy, P. 2000. *Against Race: Imagining Political Culture Beyond the Color Line.* Cambridge, MA: Belknap.

Glissant, E. 1989. *Caribbean discourse: selected essays.* Charlottesville: University Press of Virginia.

Goldin, Ian. 1987. *Making race: the politics and economics of coloured identity in South Africa.* New York: Longman.

Gronow, Pekka and Ilpo, Saunio. 1998. *An International History of the Recording Industry.* London: Cassell.

Hamm, Charles. 1991. 'The Constant Companion of Man': Separate Development, Radio Bantu and Music. *Popular Music* 10 (2): 147-173.

_____. 1988. *Afro-American Music, South Africa, and Apartheid.* US: Institute for Studies in American Music.

Harris, Iain. Guerrilla hop – explorations in Cape Town's musical underground. Native Sons – Two turntables and a microphone, one laptop many voices. <http://home.worldonline.co.za/~afribeat/beatroutes_nativesons.html>. Downloaded December 10 2004

Hesmondhalgh, D. 1996. Flexibility, post-Fordism and the music industries. *Media Culture & Society* 18 (3): 469-488.

Hurston, Zora Neale. 1995. "Characteristics of Negro Expression." *Zora Neale Hurston: Folklore, Memoirs and Other Writings.* Ed. Cheryl Wall. New York: Library of America, 1995. 830-46.

Jensen, Emile. 1995. *What is Hiphop?* Self published booklet.

Karis, Thomas and Gerhart, Gail M. 1997. *From protest to challenge: a documentary history of African politics in South Africa, 1882-1990.* Bloomington: Indiana University Press.

Keyes, C.L. 2002. *Rap music and street consciousness.* Urbana IL: University of Illinois Press.

Klopper, S. 2000. Hip-Hop Graffiti Art. In *Senses Of Culture: South African Culture Studies*. Eds. Nuttall, Sarah, & Michael, Cheryl-Ann. 178-196. Cape Town, South Africa: Oxford U Press Southern Africa.

Krabill, R. 2004. Dissertation. *Starring Mandela and Cosby: Television, Identity, and the End of Apartheid. Dissertation/Thesis Starring Mandela and Cosby: Television, Identity, and the End of Apartheid*.

Lombard, R. 2001. "'bustin' out"- transcending boundaries through performance: hip hop as 'lifestyle' in cape town. BA thesis dissertation, Dept of Social Anthropology, University of Cape Town.

Martin, D.C. 1998. The Famous Invincible Darkies Cape Town's Coon Carnival: Aesthetic Transformation, Collective Representations and Social Meanings. <http://www.iias.nl/host/ccrss/cp/cp3/cp3>. Downloaded April 14 2002.

McCloy, M. *Are You Ready? Rage* [ezine], Issue 12; cited at <http://www.rage.co.za>.

Nixon, R. 1994. *Homelands, Harlem and Hollywood: South African culture and the world beyond*. London: Routledge.

Pickel, Birgit. 1997. *Coloured ethnicity and identity: a case study in the former coloured areas in the Western Cape/South Africa*. Hamburg: Lit.

Pinnock, D. 1984. *The Brotherhoods: Street Gangs and State Control in Cape Town*. Cape Town: David Philips.

Reddy, T. 2001. The Politics of Naming: The Construction of Coloured Subjects in South Africa. In *Coloured by History, Shaped by Place: New Perspectives on Coloured Identities in the City*. Ed. Zimitri Erasmus. Cape Town: Kwela Press.

Ricochet Skillz One, a.k.a. Ricky Ricky Napthali Tafari. Letter on the Universal Zulu Nation. <http://www.zulunation.com/hip_hop_history_2.htm

Rivera RZ. 2000. New York Ricans from the Hip Hop Zone: Between Blackness and Latinidad. Dissertation/Thesis.

Rose, T. 1994. *Black Noise: Rap Music and Black Culture in Contemporary America*. Hanover, New England: Wesleyan University Press..

Saul, JS and Gelb, S. 1986. *The Crisis in South Africa*. Revised Edition. New York and London: Zed Books Ltd.

Scott, D. 1999. *Refashioning Futures: Criticism after Postcoloniality.* Princeton: Princeton University Press.

_____. 1991. That Event, This Memory: Notes on the Anthropology of African Diasporas in the New World. *Diaspora* 1 (3): 261-284.

Shamiel, X. <http://www.outcast.co.za/hhShamiel.htm>.

Soudien, C. 2001. District Six and its Uses in the Discussion about Non-racialism. In *Coloured by History, Shaped by Place: New Perspectives on Coloured Identities in Cape Town.* Ed. Z. Erasmus. Cape Town: Kwela Books.

Tomaselli, K, Tomaselli, R. and Muller, J. 2001. *Narrating the Crisis: Hegemony and the South African Press.* Denver, CO: Academic Books.

Walser, R. 1995. Rhythm, rhyme, and rhetoric in the music of Public Enemy. *Ethnomusicology* 39 (2): 193-218.

Warner, R. 2001. Battles over Borders. Hiphop and the Politics and Poetics of Race and Place in the New South Africa. PhD thesis dissertation. Dept of Social Anthropology. York University.

Watkins, L. 2001. 'Simunye, we are not one': ethnicity, difference and the hip-hoppers of Cape Town. *Race and Class* 43 (1): 29.

Western, J. 1996. *Outcast Cape Town.*: Berkeley: U California Press.

Worden, N. 2000. *The Making Of Modern South Africa: Conquest, Segregation And Apartheid.* 3rd edition. Oxford: Blackwell Publishing.

Worden, Nigel and Crais, Clifton. 1994. *Breaking the chains: slavery and its legacy in nineteenth-century South Africa.* South Africa: Witwatersrand University Press.

PART II

"we are africans:"
african hip-hop beyond
the motherland

CHAPTER 6
hip-hop speaks, hip-life answers: global african music

HARRY NII KONEY ODAMTTEN   With its immediate
origins in the social
and lived realities of African American life in the United States,
the influence of hip-hop as a cultural and academic phenomenon spans the globe. Hip-hop embraces the entire array of
artistic expressions of various youth worldwide. These aesthetic
manifestations encompass young people's social consciousness,
which is demonstrated through music, art, fashion, linguistic,
and literary expressions. Popular media has produced countless
attempts to explain hip-hop culture's unprecedented impact and
global reach. In the academy, books and documentaries as well
as journals have been dedicated to theorizing on the forms and
functions of hip-hop.[1]

In addition to attracting the interest of journalists and scholars around the world, hip-hop is believed to have inspired the
development of another musical genre, hip-life. The relationship between hip-hop and its Ghanaian counterpart, dubbed
"hip-life" by its first practitioners, is so multifaceted that some
hip-life aficionados argue that hip-hop's true genesis should be
located in the oral cultures of sub-Saharan Africa. The term hip-
life is a combination of the hip in hip-hop, and life in high-life.

High-life is an indigenous Ghanaian musical genre that began in the late nineteenth century with influences from West Africa and the United States and became the staple of entertainment life in Ghana during and after its independence struggle in the twentieth century.[2] However it came to be, hip-life is also well on its way to sharing hip-hop's global stage.

Global Africa has been described as "the geographically and socio-culturally diverse people of Africa and its Diaspora ... linked through complex networks of social relationships and processes."[3] Hip-hop, high-life, and hip-life may all be described as genres within African/African Diasporic music or *Global African Music*; which is music of African origin that utilizes some aspect of African musical culture. Some of the common constituents in global African music include syncopation, poly-rhythm, call and response, and particularly for hip-hoppers and hip-lifers the art of improvisation.[4]

The following is an attempt to describe the historical beginnings and evolution of Ghanaian *hip-life* as a musical form, which owes its unique style and content to Ghana's internal social milieu and its dynamic connections with the African Diaspora. The study seeks to illuminate how hip-life artists combine and transform global African cultural aesthetics within their songs. To obtain this objective, this interrogation will rely on audio recordings, participant-observation, as well as, cultural analyses to map out the verbal art of hip-life artists. I suggest that in addition to Ghanaian verbal culture, artists draw on various oral cultures of the African Diaspora: U.S. African American hip-hop slang, Jamaican dancehall patois, whose lexicon and structure favor English based West African creole languages distinctively spoken in Ghana, Nigeria, and Sierra Leone.

This treatise will periodize and historicize the emergence of hip-life as a global African musical genre in Ghanaian culture. I also offer an analysis on the most distinctive aspect of hip-life; Ghanaian orality, which will be described and assessed through the recordings of hip-life entertainers, Tinny and ASEM.[5] Tinny is known for his prosaic lyrical delivery of parables in Ga, the language of the Ga-Adangbe ethnic peoples of Ghana. In this case study, I explore how Tinny uses the Ga speech form of self-debasement in his battle with hip-life group, Buk-Bak, in what appears to be a contest between the reigning lyricist in the Ga language, and a pioneering Ga rap group.[6] Tinny's contemporary, ASEM who raps in Akan-twi, has also gained notoriety for giving ambiguous meaning to his songs by using tonal change, specifically the use of pauses in his rap style.[7] This creates a series of alternative understandings to obscene words, words that without pauses would not be allowed on radio or television. I conclude that while it is a distinct Ghanaian musical genre, hip-life is simultaneously African Diasporic in its origins, production, and performance.

The 2008 presidential and parliamentary elections in Ghana witnessed hip-life artists parading the platforms of various political parties; as politicians tried to reach the Ghanaian populace with their campaign messages. Hip-life then, served as an integral medium of communication between the politicians and civil society. Beyond the internal dynamics of Ghana, hip-life has also established an international voice, attracting inquiries from researchers and media organizations like British Broadcasting Company (B.B.C.) and Al Jazerah English whose program *Playlist* showed the documentary *The Hiplife Music of Ghana* produced by Eli Jacobs-Fantauzi in 2009.[8]

Anthropologist, Jesse Shipley's documentary "Living the Hiplife," was screened at the African Studies Association Annual Meeting and Society for Visual Anthropology Film Festival, both in 2007, as well as, a 2008 showing at the Smithsonian National Museum of African Art.[9] Also in 2008, *American Theater* Magazine published "How Hip life theatre was born in Ghana; The Youth culture in the West African Nation takes the reins to create a new form of expression. (AFRICA WRITES BACK)."[10] These samples of contemporary productions demonstrate the growing global reach of hip-life. Nonetheless, academic analyses of hip-life as a musical genre and social force have been scant. The objective of the following chapter is to begin the process of establishing hip-life's importance to the intellectual arena.

defining and intellectualizing hip-life: historiography

Of the limited scholarly treatment hip-life has attracted, much has been carried out by scholars in training, mostly undergraduate students on study abroad in Ghana who have been attracted to the hip-life scene in Ghana. These studies stem from a variety of disciplines, and encompass efforts to both describe and analyze the processes involved in producing a hip-life album. A representative study of these texts is *The New Hip-life Beat: Rooted in Ga Drumming* written by Nate Ash-Morgan.[11] In this study, Ash-Morgan explores the musical production and Kpanlogo (Ga/Ghanaian drum music) origins of some contemporary hip-life songs through comparisons of Ghanaian percussive styles and U.S. Jazz sounds.

There is also a growing corpus of articles in academic journals focused on hip-life, including Jesse Shipley's study "Aesthetic of the Entrepreneur: Afro-Cosmopolitan Rap and Moral Circulation in Accra, Ghana."[12] Drawing on anthropological literature and music, Shipley shows the relationship between hip-life performers and a variety of public arenas in Ghana. He connects this negotiation process to a Ghanaian past and present, and the human need for self-assertion. Hip-life is also the subject of a doctoral dissertation by Tara Aminah (Ama Sika) Jabbaar-Gyambrah, who conducts a comparative study of U.S. African American and Ghanaian women's roles and representations in the Bronx, U.S. and Accra, Ghana. Emphasizing the transcultural origins of both genres, Jabbar-Gyambrah draws on women's studies approaches to highlight the similarities of socio-historical experience for hip-hop and hip-life women, as pioneers of Black popular culture.[13] Jabbar-Gymbrah has also written about

"Triple M, Representin', Reconstructin', and Resistin': Ideologies of Gender and Sexualities in Hip-life Music in Ghana."[14] Jabbar-Gyambrah's studies have served as the focus of academic presentations "The Herstory of Global Sistahs in Hip-life and Hip-hop," and "Sankofian Diasporic Connections of Hip-hop and Hip-life Music."[15] Another article produced by this prolific writer on hip-life is "Empowerment and Resistance: Ghanaian Women's Roles in Mzbel's 16 Years."[16] Jabbar-Gyambrah's latter studies focus on the transcultural and circulatory production of hip-life as a musical genre and the roles of women.[17]

Hip-hop's status as the most popular international musical genre has resulted in the eclipse of the particularities and endogenous realities of musical forms like hip-life, which are subsumed under global hip-hop in academic literature. Sometimes hip-life's endogamous affiliation to hip-hop is highlighted as evinced in the work of Jabbar-Gyamarah.

As intimated earlier, hip-life incorporates diverse musical forms of African origin, including music from West African neighbors like Nigeria and Ivory Coast, the U.S., and the Caribbean. This is not meant to claim nativity for hip-life, because hip-life has gone global partly to the presence and migratory movements of Ghanaian youth and their families in the cities of the U.S., Amsterdam, Frankfurt, and elsewhere who have been exposed to a variety of musical cultures.[18] Hip-life is however, still a Ghanaian art form, produced and performed mostly by people of Ghanaian heritage. It emerges from the endogenous realities of the crannies, ghettoes, suburbs, cities and boarding high schools of modern Ghana.

Performers rap in English and/or one of many indigenous Ghanaian languages, including Ghanaian Pidgin English. Others also use or attempt to use Ghanaian inflected articulations of U.S. Black English (Ebonics) or the Jamaica and Caribbean derived patois used by reggae dancehall artists. In addition to their linguistic diversity, hip-life musicians combine Ghanaian high-life or other Ghanaian musical genres with other African/

African Diasporic musical forms, particularly hip-hop, dancehall or calypso, and occasionally with music of non-African heritage.

Hip-life music production often involves sung choruses, heavy bass and percussion, sampling of traditional African instruments, and synthesizing of a variety of other non-African musical instruments. The most distinctive attribute of hip-life is perhaps artists' use of Ghanaian oral styles in their rapping and lyrics. This characteristic will be central to the case studies of hip-life artists Tinny and ASEM that follow later on in this chapter.

hip-life in the 1ˢᵗ person: biographical notes and hip-life s social antecedents

I write this chapter as a member of Ghana's hip-life generation. I attended boarding school at Ghana National College (1989-1994) in Cape Coast for my ordinary level exams and Labone Secondary School (1994-1996) for my advanced level exams. As an undergraduate and graduate student at the University of Ghana, I worked as a deejay and broadcast journalist at two pioneering radio broadcast stations in Ghana, Radio Univers and Joy F.M., between 1998 and 2003. These stations helped launch hip-life as a new musical genre.

Ghanaian boarding high schools like those I attended were, and continue to be public spaces for the development of hip-life. I was literally present when the birth pangs of hip-life began with its etymological and musical progenitor Reggie Rockstone. Rockstone blazed the path for hip-life, what he now considers a "movement" and "the soundtrack to the nation called Ghana."[19] During my time at Labone, Rockstone, would join or form "yo yo" circles or cyphers on his way to or from home visiting our common friend "Darkman." Some of Reggie's lyrics in these circles would later end up on some of his tracks in his pioneering 1994 album *Maka Maka* (If I said it, I said it.) Later, existing groups and acts including Native Funk Lords (N.F.L.), Vision in Progress (V.I.P.), D.J. Azigizah, Ded Buddy, Lord Kenya and Akyeame created and developed hip-life styles and scenes in Accra and Kumasi as the Takoradi based SASS Squad also emerged with Simgwa laced lyrics. I have therefore been an active observer and peripheral participant in the development of hip-life; including spoken-word performances at *Bless the Mic* in 2008 while conducting academic research in Ghana. Nonetheless, this study is not an attempt to romanticize hip-life, but an effort to integrate my personal knowledge into the creation of a conceptual and historical space for further inquiries into this developing global genre.

Hip-life's diasporic ancestor, hip-hop, originated in the U.S. among Blacks and Latinos during the early post-civil rights period. Hip-hop's current global influence, particularly on African youth helped make it a co-progenitor of hip-life. Like hip-hop, hip-life claims ancestry to the oral traditions of the African past. If we are to think of hip-hop as emerging from the multiplicity of ethnic African oral cultures and the material vicissitudes and experiences of African Americans, hip-life occurred from the existential situation in Ghana and its distinctive oral cultures; modes of speech, poetry, and singing dating to pre-colonial times.

Such oral styles are to be found among the traditional social institutions of the Ewe, Ga-Adangbe, and Akan in modern day Ghana. These oral practices encompass the office of the Chiefs Linguist, court interpreters, praise singers, and religious poems. Some of these oral practices within the traditional political framework of Ghana have been extensively written about in works by linguists, poets, and litterateurs like Kwesi Yankah, Kofi Awoonor, Kofi Anyidoho, Abu Abarry, and S. Obeng.[20]

Before I arrived at Ghana National College, these pre-colonial and colonial musical and oral forms had somehow been transferred to the informal or student sanctioned "entertainment" activities within the music and art cultures of most secondary schools. Of particular note is the *Jama/Dzama* as used among the

Ga, also called *Samanbo* among the Akan.[21] *Jama* usually consists of a drum or set of Kpanlogo drums, a bell player, a lead singer and a host of choruses ranging from two to hundreds, even an entire boarding school population. *Jama* songs were used at inter-hall and inter-school competitions within a particular region of Ghana to promote school spirit or to jeer the opponent's school.

It is therefore not surprising that there has been some debate in certain hip-life circles regarding the influence of jama in hip-life. With jama laced hip-life songs somewhat viewed as inauthentic hip-life. Ironically, jama has been a part of hip-life from its nascence, and its role continued after Rockstone's first hip-life album. One way in which jama merged with hip-hop while I was a student was at *jama* jamming sessions. At Ghana National College for example, someone would start chanting the words "instrumentals." This was a cue for the drummer or drummers to start a freestyle drumming session accompanied by, or not, a bell player. At this time, the other vocal cord participants would interject with chants of "yo, yo, yo," cueing and providing a chorus for willing rappers in the group to demonstrate their abilities. Most rappers in these sessions had been exposed to the rapping and chanting performances of hip-hop, dancehall, and other diasporic artists through tapes and music videos, or through the endeavors by the Ghana Broadcasting Corporation (G.B.C.) pioneers of hip-life like Sampson Quaye and D.J. Azigizah.

I remember composing a dancehall styled song that epitomized the rebellious attitude of my peers and me toward the constraints of strict boarding school supervision. Others used what we called "slang" in their raps, mimicking the lingo and lexicon of U.S. rappers. Such attempts were sometimes looked upon favorably or deemed inauthentic depending on the performer's success.

These practices are reflective of the improvisational moments associated with most music of African origins. Such practices have continued with artists like Rockstone, Mensah, and other Ghanaian hip-hoppers who most of the time have lived abroad, and are also able to flow fluently in Ghanaian languages. Sometimes these occasions turned into "burning" jamborees. Burning in hip-life is equivalent to MC battles and dance challenges in other diasporic contexts. These challenges usually begin with one person suggesting that he or another student could dance or rap better than a second student. The victor in this drama of fun and "illegal" competition is considered as having "burnt" the challenger. What happened at Ghana National College and other schools in Cape-Coast was not exclusive, for it was replicated on a regional basis across secondary schools and youth gatherings throughout the country.

In addition to the international influences and distinctive musical practices manifested in the social art of adolescent males in Ghanaian boarding schools, other aesthetic influences abound. Rockstone and the Takoradi based SASS squad group have for example acknowledged the 1980s fast-talking high-life rhythmic style of Gyedu Blay Ambolley as an inspiration and precursor to hip-life. Others point to similar styles in the work of reggae influenced high-life singers K. K. Kabobo and Afro-Moses.

It is also claimed that Panji, the brain behind Ghanaian house pidgin music, used the term hip-life to previously discuss the work of his Talking Drums duo, Kwaku-T and Bayku, who also used choruses and hooks in local languages. Others reference Mahoney P's album *Kofi Babone* as a forerunner to hip-life.[22] Without dismissing these creative heraldic moments of hip-life, I offer the musical work of Reggie Rockstone as the watershed moment for the emergence of hip-life as a musical genre.

periodizing the history of hip-life: reggie rockstone; hip-life personified and the advent of private radio broadcast

As indicated, the term hip-life is popularly believed to have been originated by Reggie Rockstone, a member of the erstwhile hip-hop group P.L.Z. (Parables, Linguistics, and Zlang.) Variously known as Oseikrom President, Godfather of hip-life, or

Grandpapa, Rockstone coined hip-life combining the pre-fix hip in hip-hop, and the suffix life in high-life.

Inclusive of its terminological progenitor, hip-life is an art form generated from Ghanaian youth culture immediately preceding Ghana's re-entry into democratic culture in 1992. While high-life characterized the period before and after the independence movement in West Africa, hip-life epitomizes Ghana's entry into a globalized world after successive experimentation with socialist and capitalist democracies, and military rule between 1966 and 1992.

Reggie Rockstone was born Reginald Osei to Ricci and Hannah Osei in London during the late 1960s. Ricci, or Saint Osei as Ghanaians knew him until his untimely death in 1997, is credited with the advent of "patch jeans' in Europe. He established the first modern fashion studio in Africa and was also the founder of the publishing company Colour Chart Designs. "Aunty" Hannah, Rockstone's mother, trained in Britain to become a registered nurse, and has continued in the profession since she and Reggie returned to Kumasi, Ghana in the 1980s. A music lover, she returned with a variety of vinyl's with which Rockstone would begin his musical tutelage.[23] Born into an artistic family, Reggie was drawn to the performing arts, including martial arts in which he reputedly holds a Black Belt.

At the early age of eleven, Reggie was a well-known dancer and performer at his secondary school at Achimota College. Reggie's mother speaks about making trips to Achimota to ensure her son was re-admitted after skipping school to attend "discos," an old Ghanaian term for nightclubs. Rockstone himself speaks of being a beat boy.[24] His mother refers to her son as a "disco boy" and a "crowd puller."[25]

Rockstone later relocated to his birth country Britain. From the United Kingdom's cultural capital of London, Reggie would travel to and live in places like New York, and Little Rock, Arkansas. Reported to have attended drama school, Rockstone exhibited a desire to bridge the sartorial and oral aspects of hip-hop.[26] It was in London that Reggie joined with friends Freddie Funkstone, Jay, and U.K. disc jockey, D.J. Pogo to form P.L.Z. about 1992. The group recorded popular London hits "If it Aint PLZ" and "Build a Wall Around Your Dreams."

While Rockstone was in London and the U.S., a variety of events shaped his reentry into the Ghanaian entertainment scene. Following Ghana's 1992 democratic elections won by Jerry John Rawlings' National Democratic Congress (N.D.C.), an offshoot of his military government, the Provisional National Defense Committee (P.N.D.C.), the elected government was expected to fulfill all the trappings of democracy enshrined in the 1992 Constitution, under Article 162(3):

> There shall be no impediments to the establishment of private press or media; and in particular, there shall be no law requiring any person to obtain a license as a prerequisite to the establishment or operation of a newspaper, journal or other media for the mass communication or information.[27]

However freedom of speech and liberalization of the national airwaves was absent in the burgeoning democratic Ghana, encouraging the "culture of silence" that prevailed under the P.N.D.C. Before 1992 there had been attempts by others to break this culture of silence. Eminent Ghanaian historian, politician and later first presidential candidate of the New Patriotic Party (N.P.P.,) Professor Adu Boahen, initiated the first "popular" attempt to break this culture of silence. In 1989, the emeritus professor gave a lecture which questioned the culture of silence that had prevailed from the demise of Ghana's third republic until the second P.N.D.C. government in the early 1980s. Boahen achieved this tremendous feat by quoting E. A. Haizel, the executive secretary of the National Commission for Democracy: "The Culture of Silence has so entrapped the people that there is now a lot of murmuring and passivism around instead of a positive declaration of opinion."[28] Boahen went on to argue, "the situation is worsened by the luck of virile independent newspapers, a situation which again has been caused entirely by the PNDC government."[29] Boahen was joined in this task by University of Ghana colleagues Paul V. Ansah and Kwesi Yankah, who both critiqued and satired the P.N.D.C. in their columns "Going to Town" and 'Woes of a Kwatriot" in the *Ghanaian Chronicle* and the *Ghana Mirror* respectively. Thus, following the reintroduction of party democracy in Ghana, there was internal and external pressure on the N.D.C to allow for private radio and television broadcasting.

Such pressure was evidenced in the proceedings of a three day international seminar on private broadcasting in West Africa in 1993.[30] This was followed by the "surreptitious" crackling of the airwaves by *Radio Eye*; a frequency modulation station ran by then N.P.P. politician, Dr. Charles Wereko Brobbey in 1994. After symbolically breaking the monopoly of the government controlled Ghana Broadcasting Corporation (G.B.C), *Radio Eye's* equipments were confiscated and Dr. Wereko Brobbey was taken to court by the N.D.C. government. The government however later began to license private radio stations like *Radio Univers, Joy F.M.*, and *Radio Gold* in 1995.

Though the hip-life generation and hip-life itself had antecedent beginnings dating back to the 1980s, it was in this political atmosphere of radio broadcasts that hip-life and Reggie Rockstone emerged. As the new stations scrambled to satisfy a different Ghanaian audience, hip-life supplanted its Ghanaian predecessor high-life on the airwaves and became the soundtrack of the nation. Reggie Rockstone's first album, *Maka Maka* set the tone in 1997, and since then, Ghana has been "bumping" to the distinct varieties of hip-life that have emerged.

kasantwi: risks in verbal art performance

Hip-life artist Tinny, who was born Nii Addo Quaynor to Ricky Tetteh Quaynor and Naa Badu Quaynor at Osu a surburb of Accra, Ghana like many young Ghanaians attended boarding school at Okuapeman Secondary School. Tinny came to musical fame after collaborating with popular hip-life producer Hammer of the Last 2 and Abraham Ohene Djan (CEO of OM Studios). In 2003, he released his first album *Makola Kwakwe*, which earned him positive reviews and awards such as New Artist of the Year at both the Ghana Music Awards 2004 and Ghana Music Awards UK 2004, Youth Musician of the Year 2003, as well as the Best Guest Entertainment Musical Artist by Great Lamptey Mills.[31]

In his 2005 album, *Kaa Bu Ame* on which he featured Reggie Rockstone, Tiny defines rap in his native Ga as "Shi ha, shi ha, wiemo" or fast speech, a direct translation of the Akan "Kasa Hari" as used by Akan-twi lyricist Obrafour. However, as evidenced in Tinny's own body of hip-life works, rap is not always fast. Ghanaian linguist, Abu Abarry's interpretation "Wiemo Lala" or "talking song" is a more apt definition of rap in Ga oral culture, a tradition which Tinny draws on extensively in his lyrics. Abarry writes:

> Among the Gas, the term for song is "lala"; and the same term modifying is "wiemo lala" (talking song), refers to poetry. Thus, a distinction is seen to be made by the people between "lala", ordinary generic song, and "wiemo lala" (poetry), where a special demand is made on language skill, and creativity.

Abarry goes on to further explain that in Ga traditional poetry:

> the form of discourse and the meaning are fused into a higher unity. They have a tonal variability, and when musically transcribed yields metrical patterns. They have a beauty of form and also give intellectual pleasure. Such features are recognizable in all genuine poetry. Reflecting complex and interesting themes. They are replete with simple statements, multifarious allusions, stylistic repetitions, and col-

orful imagery. They are also distinguishable by their verbal and structural economies.[32]

These attributes that Abarry identifies prior to the emergence of hip-life, have found their way into hip-life songs sung in Ga by Tinny and other artists. This is most apparent in Tinny's battle with Buk-Bak, one of the early hip-life groups. On an album released in 2003, hip-life duo Buk-Bak seemingly attacks Tinny on a track about cleanliness.[33] The track is reminiscent of the establishment of town councils by the British colonial government beginning in 1858 and continued in 1875, as the colonial government sought to enforce colonial policies in its new capital, Accra.[34] One of the tasks of the municipal town council during this period was to ensure cleanliness in the Ga towns. A team of town council inspectors placed a fine on homes in Accra that were found guilty of not being clean. The severity of these fines and the Ga opposition to exorbitant fines has been etched in the social memory of Ga people. Buk-Bak draws on these nineteenth century events to reference sanitary environmental practices and personal body hygiene, in their Ga language based hip-life song "Oowo jen mudzi" meaning "you are messing up the place." However, as their track appears to conclude, the hype-man, Ronnie, also the raga-dancehall style half of the duo enters into a chorus, making indirect allusion to a Tinny sobriquet "Aletse." Aletse, Tinny's other *nom de guerre*, literally means knowledgeable person/father. Despite Ronnie's use of Aletse, it remained difficult to ascertain whether Tinny, was the target of the lyrics. Ronnie chants:

> Open up your ear, and listen up
> Now look at knowledgeable person, landlord
> You've made yourself a dirt head, yet you engage in antics.

This form of oral attack is a Ga speech form known as *Kasantwi*. Among the Ga people kasantwi denotes a type of indirect speech.[35] It is used in oral critique of an imagined yet real person or group of people with whom one is engaged in discourse. In the Ghanaian/Akan context, Kwesi Yankah, describes indirection as "veiled rhetoric in the form of indirection, metaphor, proverb, allegory, circumlocution, innuendo, locally called *akutia* and related literary devices."[36] Kasantwi in its distinctive Ga signifying form is also an implicit device that makes direct rejoinders tricky, a direct response is more or less a guilty plea of things alleged by an oral adversary. Kasantwi opponents therefore also respond indirectly making for a competitive *Mpowa* or oral challenge.[37] The challenge now facing Tinny is to determine if and how Buk-Bak referred to him, and how he should respond. Tinny counteracts the perceived oral critique by Buk-Bak also using Kasantwi and other components of Ga orality such as self-demeanization, re-signification, stylistic repetition, deferential addresses, as well as unleashing an array of Ga proverbial and allegorical sayings, tales, and riddles. Tinny's response is set to an allegorical chorus, which explains what has been allegedly said and done to him, Tinny:

> Someone was doing it before you came
> Someone was doing it before you came
> Knowledge head they calling me dirty head
> Knowledge head they calling me dirty head

Tinny, using Ga idiomatic expressions continues with some self debasement:

> Now, as for me I know when others are going, I don't
> go
> And I don't have legs, don't have legs
> Now, beauty/handsomeness also I don't have
> The women know
> So when called, I don't even know I've been called

I don't get near

This act of self-humiliation as drawn from the Ga oral rhetoric, Kasantwi is meant to render a response by an opposing interlocutor useless. In other words, Tinny's response poses the rhetorical question to Buk-Bak: "What invectives could you employ about me that I or others do not already know?" Following this, Tinny warns "but you will cry, tearfully, you will cry."

Next, Tinny distinguishes between his virtues of friendliness and then hits hard at the underlying cause of Buk-Baks rudeness, using a Ga proverb about drunkenness, and then ends with a circumlocution of the said proverb:

> I am cool with everyone; I have no beef with anyone
> But it is the alcoholic, drunkard who breaks bottles
> Bottles would be broken, I will break a bottle

Tinny is here also re-signifying a signature statement often used by Buk-Bak's Ronnie before and after a Buk-Bak song. The statement "Nye momi na adzwa to" translates literally as "Hold/help lets break this bottle," also meaning a toast to drink up. Its social signification is based on the sharing of drinks and fun by friends or acolytes, not necessarily actually getting drunk. Tinny however re-signifies the literal meaning of this saying by suggesting another proverb "that it is only a drunk who breaks bottles." To reinforce his re-signification of the statement used by his antagonists, Tinny uses the imagery of the recording studio and the process involved in recoding a song for effect. He asks his producer/engineer, Hammer, in Ghanaian pidgin English:

> Tinny: You dey record me Hammer?
> Hammer responds: Nah, taking it again.

In redoing it as Hammer suggests, Tinny in the next verse is able to use repetition, another typical Ga oral device for invectives:

native tongues: an african hip-hop reader

I am cool with everyone; I have no beef with anyone
But it is the alcoholic, drunkard who breaks bottles

Tinny continues with another Kasantwi style, this time using double coded lines laced with a tale of what has been negatively and erroneously said about him. He begins with a definition of what music should be about and ends with claims of originality, and the right to speak:

> Music making is no fight, jiving, a little thought, and knowledge
> Foolish elderly man, his bed is wet with urine, bed wetter.
> Foolish old man, his bed is wet with urine; you have peed in your bed
> Look, Knowledge head, they calling me dirty head, it makes me laugh
> Little kid Tinny, I come out during harmattan season
> When did I even get here to be called landlord
> And Ghanaian women are all over my dirt
> I love them with their scented mouths and beauty
> Who loves nasty things, far from here
> Did you say you loved that?
> Look when did I get here to be called landlord
> Day by day I will speak, not grown but been around long enough

In the lines that follow, Tinny, demonstrates his authenticity and autochthony as a Ga and hip-life rapper, and points to both his Ghanaian royalty and upbringing and respect for Ga lore and values. Drawing from this knowledge Tinny shows how an elder who has no respect of his own status, and disrespects youth leaves him/herself liable for critique and disrespect from said youth:

> From long, Ghanaians made me King

Tinny, it's him, knowledge head, Nii Addo, Son of Ga
Don't forget, knowledge head
I have good upbringing, I have respect, and am per-
ceptive
So Ricky, Naa Badu, Thank you/Long life
The one advice mother and father gave
When someone slaps my cheek, turn the other cheek
for another slap
So am very respectful of you
But an elder is an elder
And a child is also a child, but you did this to me
Everyone licks the crannies of their mouth

After this verse of proverbs, allegories, and caution, Tinny moves on to invoke Ga and Christian ontological values, including the sacredness of day-names and Ga deities. Day-names signify a day-naming pattern used by most Ghanaian ethnicities including Tinny's ethnic group the Ga-Adangbe's, as well as, the Guan, Ewe, and Akan.

Kwabena Tinny, I don't desecrate Tuesday.[38]
Yours is in the Koole River, go take it, Sampson 12:2

Naa Koole is a Ga female deity representing the Koole River, and is one of the principal deities of the Ga-Adangbe people. It is unclear whether Tinny himself understood the full meaning of invoking Naa Koole as such a summons in Ga invites cataclysmic punishment for culpable parties in a dispute like that between Tinny and the Buk Bak duo. After the chorus, Tinny continues his references to celestial beings:

Oh Head Creator you are the anchor
God help your child, your child is crying

Tinny's use of these Ga oratorical styles has endeared him to Ga language speakers in particular and hip-life enthusiasts in general. But, he is not the only person utilizing Ghanaian oratorical skills. Tinny's contemporary hip-life artist, ASEM, whose name literally means issue, matter, or subject, also utilizes Ghanaian oratorical skills in his music. For instance, ASEM often deploys a set of Ghanaian or Akan based tonal ambiguous words as part of the issues (*nsem* in Akan) that he raps about in his single, "Give me Blow." An example of this is the way in which he staggers and stammers his way into asking his listeners to give him blow, that is, raise their clenched fists. In addition to his use of the English phrase "give me blow," ASEM uses the Akan word *twediem*. He, however, staggers the pronunciation of *twediem*, meaning clenched fist. As I explain below, in using such tonal ambiguity, ASEM manages to establish a series of alternative meanings for the issues that he raps about. The name ASEM itself is a reflection of such stuttering of words. ASEM seems to be a contraction of the rapper's surnames, Asante Mensah. Born Nana Wiafe Asante Mensah, ASEM attended St. Peters Secondary School (Pesco) in the eastern region of Ghana. He holds a diploma in communication studies from the Ghana School of Journalism and is currently attached to Lynx Entertainment managed by Richie, also a singer, producer, sound engineer and CEO of the label.[39]

ASEM's single "Give me Blow" on his 2008 Album, *Betta late than Neva* starts off with the chorus: Give me blow, Give me blow, Give me blow, blow blow bloblow. A.S.E.M. (SPELLED OUT), ASEM (PRONOUNCED). This beginning establishes a clear meaning with ASEM seemingly suggesting as he does with his stage performance, that it means putting a fist into the air.

ASEM in a 2008 performance also wields a boxing glove on his right arm, demonstrating machismo or prowess. Such gesticulations also evoke memories of the Black Power Movements trademark fist salute which came into the international limelight at the 1968 Olympics. This was when U.S. black athletes, Tommie Smith and John Carlos, respectively gold and bronze medalists for the men's two-hundred meters, put their fist in the air when they received their medals at the Olympics in Mexico City. In the context of Ghana, Black Power achieved further national popularity when Ghanaian politician Komlah A. Gbedemah representing the National Alliance of Liberals (NAL) during the 1969 elections used "Say it Loud, I am Black and Proud" as his campaign slogan. He subsequently earned the nickname Afro-Gbede. ASEM's rendition of "give me blow" may therefore appeal to multiple Ghanaian audience. Youth familiar with hip-hop slang may see it as a creative re-imagination of "Put your hands in the air and move from side to side" used in most hip-life and hip-hop concerts. Ghanaians who witnessed the 1968 Olympics and the 1969 elections, or any person with some historical memory may attribute "Give me blow" to the global reach of the Black Power Movement. Black nationalists around the world may also see ASEM's act as a celebration of the global black freedom struggle.

Having established these singular and multiple meanings ASEM follows up with others:

> You'll sleep, You'll sleep, You'll sleep early
> A.S.E.M.(spelled out alphabetically) ASEM

Without explicitly suggesting any sexual conations ASEM has called to mind the act of sleeping and its multiple connotations. For instance, sleep, *eda* in Akan, could also mean amorous sex. Thus, while the verse's literal meaning could be said to be the act of sleeping, for Akan speakers this could also mean the masculine ASEM articulating his sexual prowess. This is made clearer with the following:

> If you love your lover and your lover also loves you
> And If you look at her face, but you see her back
> And now if she gives you a sign that gentleman come ride
> Give me blow, give me blow, give me blow, blow blow

Here, the manifold interpretations of "give me blow" that listeners were subjected to have been suddenly transformed into a love relationship between a man and a woman. Yet, he returns his listeners back to guessing about the precise meaning when he raps the following line three times:

> Put your "twe, twe, twe", twe-diem in the air

One is left wondering whether ASEM means clenched fist rather than "twe" an Akan term for the female sexual organ. In this instance, ASEM pauses and staggers the unity of *twe* and *diem* to form "twediem". With this ASEM draws his listener's attention momentarily to *twe*, the female sexual organ. An explicit use of this term in Akan and Ghanaian culture is absolutely forbidden, and ASEM would have faced some censorship had he just left it at the expression *twe*. He manages to evade censorship and moral scorn by immediately following up with the *twediem* or fist.

ASEM and Tinny's use of indigenous Ghanaian oral styles, which also on occasion incorporates African American slang, is symptomatic of the distinctiveness of Ghanaian hip-life as compared with its endogenous predecessor high-life and its exogenous antecedent hip-hop.

conclusion

At present, there are a variety of hip-life musical schools. This includes old school hip-life as it began with the classics of hip-life's pioneers, Rockstone, Lord Kenya, Tic-Tac, Nananom and others who rap in local languages over sampled hip-hop and African beats. These old school artists have themselves in many cases transcended this formative stage of hip-life. Members of this group heavily utilize the older high-life rhythms in their music. This is evidenced in hip-life artists who feature high-life musicians on their tracks. Some examples include erstwhile member of Nananom, Omanhene Pozo's remix of C.K. Man'S high-life track Afa, and Alhaji K. Frimpong's *Kyenkyen bi adi mawu*, the same track Rockstone sampled for his 2000 track "Keep your eyes on the road."

Another hip-life sub-group may be identified by their use of heavy instruments. These instruments are mostly drum based or percussive styles, which are weaned off sounds and rhythms of traditional Ghanaian musical genres like Kpanlogo, Adowa, Kundum, and others. This style is associated mostly with hip-life groups Buk-Bak, 4x4, FBS, and Obour. The percussive styles allow for a dance-based type of hip-life leading to the recreation and invention of hip-life dance styles such as *Gbee ohe* (open up yourself,) and *Ko Gon* (climb the hill). There is also GH (Ghanaian) rap or GH hip-hop. Some members of this school mainly see themselves as hip-hop artists and not hip-life artists. This style has neither been commercially successful locally nor particularly popular worldwide. Despite these failures, old school hip-life artists such as Rockstone and Mensah, and new artists such as Jayso, Killbeats, Kevin Beatz, Trigga, Pappi Props, together with other less popular rappers are all exemplified by their emphasis on verbal skills. These skills utilized in GH rap, including lyrical dexterity, flow, and battle abilities are less appealing to commercial hip-life producers. While the hip-life genre is still growing, GH rap artists such as DR Cryme and Macho Rapper have attempted to distinguish themselves from others by labeling their brand of music Twi-pop, a style delivered in Twi, one of the many Akan languages.

The rag-life sub-genre is the distinct approach used by hip-life artists who are enamored with roots reggae.and dancehall rhythms derived from the Caribbean, particularly Jamaica. Some of the classical works in this hip-life school were initially created by Yogi Doggy, Kokoveli, Borax, and Sonni Bali. This tradition has been carried on by Screwface, Wutah, and lately, the more popular "Batman" Samini. Like all the others in this cohort, Samini, who has gained international notoriety for his rag-life lyrics, combines various Ghanaian languages with Ghanaian tinged approximations of Jamaican or Caribbean patois. Samini's official Myspace page lists his musical genres as Afrobeat, reggae, and zouk.[40] Samini in 2008 was the Best African Artist at Nigeria's Hip Hop World Awards. He was also nominated for the MTV EMA Awards in 2007, the Channel O Awards and the Radiophonie prize in France, as well as, the Best African Musician at the MOBO awards in the U.K. in 2006. The aforementioned hip-life forms are not exclusive, but rather mutually inclusive, which is not meant to suggest that an artist listed in the various categories has one style. In reality, some artists like Wanluv the Kubolor are developing distinctive and original styles that are hard to categorize because the authenticity of their work transcends genres including hip-hop, high-life, and hip-life.

The hip-life generation grew up on high-life and a variety of Ghanaian musical cultures that were available in the late 1980s and early 1990s. Eventually, as hip-hop spread throughout the world, Ghanaian youth became enamored with hip-hip culture and its music. However, when Rockstone and Brooklyn raised D.J. Rab met in Accra in 1994, the Ghanaian youth adulation for hip-hop and their own indigenous musical history and lived realities would merge to birth of a new musical genre. A decade and half after this not so fortuitous beginning, hip-life is reaching the same heights as its African American progenitor. Yet, the global expansion of hip-life depends on the continued production of the eclectic sounds of its godfather Rockstone and his versatile acolytes like Mensah, Samini, and Kubolor. With Ghanaian representation at the 2010 BET Hip-hop Music Awards Ghanaian hip-life seems to have come full circle.

notes

1. For studies on hip-hop in general and works related to hip-hop see for example Pero Dagbovie, *Black History : "Old School" Black Historians and the Hip Hop generation* (Troy, Michigan: Bedford Publishers, 2006); Tricia Rose, *Black Noise: Rap Music and Black Culture in Contemporary America* (Hanover, N.H. : University Press of New England, 1994); *The Hip Hop Wars : What We Talk About When We Talk About Hip Hop--and Why It Matters* (New York : Basic Civitas, 2008); Bakari Kitwana, *Violence The Rap on Gangsta Rap: Who Ran It?: Gangasta Rap and Vision on Black* (Chicago: Third World Press, 1994); *The Hip Hop Generation: Young Blacks and the Crisis in African American Culture* (New York: Basic Civitas, 2002); In addition to various articles in other journals including the *Journal of Black Studies, Art Journal, Popular Music, Social Text,* and *African American Review* specially dedicated to Hip-hop are *Journal of Hip Hop* and *Hip Hop Business Journal.*
2. On the beginnings and social aspects of high-life see John Collins, "Ghanaian Highlife," *African Arts,* 10 (1976); "Postwar Popular Bands in West Africa," *African Arts,* 10, no. 3 (1977); "The Early History of West African Highlife Music," in J. Farley and S. Rijven (eds.) *Popular Music,* (Cambridge: Cambridge University Press, 1989); *Popular Music in West Africa* with Paul Richards in *World Music, Politics and Social Change,* ed. S. Firth (Manchester: Manchester University Press, 1989); *The Evolution of West African Popular Entertainment* in *The Encyclopedia of Sub-Saharan Africa,* ed. J. Middleton (New York: Charles Scribner and Sons Reference Books, 1999).
3. Ruth Simms Hamilton, *Routes of Passage: Rethinking the African Diaspora* (East Lansing: Michigan State University Press, 2007), 1.
4. For some of these commonalities in African music see John Collins, *African Musical Symbolism in Contemporary Perspective - Roots, Rhythms and Relativity,* (Berlin: Pro Business, 2004); *African Pop Roots* (London: W. Foulshams, 1985); *West African Pop Roots* (Philadelphia: Temple University Press, 1992); *The Importance*

of African Popular Music Studies for Ghanaian/African Students (Dakar: Codesria, 2008).

5. All the texts are in English; I translated them respectively from Ga and Akan-Twi.

6. For some works on Ga speech and songs, see Marion Kilson, *Kpele lala; Ga religious songs and symbols* (Cambridge, Harvard University Press, 1971); Abu Abarry, "A Traditional Poetry of the Ga of Ghana," *Journal of Black Studies*, 14, no. 4 (1984): 493-506.

7. For Akan Speech form and verbal art see the works of Kwesi Yankah, "Proverbs: The Aesthetics of Traditional Communication" *Research in African Literatures* 20, no. 3 (1989): 325-34; "To Praise or Not to Praise the King: The Akan "Apae" in the Context of Referential Poetry," *Research in African Literatures* 14, no. 3, Special Issue on Epic and Panegyric Poetry in Africa (1983): 381-400; "Risks in Verbal Arts Performance" *Journal of Folklore Research*, 22, no. 2/3, Folklore and Semiotics (1985): 133-153; "Proverbs Rhetoric and African Judicial Process" *The Journal of American Folklore*, 99, no. 393 (1986): 280-303.

8. *HomeGrown: Hiplife in Ghana*, produced by Eli Jacobs Fantuzzi, 110 minutes, Clenched Fist Productions, 2009, DVD.

9. *Living the Hip-Life*, produced by Jesse Weaver Shipley, 63 minutes, Evidence Films, Coltan Media , 2007, DVD.

10. Daniel Banks, "How Hip Life Theatre was born in Ghana; Youth Culture in a West African Nation takes the reins to create a new form of expression. (Africa Writes Back)," *American Theatre*, November 1, 2008.

11. Nate Ash-Morgan, "The New Hip-life Beat: Rooted in Ga Drumming" (B.A. Hons. Wesleyan University: Connecticut, 2008).

12. Jesse Weaver Shipley, "Aesthetic of the Entrepreuner: Afro-Cosmopolitan Rap and Moral Suasion in Accra, Ghana," *Anthropological Quarterly* 82, no. 3 (2009): 631-668.

13. Tara Aminah (Ama Sika) Jabbaar-Gyambrah, "Hip-hop, Hip-life: Global Sistahs" (Ph.D. diss., Buffalo State University of New York at Buffalo, 2007).

14. Tara Aminah (Ama Sika) Jabbaar-Gyambrah, "Triple M, Representin', Reconstructin', and Resistin': Ideologies of Gender and

Sexualities in Hip-Life Music in Ghana," *Journal of Race & Policy* 4, no. 1 (2008).

15. Paper presented at the annual meeting of the Association of African American Life and History (ASALH) 93rd Annual Convention, Sheraton Birmingham, Birmingham, Alabama, 2009-05-23. <http://www.allacademic.com/meta/p275116_index.html>

16. Paper presented at the annual meeting of the National Women's Studies Association, Millennium Hotel, Cincinnati, OH June 18-22, 2008.

17. Tara Aminah (Ama Sika) Jabbaar-Gyambrah, "Triple M, Representin', Reconstructin', and Resistin': Ideologies of Gender and Sexualities in Hip-Life Music in Ghana" in *Journal of Race & Policy*, 4, no. 1 (2008).

18. This fact can be easily ascertained through a quick search of various social network search engines in the named locations. A search of hip-life and New York yields over a hundred search results.

19. Disastrous and Reggie Rockstone, " Interview," http://www.youtube.com /results?search_query=Disastrous+and+Reggie+Rockstone +interview+&aq=f

20. See Kofi Awoonor, *Guardians of the Sacred Word: Ewe Poetry* (New York: Nok, 1974); Kofi Anyodoho, *Praise Song for the Land : Poems of Hope, and Love and Care* (Accra : Sub-Saharan Publishers, 2002); Marion Kilson, "The Structure of Ga Prayer" *Journal of Religion in Africa*, 9, fasc. 3 (1978): 173-188; and for Kwesi Yankah, see note 6.

21. Somebody like Ishamel Odamtten earned the sobriquet Jama Banton by his school mates at Accra Academy in the mid 1990's for his abilities on the drums and his compositions of *jama* songs to merge with contemporary dancehall music. His guerre de nom Banton was taken from Jamaican Dancehall artist Buju Banton.

22. Conversations with colleague D.J.'s and presenters at Radio Univers including Ice Cream (Onasis Cyriano), Elvis Lawer, D.J. Rufus (Mills), and D.J. Black (Kwadwo Ampofo). Elvis Lawer offered the information on Mahoney P.

23. Cultural Caravan Diaries, "Reggie Rockstone's Entry," http://www.youtube.com /watch?v=mtGY_UeUP9g; Cultural Caravan

Diaries, "Reggie Rockstone Visits Mum," http://www.youtube.
com/results? search_query=reggie+rockstone+visits+mum+&aq
=fhttp://www.youtube.com/watch?v=TuiP6pOD4rc
24. Museke.com, "Chit-Chat: Reggie Rockstone," http://museke.com /
en/ node /2201
25. Cultural Caravan Diaries, "Reggie Rockstone's Entry"; Cultural
Caravan Diaries, "Reggie RickstoneVisits Mum."
26. Museke.com, "Chit-Chat: Reggie Rockstone," http:// museke.com
/en/ node/2201
27. Ghana, *The Constitution of the Republic of Ghana* (Accra: Ghana
Publishing Corporation, 1992).
28. Albert Adu Boahen, *The Ghanaian Sphinx: The Contemporary
History of Ghana 1972-1987* (Accra: Ghana Academy of Arts and
Sciences, 1989), 54.
29. Boahen, *Ghanaian Sphinx*, 55.
30. K. Karikari. (ed.) *Independent Broadcasting in Ghana: Implications and Challenges: Proceedings of the National Conference on
the Promotion and Privatization of Radio and Television Broadcasting in Ghana, 1993.* (Accra: Ghana Universities Press, 1994).
31. Nii Atakora Mensah, *"Tinny The Hit Maker,"* http://www.
ghanaweb.com/ GhanaHomePage/audio/artikel.php?ID=191793
32. Abarry, "A Traditional Poetry": 493-494.
33. Buk-Bak, *Muji/Tankase, Gold Coast 1662*, Bright and Ronnie 2004
34. PRO CO 96/43, Pine to Labouchere, No. 44, dd. James Fort, 7 May
1858; PRO CO 96/115, Strahan to Carnarvon, Conf., 5 Mar. 1875;
PRO 97/2, Towns, Police, and Public Health Ordinance, No.10 of
1878, 5 July 1878.
35. For universal, African, and Ghanaian forms of indirection see
James C. Scott, *Domination and the Arts of Resistance* (New
Haven: Yale University Press, 1990); Roger Abrahams, *Singing the
Master,* (New York: Pantheon Books, 1992); Kwesi Yankah, *Free
Speech in Traditional Society: The Cultural Foundations of Com-
munication in Contemporary Ghana* (Accra: Ghana Universities
Press, 1998)
36. Kwesi Yankah, "The Sung-Tale Metaphor and Protest Discourse in
Contemporary Ghana" in Joseph Adjaye and Adrianne Andrews
Eds., *Language and Rhythm, and Sound: Black Popular Cultures*

into the Twenty-First Century (Pittsburg: University of Pittsburg Press), 54-73.

37. Similar or homologous forms of indirection exist among U.S. African-Americans and other cultures, for academic inquiries into these see William Piersen, "Putting Down Ole Massa: African Satire in the New World." in *African Folklore in the New World* (Austin: University of Texas, 1977); Claudia Mitchell-Kernan, *Language Behavior in a Black Community*, (Berkely: University of California, 1974).

38. Tinny is here referencing the sacredness of the day naming tradition in Ghana, used by the Ga, Akan, and Ewe of Ghana. Tinny by this convention was born on Tuesday, hence Kwabena.

39. ASEM Profile, http://www.ghanaweb.com/ GhanaHomePage/ people/ person.php?ID=625

40. Batman Samini, http://www.myspace.com/samini1

bibliography

Abarry, Abu. "A Traditional Poetry of the Ga of Ghana." *Journal of Black Studies*, 14, no. 4 (1984): 493-506.

ASEM. "Profile." http://www.ghanaweb.com/ GhanaHomePage/ people/person.php? ID =625.

Ash-Morgan, Nate. "The New Hip-life Beat: Rooted in Ga Drumming." B.A. Hons. Wesleyan University: Connecticut, 2008.

Atakora Mensah, Nii. "*Tinny The Hit Maker*http://www.ghanaweb. com/Ghana Home Page/audio /artikel.php?ID=191 793.

Awoonor, Kofi. *Guardians of the Sacred Word: Ewe Poetry*. New York: Nok, 1974.

_____. *Praise Song for the Land : Poems of Hope, and Love and Care*. Accra : Sub-Saharan Publishers, 2002.

Boahen, Adu Albert. *The Ghanaian Sphinx: The Contemporary History of Ghana 1972-1987*. Accra: Ghana Academy of Arts and Sciences, 1989.

Buk-Bak, *Muji/Tankase, Gold Coast 1662*, Bright and Ronnie 2004.

Collins, John. "Ghanaian Highlife." *African Arts*, 10, (1976)

_____. "Postwar Popular Bands in West Africa." *African Arts*, 10 (1977).

_____. *African Pop Roots*. London: W. Foulshams, 1985.

_____. "The Early History of West African Highlife Music." *Popular Music*, Edited by J. Farley and S Rijven. Cambridge: Cambridge University Press, 1989.

_____. *Popular Music in West Africa*. With Paul Richards. In *World Music, Politics and Social Change*, edited by S. Firth. Manchester: Manchester University Press, 1989.

_____. *West African Pop Roots*. Philadelphia: Temple University Press, 1992.

_____. *The Evolution of West African Popular Entertainment*. In *The Encyclopedia of Sub-Saharan Africa*, edited by J. Middleton. New York: Charles Scribner and Sons Reference Books, 1999.

_____. *African Musical Symbolism in Contemporary Perspective - Roots, Rhythms and Relativity*. Berlin: Pro Business, 2004.

_____. *The Importance of African Popular Music Studies for Ghanaian/African Students*. Dakar: Codesria, 2008. Cultural Caravan Diaries. "Reggie Rockstone's Entry." http://www. Youtube.com / watch?v=mtGY_UeUP9g

_____. "Reggie Rockstone Visits Mum." http://www.youtube.com / watch?v=TuiP6pOD4rc

Dagbovie, Pero. *Black history : "old school" Black historians and the Hip Hop Generation*. Troy, Michigan: Bedford Publishers, 2006.

Disastrous and Reggie Rockstone Interview. http://www.youtube.com/results? Search query=Disastrous+and+Reggie+Rockstone+interview+&aq=f

Ghana, *The Constitution of the Republic of Ghana*. Accra : Ghana Publishing Corporation, 1992.

Hamilton, Ruth Simms. *Routes of Passage: Rethinking the African Diaspora*. East Lansing: Michigan State University Press, 2007.

Jabbaar-Gyambrah, Tara Aminah (Ama Sika.) "Hip-hop, hip-life: Global Sistahs." Ph.D diss. Buffalo State University of New York at Buffalo, 2007.

_____. "Triple M, Representin', Reconstructin', and Resistin': Ideologies of Gender and Sexualities in Hip-Life Music in Ghana." *Journal of Race & Policy* 4, no. 1 (2008).

Karikari, K. (ed.) *Independent Broadcasting in Ghana: Implications and Challenges: Proceedings of the National Conference on the*

Promotion and Privatization of Radio and Television Broadcasting in Ghana, 1993. Accra: Ghana Universities Press, 1994.

Kilson, Marion. *Kpele lala; Ga Religious Songs and Symbols.* Cambridge, Harvard University Press, 1971.

_____. "The Structure of Ga Prayer" *Journal of Religion in Africa*, 9, fasc. 3 (1978): 173-188.

Kitwana, Bakari. *The Rap on Gangsta Rap: Who Ran It?: Gangasta Rap and Vision on Black Violence.* Chicago: Third World Press, 1994.

_____. *The Hip Hop Generation: Young Blacks and the Crisis in African American Culture.* New York: Basic Civitas, 2002.

Museke.com. "Chit-Chat; Reggie Rockstone," http://museke.com /en/ node/2201

Mitchell-Kernan, Claudia. *Language Behavior in a Black Community.* Berkeley: University of California, 1974.

Piersen, Williams. "Putting Down Ole Massa: African Satire in the New World." in *African Folklore in the New World.* Austin: University of Texas, 1977.

PRO CO 96/43, Pine to Labouchere, No. 44, dd. James Fort, 7 May 1858; PRO CO 96/115, Strahan to Carnarvon, Conf., 5 Mar. 1875; PRO 97/2, Towns, Police, and Public Health Ordinance, No.10 of 1878, 5 July 1878.

Rogers. Abrahams. *Singing the Master.* New York: Pantheon Books, 1992.

Rose, Tricia. *Black Noise: Rap Music and Black Culture in Contemporary* America. Hanover, N.H. : University Press of New England, 1994.

_____. *The Hip hop Wars: What We Talk About When We Talk About Hip Hop—and Why it Matters.* New York: Basic Civitas, 2008.

Samini, "Batman." http://www.myspace.com/samini1

Scott, James C. *Domination and the Arts of Resistance.* New Haven: Yale University Press, 1990.

Yankah, Kwesi. "Proverbs: The Aesthetics of Traditional Communication." *Research in African Literatures* 20, no. 3 (1989): 325-34.

_____. "To Praise or Not to Praise the King: The Akan "Apae" in the Context of Referential Poetry" *Research in African Literatures* 14, no. 3, Special Issue on Epic and Panegyric Poetry in Africa (1983): 381-400.

_____. " Risks in Verbal Arts Performance" *Journal of Folklore Research*, 22, no. 2/3, Folklore and Semiotics (1985): 133-153.

_____. "Proverbs Rhetoric and African Judicial Process" *The Journal of American Folklore*, 99, no. 393 (1986): 280-303.

_____. "The Sung-Tale Metaphor and Protest Discourse in Contemporary Ghana" in Joseph Adjaye and Adrianne Andrews Eds., *Language and Rhythm, and Sound: Black Popular Cultures into the Twenty-First Century*. Pittsburg: University of Pittsburg Press, 1997.

_____. *Free Speech in Traditional Society: The Cultural Foundations of Communication in Contemporary Ghana*. Accra: Ghana Universities Press, 1998.

CHAPTER 7
le cauchemar de la france:
blackara's postcolonial hip-hop critique in the city of light

J. GRIFFITH ROLLEFSON

O-Dog c'était le negro le plus barge de la terre. Le cauchemar de l'Amérique: jeune, black et qu'en a rien à branler.[1]
– Menace II Society, 1993 (French Dubbed Version)

It was early April in Paris when I received a reply from the rap duo Blackara in my MySpace inbox. I had met the two MCs, Xiao Venom and Mani Peterson, a week earlier at the studios of *Radio Plurielle* [Pluralist Radio] in Paris's 19th *Arrondissement* where they dropped in to promote an upcoming concert. The community radio station in the ethnically diverse working-class neighborhood of Jaurès featured a weekly hip-hop show called *Marché Noir* [Black Market] which showcased the freestyle skills of local underground MCs such as Xiao and Mani.[2] The studio was sparsely decorated and the program's format straightforward. From the control room the show's host, Tarik stood at a

mixing board introducing the MCs. Behind him DJ Dirty Swift dropped the beats from his two-turntable and laptop setup. From his position at the board, Tarik looked through a large window into an adjacent live room containing a round table with four microphones and six chairs, twenty or so rappers, one overflowing makeshift ashtray, and an asthmatic looking plant. [see Fig. 1][3] Much like a jazz jam session, the rappers would rotate in and out of the seats to freestyle, some staying longer than others. Xiao and Mani—first-generation Parisians from the Democratic Republic of Congo and Cameroon, respectively—were among the handful of MCs that spent a good deal of time on the microphone, effectively promoting themselves.

Over the previous months studying hip-hop communities in Berlin, I had come to count on freestyle sessions as the best points of entry into local scenes. I attended numerous formal concerts, contacted local recording labels, and checked out the best record stores, but for sheer ease of accessibility

figure 7.1: taping of *marché noir* in the studios of *radio plurielle*. top: xiao (rapping) and mani bottom right, upper left; host tarik at board in control room (in white). bottom: dj dirty swift producing live beats for the mcs from the control room.

and cultivation of contacts nothing could beat a good weekly freestyle session. In her *Rap Music and Street Consciousness*, Cheryl Keyes describes such meetings in which "a circle of three or more people" come together to perform, challenge, and feed off of one another as "ciphers" (or "ciphas").[4] Indeed, this was the preferred nomenclature in Paris, as it had been in my experience of Berlin and would later prove to be during my fieldwork in London. In each of the three cities, such circles formed the basic units of hip-hop community. These musical sites contained the most collective knowledge about local scenes and were entry points to information about local artists, upcoming concerts, recording labels, and the best record shops.

In all three cities I found tight knit but fluid, supportive yet competitive communities of rappers that were happy to show an American hip-hop fan and researcher the ins and outs of their local music. In each cipher I would come to know a core of rappers that were regulars, returning week after week. Some were mentors, usually slightly older rappers offering advice and challenges to younger MCs and newer arrivals, while others were upstarts, young men with ravenous appetites for freestyle competition. Most ciphers were comprised predominantly of young men from sixteen to thirty with a handful of young women, some of whom would rock the mic as well. Stylistically, the makeup of these core groups ranged from the musically stripped down aggression of gangsta rap to the aurally nuanced and expressly political language of conscious hip-hop.

In all cases, from Paris and Berlin to London, the racial makeup of the ciphers were more diverse than their respective societies, mixing majorities of young men and women of non-European backgrounds together with their peers of European backgrounds to form musical communities. *Marché Noir* was no exception, comprising a diverse assemblage of both ethnically French MCs and rappers of postcolonial origins from sub-Saharan Africa and the Maghreb to Southeast Asia. While the musical styles and ideological perspectives varied wildly from MC to MC, the resultant ciphers shared a notable opposition to their respective national societies, both voicing and embodying the ideas of an alternative public sphere. As I will argue, in making music these young Europeans were also making themselves—formulating their politics, expressing their opinions, and otherwise fashioning their identities in explicit contrast to their cultural mainstreams.

The case of *Marché Noir* serves as just one example of this point. Indeed, the name of the cipher implies opposition, modeling itself as an alternative economy. The radio show is both a "black market" of underground music that is not available in record shops and a black market of marginalized ideas and viewpoints not commonly available in national media debates. Furthermore, it is no mistake that the idea of blackness is central to this construction. Not only does the term "black market" imply the non-transparency of underground economies, it gestures to racial blackness and to a particular black masculinity of hip-hop music. As we will see, uses of racialized discourses are central in the musical politics of the rappers with whom I spoke in Paris—"the City of Light." Thus, I will also argue that as the central form of hip-hop culture, music is the key mode of articulating such alternative public spheres and bringing to life the expressive communities that voice the truth of an ethnically diverse Europe. As I will demonstrate, this mobilization led by European minority youth takes its lead from the ways in which music has served as the key site for African American formulations of cultural and political identity.

As a cipher, the *Marché Noir* radio show was unique to me in the respect that it was held in a radio studio rather than at a concert venue, but both the feel of this artistic community and its function as an artistic outlet and training ground for MCs was identical with the many "live" events that I had attended. Indeed, the most common criticism of such cipher-styled live freestyle concerts is that the participants seem to be performing for themselves and their peers rather than for an audience. Even at larger staged events it was not uncommon for rappers to form a circle, with a number of the rappers literally turning their backs to the audience. In this respect the feel of the freestyle radio format of *Marché Noir* was nearly indistinguishable from the freestyle concert format, as audience feedback came from the gathered crowd of MCs in the studio just as it would in a club. While individual rappers put together lines of verse over DJ Swift's instrumental beats, MCs at other microphones and throughout the studio would voice their approval by interjecting shouts of "*ouais*" [yeah], echoing quality lyrics, and speaking the featured MCs name. Conversely, and less often, they would voice their disapproval by whistling, booing, talking to each other, or directly responding to the MC in question when they stepped to the microphone. The effect was that of a community that provided instant feedback, rewarding perceived stylistic or lyrical quality and deriding underdeveloped skills—but all in the context of a shared artistic community.

After the taping of *Marché Noir* I talked to Xiao, Mani, and a number of the other twenty or so MCs who were crammed into the two small rooms comprising the studio. As I had also learned over the previous months in Berlin, the preferred networking apparatus for rappers, DJs, and their promoters was MySpace.com. This held true for Paris as well, as I collected URLs from around the room that would provide a conduit for communication with each individual or group of rappers, in addition to giving me a taste of their recorded music, videos, performance activity, promotional strategies, influences, and often even biographical information. Indeed, such online pages broaden the circle of such freestyle ciphers to include a seemingly limitless network of artists who share information about other upcoming ciphers, concerts, and recordings. I sent messages to a number of the MCs from *Marché Noir* the following day, and was beginning to examine the music and information on their web pages. At that time Blackara's MySpace page featured two tracks, "Bang Bang" and "*Arrivistes*" [Go-Getters/Social Climbers], including a video for the latter.[5] As Xiao and Mani explained to me later, the two tracks were central to their oppositional self-empowerment ideology.

blackara: *le cauchemar de la france*

When I received the reply from Blackara a week later, Xiao left a mobile phone number for me to reach them and indicated they would be free later that night. When I called, Xiao said they could meet me at the Bastille McDonald's in a couple hours. As he explained, their continuing promotion efforts had them flyering in and around the many clubs in the Rue de la Roquette area east of Place de la Bastille and the golden arches provided an easily recognizable sign. I replied that I was happy to meet them there as the apartment that I had found for my stay was not far south of Bastille in the direction of Gare de Lyon. Although I had hoped to find a location in the more diverse 18th, 19th, or 20th *Arrondissements* during my housing search, the location in the central 11th proved handy in its proximity to Rue de la Roquette. As I would later find, the location was also within walking distance of the *Capitale Sale* [Dirty Capital] record label office and recording studio operated by DJ Swift, Tarik, and a number of the MCs I had met at *Marché Noir*.

I arrived at the Bastille McDonald's at the appointed hour of 11 pm and after a bit of waiting, walked to the small cinema next door to browse the line up of an upcoming Scorsese festival. Shortly after I had resolved to see *Taxi Driver* the following week, a sunglassed and dapper-looking Mani emerged from a beat-up hatchback and flipped the seat to let me into the back of the two-door. It turned out that the duo had been to the barber earlier in the day in preparation for their upcoming show. Xiao's cut was especially interesting featuring a perfectly rendered argyle design arcing over his head. As I leaned forward between the seats to inquire about our destination, I also realized that both of them were equipped with the custom-fit tooth cap jewelry known as "grillz." They were dressed for hip-hop success.

Xiao drove us several blocks east to the Twentyone Sound Bar, a familiar location that DJ Swift had introduced me to a couple weeks prior. The small venue was one of the few bars in Paris that was dedicated to hip-hop according to Swift, who holds a regular engagement there. As we got out of the car I inquired about one of Blackara's tracks that I listened to online. The track featured a number of familiar home studio production values that I had encountered among the underground artists I was interviewing. The beat was something of an aural assault, comprised of a Moog emulator playing an octave-sweeping minor key hook, a parallel motive of electronic blips, and a synthesized trumpet line in a martial staccato style that was fast becoming ubiquitous in underground productions [Ex. 1].

The scene in Paris, I would learn, was currently under the heavy influence of "crunk" an Atlanta-born hip-hop subgenre featuring the punchy electronic sounds and drum machine beats of the ubiquitous Roland TR 808—an historically important tool for hip-hop producers, especially the West Coast gangsta rap, or "G-funk" pioneers. Unlike the 1990s gangsta rap producers like Dr. Dre, however, contemporary producers of crunk beats such as Lil Jon and Develop use such digital technologies to layer strident tones one on the other rather than creating the laid back grooves of "G-funk." Although the dense musical texture of Blackara's "Bang Bang," is more akin to crunk, the track includes compositional features of both subgenres, fusing the slow tempo and signature portamento moog gestures of G-funk with crunk's bright and active snare hits and piercing synthesized timbres.

example 1: transcription of the crunk-styled sonic barrage of the "bang bang" loop.

The vocal delivery of "Bang Bang," however, establishes the track as explicitly crunk-inspired. The voices of Mani and Xiao are mixed front and center to cut through the bright timbres and crowded musical texture. Furthermore, where G-funk vocals are commonly fluid and easy, crunk vocals are consistently punchy, clipped, or otherwise aggressively delivered. This is the case with the rapping style of the two on all of their recent tracks, which aurally convey a sense of urgency. Finally, the track also includes the loud and diffuse bass tones of both G-funk and crunk, designed for the car cultures of both Southern and West Coast American hip-hop scenes. Although Mani and Xiao did not seem to have invested a great deal in their car's audio system, I would later learn that they were, in fact, interested in such car culture.

More distinctive than either the sweeping moog lines or the booming bass gestures in "Bang Bang," however, is a spoken sample at the outset of the track. "The beginning of 'Bang Bang,'" I asked in my fast improving French as we approached the club, "what's that sample from?" "C'est Menace II Society" came the

"Bang Bang" Densely Layered Loop

response from Mani.[6] "*Le cauchemar de l'Amérique*" [America's nightmare] he continued, switching to quote the line in English: "young, black…" here Xiao joined in, "and don't give a fuck!"

Blackara's track "Bang Bang" opens with this line as sampled from the film's French dubbed version, "*Le cauchemar de l'Amérique: jeune, black et qu'en a rien à branler.*" On their recording, the line quickly segues into Xiao and Mani rapping "*Blackara, Blackara: Offensive Records,*" an exposition comprising the name of their group and the name of their self-run record label.[7] The sample from the Hughes brothers' 1993 ghetto epic is taken from a voiceover of the main character describing his best friend O-Dog who shoots and kills a Korean storeowner over a disrespectful and paternalistic comment. As I learned in the interview that followed, Xiao and Mani did not consider themselves gangstas, but something resonated with them in this now-famous image of the young black man as America's nightmare. Indeed, by highlighting the *Menace* sample and declaring themselves "offensive" in the first seconds of "Bang Bang," the two postcolonial subjects purposefully entangle themselves in W. E. B. Du Bois's hundred-year-old question "How does it feel to be a problem?"[8] The two central Africans making a life for themselves in the former colonial center thus gesture to the African American experience for their critical tools and, by way of analogy, declare themselves *France's* nightmare. Such a triangulation of postcolonial identity was a common feature among MCs and DJs with whom I spoke in Berlin and London as well as Paris. Indeed, the historical forces that brought Xiao and Mani to Paris continue to resonate in the contours of Black Atlantic music.

menace ll the west

In his 1903 *Souls of Black Folk*, Du Bois wrote that "the problem of the twentieth century is the problem of the colorline," but as his work indicates he did not intend for this to be understood as a uniquely American problem. In his 1906 article "The Color Line Belts the World," published in *Collier's Weekly*, Du Bois explained how "The Negro problem in America is but a local phase of a world problem."[9] Indeed, after publication of the landmark *Souls of Black Folk*, Du Bois became increasingly invested in anti-colonial projects, traveling around the world to work with international antiracist movements that linked anti-black racism in the United States with racisms and economic inequities around the world. Nonetheless, the "problem" of race relations was cast as a uniquely American problem over the course of Du Bois's century—the unseemly counterpart to American exceptionalism known the world over. In their appropriation of the "nightmarish" black masculinity of *Menace*, Blackara is referencing this most American of problems to reassert the "local phase" that they are enduring in Paris. But as I demonstrate, in this transaction the exemplary articulation of African American political struggle and cultural pride has become something more than just a phase, it has become something iconic and universally assimilable to a degree that the dominant modalities in which blackness are now lived are American ones.

In the introduction to his collection of essays *Small Acts*, Paul Gilroy gestures to this development, including the following observation about the impact of African American political models on the black British context:

> The social memory of the black movements of the 1960s is important for other reasons too. Its creative appropriation marks black Britain's sharp turn away from the Caribbean as its major source of inspiration. Black political culture in this country now looks to African-American history for guidance, pleasure and raw material for its own distinct definitions of blackness. The appeal of the heroic figure of Malcolm X has been central to this development.... It represents the latest triumph of outer-national and intercultural political forms that make their local equivalents, still bolted to the decaying chassis of a nineteenth-century nation-state, look tame, redundant and outmoded by comparison.[10]

The motivations and mechanisms that Gilroy points to are today evident in minority communities—both black and non-black—throughout the West. The American Civil Rights Movement, along with Black Power and other black nationalisms, established the dominant paradigms for discourse about race and racism due in no small part to the power of American media and the ability of civil rights leaders and social activists to mobilize those media to serve their ends. As Gilroy argues, the black American identities that grew out of the sixties developed through the Black Power Movement and found guidance in figures like Malcolm X. They also provided alternative structures of feeling to the historically racialized and exclusive concept of the nation-state.

In hip-hop we can hear European minorities relating themselves in both style and substance to the African American experience of double consciousness. Both implicitly and explicitly, these expressions of double consciousness share with African

Americans the cultural memory of slavery and colonialism and the lived legacy of racial exclusion and oppression. As an artistic movement and popular cultural form, hip-hop positions minority life within the context of the nation-state like nothing else. Yet despite the historical marginalization of black Americans, African American culture—especially music—is undeniably at the core of American culture.

Ralph Ellison expresses this point in his 1970 article "What America Would Be like Without Blacks." His argument, of course, concludes that it would be unrecognizable. Indeed, it would not be America. Ellison writes:

> The problem here is that few Americans know who and what they really are. That is why few [white ethnic] groups—or at least few of the children of these groups—have been able to resist the movies, television, baseball, jazz, football, drum-majoretting, rock, comic strips, radio commercials, soap operas, book clubs, slang, or any of a thousand other expressions and carriers of our pluralistic and easily available popular culture. It is here precisely that ethnic resistance is least effective. At this level the melting pot did indeed melt, creating such deceptive metamorphoses and blending of identities, values and lifestyles that most American whites are culturally part Negro American without even realizing it...
>
> Despite his racial difference and social status, something indisputably American about Negroes not only raised doubts about the white man's value system, but aroused the troubling suspicion that whatever else the true American is, he is also somehow black. Materially, psychologically and culturally, part of the nation's heritage is Negro American and whatever it becomes will be shaped in part by the Negro's presence.[11]

Ellison reminds us of the fact that the African American is constitutive of the American, and yet is commonly subjected to erasure in national and international discussions. Following Ellison, I suggest that the parenthetical construction of "(African) Americanization" might help to draw out and highlight the centrality of African American culture to American culture while simultaneously speaking to the marginalizations, occlusions, and erasures at play. To use W. E. B. Du Bois's noted metaphor of double consciousness, the parentheses in this figure are "the veil."

Read in tandem with Ralph Ellison's thoughts on the inherent hybridity of American culture in his "What America Would Be Like Without Blacks," Gilroy's above thoughts provide an evocative political corollary. The (African) American example has facilitated both Ellison's irresistibly "pluralistic and easily available popular culture" as well as Gilroy's triumphant "intercultural political forms" that together guide today's minority identity politics across the Western world. Historically, music has been the key to crafting and expressing these political forms among African Americans. Fittingly, in today's demographically changed Europe, African American music is increasingly the key to developing new intercultural political forms. To paraphrase Ellison, 'whatever the true Frenchman is, he is also somehow Congolese, Cameroonian, Algerian....' Today, this truth is voiced loudly and clearly in hip-hop.

les "arrivistes"

When I sat down with Xiao and Mani at the Twentyone Sound Bar one of my first questions was about the name "Blackara," which seemed to articulate an African *American* perspective through the use of the English term "black." Indeed, such a word choice eschews francophone articulations of African diasporic identity, most notably the *"Négritude"* movement promoted by intellectuals such as Léopold Senghor and Aimé Césaire. Mani explained that the name reflected a "pro-black" agenda, while the suffix "ara" referenced gold "like 18 karat or 24 karat" he said pulling his chain from his chest. "Blackara shines! It has to be real. If you want diamonds and gold, you've got to work. If you sleep, you get fake gold and fake diamonds." "By any way necessary," added Xiao in English. As Gilroy indicates, Malcolm X remains a heroic figure for blacks in the English-speaking world and a powerful signifier of African American struggle, but here we see the global reach of Malcolm's words and of African American political culture writ large. Xiao's shorthand reference to Malcolm's politics easily conveyed his meaning to his American interviewer and cleared the way towards an understanding of Blackara's particular cultural politics.

As their explanation of the name indicated, Blackara's politics is expressed through the articulation of blackness and the symbol of gold.[12] For them, gold has a deep meaning that represents the material results of hard work and self-reliance. In their formulation of the name Blackara, Xiao and Mani are also expressing a postcolonial perspective on the exploitation of Africa's natural resources—most notably the continent's once rich gold reserves which were mined and exported back to Europe's colonizing nations.[13] In the symbol of African gold, the two thus establish a diasporic link to Africa as well as a motivating force for themselves in Paris. Importantly, for Xiao and Mani this motivating factor is not couched in terms of reparations for colonial exploitation, but viewed as both a means and an end.

Expanding on this idea and the central concept of their track "*Arrivistes*" [Upstarts/Go Getters/Social Climbers], Xiao and Mani described their goals of material improvement and self-reliance in Paris as follows:

> Xiao: Here it is not possible for us to succeed [*arrive*]. People always tell us: "you cannot." But we've got to make it by any way, because there is no way for us. There is no way. Because the life we are living is not a vacation. When you go back home and you see your

mother and father in trouble—you know if you don't
do something now, it's going to be you at home with
trouble.

Mani: And you know in France people always say:
"yeah, there's some help." You know for hospital and
everything. There's a lot of help, of course, but it's a
way for the government to know you and to keep you
down. When you aren't working you earn—maybe
about 700 euros [per month]. You know? And when
you work, you're up every morning you earn about
1000.

Xiao: Or more.

Mani: More, but you're working. So people always
think, okay I'll sleep and I'll take my money, but it's
the new...

Xiao: Chains. The new slavery.

Mani: The new slavery. Because you have to say: "give
me, give me, give me." It's why in France it's more
difficult to blow up [achieve success], to blow up
for real... You know, because the government, they
keep you down. Giving you food. Feeding you. So
you cannot be intelligent here. In the United States
they say you are rich or you are poor. There are two
ways. Here they make you think you can do anything
you want. But really you cannot do anything when
you go somewhere and people see you're black. Of
course there's not racism everywhere, everywhere,
everywhere...

Xiao: No KKK here...

Mani: But the real problem is when you go out and
you see the world is not like you're living in the 'hood.

It is clear that the two do not fully idealize the United States, but
a pronounced free market logic underscores their critique of the
French welfare state. In their view of the French social safety net
as new from of slavery, Xiao and Mani express a nuanced view
that critiques welfare as a method of keeping black Parisians in

a hand to mouth cycle of poverty. In addressing the symptoms of poverty rather than the causes—racism and lack of economic opportunity—they view French policies as ways to keep black Parisians dependent. Demonstrating a novel, if under-informed view of U.S. policy, Mani suggests that at least in the U.S. the government will not pretend to take care of you.

When I later asked them about the upcoming presidential election touted as the most important in a generation, the two responded that they are no more impressed with the Socialist Party's Ségolène Royal than with the conservative free-marketeer Nikolas Sarkozy. They explained:

> Mani: Me I can vote, so I'm gonna vote. But really... Sarko is gonna do things for his friends and Ségolène for her friends, and everybody's got friends, but it's not for us really. But remember, they are all friends.
> Xiao: The shit is for them not for us. They keep the poor poor. We think the real thing is that they have the money and the power—and the people, we're fighting for respect.
> Mani: I make my money. I make my things. We make ours.
> Xiao: If you don't teach something to us we're going to take it. We have to take it. Life is like this: if you are waiting for the sky to give you bread you're gonna die.
> Mani: You're gonna die. We prefer dying trying to get rich.

In addition to harboring a distrust of the political class at large, they went on to describe in detail their distrust of Royal because of her paternalistic politics and "Sarko" because of his racism. Interestingly, however, their own economic politics echoed those of the latter, the pro-business "Americanizer" who would soon be elected president. Notably, their comments also reference the American gangsta rapper 50 Cent's 2003 album *Get Rich or Die Tryin'*.[14] As we will see, the reference was likely intended.

Mani and Xiao, it turned out, grew up not far from the studios of *Radio Plurielle* in the neighborhood between Jaurès and Stalingrad Metro stations. The area in the northwest corner of Paris, in which the two still live, is home to some of the largest housing projects (known as *cités*) within the city proper and is also one of the most ethnically diverse quarters. Together, Mani and Xiao recounted a story about asking for financial assistance from the city for a block party that they were organizing. The tale served as a sort of Genesis story of their current self-reliant worldview.

> Mani: We don't wait for our people. Because we have had some problems. In the 'hood in Jaurès there is no organization to help the young and the old.
> Xiao: The youngsters, they're on the street, you know, and they can be hit by a car any time, and no one does anything. So a long time ago we went to see the mayor and he said that...
> Mani: In his office...
> Xiao: and he said that in our 'hood there are not enough problems, so I cannot help you. I said okay. So after that we decided to make our money by any means necessary—in good ways, bad ways, we don't give a fuck. Because, our people deserve to be happy. So with this money we organized a 'hood party for the young and the old. For all the people: black, white, Arab, everybody. And then later the mayor said to us, oh we can do this together and we said "no!"
> Mani: We can do it on our own.
> Xiao: Because when we came to you, you said "fuck you" so don't come to us now. Because now we are independent. So, a kind of power. We can do something for the people. The people believe in us. And we got the solution for the whole problem.
> Mani: We'll make our money and after we have our party we'll live on our own. It's like in the film *The*

Village. Our 'hood is a village. The village is closed and there are monsters, but in the village everything is good. It's how we live. We've got our own course and way of life. And we say to everybody, we speak for you telling you to keep your own people. We keep ours. And after everybody is the same we can be really linked.

Mani's analogy to *The Village* proved to be a reference to M. Night Shyamalan's 2004 thriller about a small town insulating itself against modernity by creating a myth about monsters in the woods surrounding them.[15] Although he had earlier compared Sarkozy to Hitler (and George W. Bush), his point did not concern monsters, but rather the vision of self-reliance he had for his community. As Mani had noted earlier, he sees the main problem as the imbalance between life in his economically depressed and ethnically diverse 'hood, and life in Paris's extremely wealthy and expensive city center. Additionally, his point of reference again turned out to be an artifact of American popular culture. While there were many cases in which the two searched for metaphors that might better convey their meanings to an American researcher with imperfect French skills, the case of Mani's reference to *The Village* was quite clearly pre-conceptualized as something that resonated with him regarding this exact point.

figure 7.2: "les arrivistes" xiao and mani exhibiting their "personalized" styles.

The hopeful gesture of solidarity that Mani closes with here is also reminiscent of Du Bois's 1897 entreaty for African Americans "to maintain their race identity until the mission of the Negro people is accomplished, and the ideal of human brotherhood has become a practical possibility."[16] Indeed, his statement that "after everybody is the same we can be really linked," while grounded in the language of self-determination, is a very clear argument for equality through difference rather than through assimilation—as French governmental conceptions of naturalization would have it. Although Xiao is clear about the multiethnic inclusiveness of their project, their larger message and a second nod to Malcolm X makes manifest the explicit linkages between their political project and African American models of opposition, resistance, and ultimately, relation.

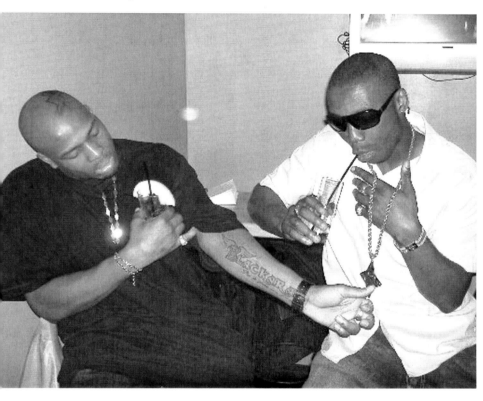

Xiao further explained the self-empowering "*Arriviste*" ideology as an individualizing one, displayed through the gold on their necks, the jewelry in their mouths, the "Blackara" tattoos on both of their forearms, and the patterns in his hair [Fig. 2]. The two even have signature "hooks," that appear in every track. Xiao's is a call of "Xiao i-*ci!*" [Xiao here!], with an emphasis on the second syllable of the word and Mani's is a quasi-Latino call of "aye, aye, *aye!*," again with the emphasis on the final syllable.

As he pointed to his personalized and consciously ostentatious markers of success and conspicuous consumption Xiao explained:

> Like we say in "*Arrivistes*": "personalized for your personality" [*personalisé pour sa personalité*]. It means we have our own customized character. Because today in France everybody wants to look like everybody else. But we don't want to be just anybody we want to be somebody. You know? So we have to be personalized, custom. We like to show off our jewels, our hairstyle. You see: "personalized," because when you see us you know: "ah, that is Blackara."

As Xiao and Mani explained, they take a great deal of pride in community and yet seek to express a strong sense of individuality within that sphere. Further, they are working towards the goal of a better-integrated and more equitable society but remain opposed to the assimilationist and paternalistic welfare policies of the Socialist party, dismissing Socialist political activists as "sheep." On the flip side, although they are sworn enemies of Nikolas Sarkozy, Blackara's neo-liberal politics closely parallel his. Blackara's *Arriviste* ideology thus seems wholly unexpected if not paradoxical.

On the track "Bang Bang," Xiao gives musical voice to these signifiers of individuality and work, when he raps the lines:

> *Nous grande pointure, gros bonnet / Les boss c'est nous*
> *Faut pas que tu te trompes / Grande voiture, gros bijoux*
> *Rajoute des crômes / C'est sur une pyramide de MCs que le blackara trône*
> [Our baggy clothes, fat caps / We are the boss
> Make no mistake about it / Big car, big jewels

Covered in chrome / Atop a pyramid of MCs sits
Blackara's throne][17]

Although such lyrics are easily dismissed as effects of the worldwide spread of American consumer culture and the influence
of commercial hip-hop's increasingly "bling"-focused lyrics, we
must also take into consideration Mani's point that: "the real
problem is when you go out and you see the world is not like
you're living in the 'hood." Indeed, critiques of conspicuous
consumption are most commonly directed not at wealthy consumers of *haute couture* but at the social climbers that Blackara
fashion themselves. While few of the underground rappers that
I spoke with in Paris shared Blackara's explicit *Get Rich or Die
Tryin'* mentality, the logic of their ideology was striking.

In addition to the bling imagery of "Bang Bang," the track
also expresses an oppositional anger couched in terms of their
neighborhood's "soldiers" and their "enemies." Supporting the
track's violent title, both the beat and the lyrics are delivered in
an aggressively hypermasculine and "raw" manner throughout.
As described above, the high vocal mix is designed to match
the intensity of the heavily layered texture of sweeping moog
lines and martial trumpets over a relentless drum track [Ex. 1].
Through the use of vocal overdubs, the texture of Xiao's baritone
voice grows thick in the above stanza, and is positioned prominently in the mix. The imperfect matching of vocal takes in the
overdubbing also creates a level of tension as the rapper gasps for
air at unequal intervals. As such, the track crafts an underground
aesthetic of struggle that implies the earned reward of such material wealth. And despite the low-fidelity production values and
bling subject matter of "Bang Bang," the poetic structure is quite
elegant with rhyme schemes emerging not only at the end of
lines (*nous/bijoux, crômes/trône*), but also across lines (*pointure/
voiture*) and with internal assonances (*nous grande pointure*).

The video for *"Arrivistes"* is a visual representation of the
track's message and embodies many of the themes that arose

in the interview. Yet, it also raises a number of questions about what their ideology of uplift looks like in practice. It begins with a shot of Mani on the street, transacting some sort of deal with another young man. Indeed, the opening image suggests another translation of *arrivistes* as "hustlers." The word is, of course, commonly associated with drug dealing and other illegal business in the hip-hop lexicon, but the "by any means necessary" ideology that Blackara espouses flips the script on the value judgment, arguing that their entrepreneurial spirit in unregulated markets will be rewarded.

In the scene that follows, their discussion of welfare as the "new slavery" is visually narrativized as Mani calls Xiao to rouse him out of bed and out of inaction. Xiao's cell phone rings with the lush strings of the opening phrase of Nino Rota's *Theme from The Godfather*—a gesture to Blackara's valorization of (mediatized) organized crime, here symbolized by the infamous Italian American social climbers. Xiao answers the call and Mani tells him to wake up because they have to meet Mac Manu, a female vocalist who will perform the chorus for the track. Xiao gets up from bed to attend to his business of underground hip-hop production, and the video begins in earnest.

The body of the video reads like a catalog of American rap video conventions. The first scene establishes their neighborhood, depicting Blackara and guest artist Mac Manu beneath the platform of their home Jaurés Metro station. In one shot, Xiao lifts his trademark gold medallion from his neck and the next tight shot focuses on **example 2: descending natural minor scale with lowered 2nd scale degree.** Mani's gold-filled mouth. As Mani rhymes that he is an expert in the "parallel economies" of the black market, we see images of high stakes hustler life borrowed from Hollywood cinematic conventions. Closely emulating the visual grammar of crime films, Mani descends into a parking garage to conduct a transaction—presumably a drug deal—sliding a briefcase to a business associate or rival hustler. From these opening images Blackara fashions a criminal authenticity that provides the logic for the *arriviste* images of wealth in the scenes that follow.

The English cognate of the term "*arriviste*" is of course, "arrive," and in the next section of the video the three literally arrive at a posh dance club in a large, albeit older model American car. Reflecting their knowledge of and engagement with U.S. hip-hop car culture, we see a customized white Chrysler Le Baron roll up in front of the "Jet Club" with the name Blackara on the car's grill and their initials, XV and MP on the sides. The scene inside the club presents the three in a VIP lounge with a group of friends, many who are scantily clad women. The VIP scene—established by the visual markers of red walls and dancing women—thus serves as an arrival in terms of wealth and prestige. It is the presumed goal of the high stakes underground transactions and "hard work" established in the previous tableau.

With the first iteration of the chorus, the VIP scene also serves to demarcate a musical arrival. Although the primary musical loop is constant throughout the track's verses and chorus, it contains within it highly teleological trajectory that reinforces the narrative of both the lyrics of the song and the images of the video. Indeed, the melodic shape of the line of continuous sixteenth notes is that of a countdown, outlining a falling natural minor scale with a lowered second degree [Ex. 2].

"Arrivistes" Melodic Loop

Although the tonal goal of E-flat is constantly reinforced on every beat, the gesture is nonetheless one of impending doom. The loop resonates with the narrative of Mani's high stakes criminality as the lowered second acts an especially powerful musical signifier of proximity to danger.[18] The falling gesture resonates with Mani's descent into the dark parking garage and its F-flat conveys the danger of this type of descent. Indeed, where a leading tone on ascent is pleasing in a functionally tonal setting, this type of leading tone on descent is fundamentally upsetting despite its established inevitability in this Phrygian modal environment. The musical and narrative message here seems to invert this pleasure/displeasure binary, however, as Mani and Xiao take pride in their stated ability to *arrive* in desperate circumstances—to step up and succeed in turning such situations to their financial advantage.

Over the continuing loop, Blackara's vocalist Mac Manu sings the track's chorus of: "*Les Arrivistes... Personalisé pour sa personalité*" in a Jamaican dancehall idiom of rapidly repeated eighth notes on E-flat, with interjections of major seconds and minor thirds at structurally important points. While the half-sung half-spoken idiom is not especially common in Parisian hip-hop, the musical connections between hip-hop and dancehall are historically well established and very active in other European scenes, including London's heavily Caribbean influenced scene and Berlin's surprisingly robust dancehall underground which regularly features Kingston-based performers in its clubs.

In the verse that follows, Xiao plays the role of pimp rather than drug dealer. Set somewhat awkwardly in a McDonalds, we see Xiao sitting in a booth between two women. After establishing his power of attraction in the verse's opening lyrics, he points to his personalized style as the source of his prowess. Here, his signature argyle hairstyle is mirrored on the hood of an argyle emblazoned red sweatshirt and matching pants, yielding a striking visual effect. In the main dramatic device of the scene, we see him imagine himself as something other than an attractive and customized ladies' man. In a brief dream sequence we see him in a conservative dark-colored sweater and khakis with a primly dressed woman on his arm. Notably, while the woman in the dream sequence is also dressed conservatively in a black sweater and plaid skirt, the women in the booth are dressed in revealing red and leopard print dresses, respectively. Furthermore, the conservatively dressed woman happens to be white, while the women in the booth are black. This moment of racialized difference is quickly injected with misogynistic overtones as well, as Xiao makes one of the women in the booth take a note to the white woman, who, now out of the dream sequence and into the present, is instructed to call Xiao. In the end, the scene serves to establish Xiao's power over all of the women, simultaneously characterizing him as a pimp and objectifying all three of the women as obedient prostitutes. Rather than joining mainstream society—as portrayed in the dream sequence—Xiao's character endeavors to bring the mainstream (white) woman into his world. After the verse is complete, the chorus and its VIP lounge scene resumes, now with the added implication that all of the dancing women there too are prostitutes.

Through the two fictionalized scenarios of Mani as drug dealer and Xiao as pimp, Blackara completes the narrative that crime does indeed pay. Although Mac Manu sets herself apart from the rest of the women in the VIP lounge by sitting and wearing even more gold than Mani and Xiao, the remainder of the video features objectifying close-ups of the dancing women. Indeed, the chasm between the self-empowering *arriviste* ideals that Xiao and Mani described to me and the debased narrative with which they chose to illustrate this ideology is wide. Where the mantra of "by any means necessary" rang true as a response to structural racism and economic inequality in our interview, the video for "*Arrivistes*" threw cold water on their righteous indignation.

In his article, "The Cosmopolitan Nativist: Fela Anikulapo-Kuti and the Antinomies of Postcolonial Modernity" Tejumola Olaniyan describes another musician's ideological paradoxes as indicative of a wider postcolonial dilemma.[19] Olaniyan illustrates how the father of Afro-Beat music, the Nigerian Fela Kuti, matched a cultural traditionalism replete with separatist politics to a musical style that drew on global popular culture, arguing that the disjunctures of postcoloniality make such antinomies possible, if not necessary. In brief, Olaniyan argues that the collision of first and third worlds on the same soil and in the same minds has brought about a new paradoxical system in which rational ideals such as universalism and equality are challenged by the manifestly illogical realities of white supremacy and structural racism. As such, the argument also closely parallels the mental two-ness of Du Bois's "double consciousness."

While Olaniyan's primary consideration is of the antinomies of Euro-American cosmopolitanism and African tradition, he also interrogates the unexpected misogyny of Fela's otherwise liberating cultural politics. Indeed, the antinomy is heightened in light of the fact that the famed bandleader's mother was at the forefront of African women's movements. Olaniyan theorizes these antinomies through the paradox of a "cosmopolitan nativist," who "borrows tools from wherever in defense of African ways of knowing and being conceived as embattled by Euro-American cultural imperialism. In this conception, postcolonial musical modernity, indeed postcolonial modernity, is best theorized as an aporia pulling together two apparently contradictory paradigms."[20]

Though I will not attempt to offer an apology for Blackara's sexism—or staged criminality, for that matter—we might follow Olanyian's lead in working towards an understanding thereof. We have in the video's figure of the conservatively dressed white woman, an image of white European normativity. Though he does not explicitly espouse sexism, here we see Xiao militating against his stated enemy, white French normativity, but doing so in a sexist mode. As a widely available, if destructive, way to feel empowered, the sexist discourses embodied in the video function as "tools" with which to do violence against a straw (wo)man for class and race discrimination in France, albeit a manifestly misguided one.

In his book-length study of Fela, *Arrest the Music*, Olaniyan describes the genesis of Fela's mature ideology as the result of his exposure to the Black Power Movement while working with musicians in the United States in the late 1960s. Therein he writes of the "radicalizing effect of the ten-month U.S. trip on Fela...

which forcefully catalyzed and definitively shaped" his "cultural nationalism."[21] While the early Black Power Movement was characterized by a relatively positive record of gender equality and women's empowerment, many ideas that have filtered down to hip-hop in the intervening years have sustained certain liberating aspects, while subverting others. The case of Public Enemy is instructive as a widely cited example of the politically liberating potential of Black Power influenced hip-hop. However, in order to make celebratory claims about the seminal group, critics are forced to downplay or all together write out the group's sometimes violently antisemitic views. As their music and video illustrate, Blackara has found in the expressive culture and media of American hip-hop a deep legacy of black cultural pride and self-reliance on which to draw, but they have also fallen into many of the same traps as African American artists.

community memory and the resonance of africa

Later in the interview, I asked Xiao and Mani if they had a strong connection to Africa. Xiao responded: "Yes, it is natural, it's an obligation. Because we are Africans. When you turn on the TV and you see something about Africa—it touches us. We see our family in Africa. And in our community [in Jaurés] they speak my language." Xiao went on to explain that they were both first generation immigrants having arrived in Paris as infants. Mani was born in Cameroon and he in "Zaire, Congo..." adding "where Muhammad Ali beat George Foreman." The reference to the famed "Rumble in the Jungle" was likely intended to help orient me to his place of origin, but it was also spoken with a great deal of pride. The momentous boxing match was promoted by Don King and Zaire's strongman president Mobutu as a pan-Africanist event imbued with an air of Black Power at the height of the movement. Of course, the fight also featured the Nation of

Islam's highest profile member, an associate of Malcolm X and another prominent symbol of the Black Power Movement—Ali.

When I asked the two for their takes on the legacy of colonialism in France and in Africa, the first response came from Xiao, who explained with conviction:

> The problem is that people forget *everything.* That's the problem. We have got to have *memory.* It's what kills black people, you know? The memory. When we went to school they taught us about a lot of important things, really important things. But you have to speak to me about *my* history, what you have done to my people.

The words echo those of countless African Americans confronted with curricula in which black history is relegated to a special case (and month) and otherwise marginalized. They also share a commonly used discourse in American rap lyrics, including a particularly poignant line from the New York hip-hop group De La Soul: "I make you feel lost like high school history."[22]

In a mocking tone, Mani continued on the point, explaining that in Parisian classrooms they teach colonialism saying: "Maybe some people have done bad things but we went over there to do good things. We taught you to eat with a spoon!" They continued:

> Xiao: In education, the government has a law that you have to teach about the good side of colonization.
> Mani: That is really shit! And you can't speak back to the teacher. So: "okay, okay, okay okay." But afterwards you look to your continent, to your country, and you say "look they speak that language in that part of the country, and here is another country, but they speak the same." Who cut—who made it that way? It's colonialism.
> Xiao: And they just say they taught you how to eat with a spoon!

Mani: Look I have a pen!

Mani's point about social memory and the shortcomings of their school's African history curriculum was clearly an important one for him, as he kept returning to memory as a theme throughout the interview. Indeed, the symbol of gold served as reclamation of African natural resources for which colonizers "gave us some guns, some drugs, and cigarettes." This sentiment is given dramatic shape in a postcolonial revenge scene at the end of Blackara's track "Bang Bang." After giving shout outs to a number of their friends, their neighborhood of Jaurès, and their 19th *Arrondissement* with calls of "Bang Bang," they lower their figurative saluting guns from the sky to the colonizer, closing the track with the line: *"Général colonial: bang, bang, bang, bang"* [Colonial general: bang, bang, bang, bang].

As Blackara's responses indicate, the two are genuinely engaged in postcolonial, national, and international politics and acutely aware of the histories thereof. However, when I asked what their school had taught about black Francophone intellectuals such as the Martinicans Aimé Césaire and Frantz Fanon, and the Senegalese Léopold Senghor, they shrugged off the question. Whether through disinterest or because the anti-colonial leaders were not taught in their school curricula, Mani and Xiao found their resources for postcolonial opposition and self-improvement elsewhere. Like Fela before them it was the African American models of Black Power and self-reliance that provided the most puissant models of black identity and community solidarity. Furthermore, through their engagement with, and reference to, elements of American popular culture it became clear that electronic media were central to both imagining their worlds and themselves. Indeed, the gangsta rap narrative and commercialized images of the *"Arrivistes"* video seemed to confirm this influence. For better and for worse, American hip-hop music in particular provided the primary way to formalize their ideas, represent themselves, and achieve their goals.

saying something

When I asked the two how they make musical choices on their tracks, Xiao described their compositional process as follows:

> It's like a story. It's why for us, you can't use our lyrics, you know, to make a shaker (a simple dance track). There's a lot of people who can make a shaker of a song. But it's the same song. Always the same song. In our songs we have to say something. Maybe it's about parties, maybe drugs, maybe music, maybe problems, maybe about our parents, maybe about history, maybe about school, but we say something from the beginning to the end of all our lyrics.

When I followed up, pressing them about the actual musical processes of crafting a beat, Mani said that they produced the beats on a computer at home but returned to the same point, finding himself at a loss for words: "It depends on the track. If it is about something sad, then we have sad music; something serious, serious music; something fun, party music. But we always say something."

For Blackara the sonic elements of their tracks were foremost a vehicle for the communication of lyrics, ideas, and feelings. As Ingrid Monson describes in her *Saying Something: Jazz Improvisation and Interaction*, the jazz tradition is part of an "aural legacy" of African American tradition that has historically employed such musical communication as a form of cultural memory.[23] Musical storytelling has been an especially useful vessel for both establishing dialogue and sustaining and developing traditions and memories. Just as Xiao and Mani note that their instrumental tracks must establish the tone for their rhymes to have meaning and power, Monson writes of the fundamental importance of the rhythm section for the jazz soloist at the outset of her study:

> An imaginative rhythm section can inspire a soloist to project his or her most vibrant voice, while disinterested accompaniment can thwart even the strongest artist...When a musician successfully reaches a discerning audience, moves its members to applaud or shout praises, raises the energy to dramatic proportions, and leaves a sonorous memory that lingers long after, he or she has moved beyond technical competence, beyond the chord changes, and into the realm of "saying something."[24]

To be sure, in hip-hop the live freestyle cipher format more closely echoes the improvisational interaction of jazz soloist and rhythm section. Countless MCs at freestyle ciphers have indicated to me that when the DJ's beats are not *just right* it is impossible to establish a "flow," either stylistically, musically, or lyrically. Blackara's emphasis on the importance of the musical context in the studio, however, conveys the idea that without a good beat the lyrical delivery will not only keep them from flowing, but that without an appropriate musical feel their ideas will certainly fall on deaf ears. In the context of their remarks about their community in Jaurés, it is clear that Xiao and Mani are interested not only in speaking, but in communicating ideas or feelings to a receptive audience. In their view, if nothing is communicated, nothing is said. As such, the act of "saying something" is more akin to dialogue than monologue. Despite Blackara's highly individualizing lyrics and style choices, their ideology works dialectically through hip-hop as a simultaneously communicative, community building, and empowering musical and cultural form.

At the end of our interview Xiao pointed out the t-shirt that he had designed for their record label, Offensive Records. It represented another "personalized" affect that he was wearing for their promotional activities, and was in this case a truly personal and powerful one, which he was especially proud of. [see Fig. 3]

The poetry, beginning on the shirt's back, is his own and reads:

For THEM I am:
less than nothing,
a robber, lazy,
a delinquent, a savage,
an outcast, a coward,
a prisoner, the bad guy,
an ignoramus, an imbecile,
a problem, a good for nothing,
a MODERN SLAVE
But when I look at myself in my
mirror, I see:
a father, a son, a brother,
a fighter, a genius,
the future, an upstart,
a hard worker, a thinker,
a visionary,
A FREE MAN.
THEY judge us but...

figure 7.3: xiao s design for the offensive records t-shirt: "they do not know who we are."

Xiao then pointed out how the final ellipsis on the shirt's back leads to the shirt's front, which reads in much larger letters: "They do not know who we are."

The list of stereotypes, including "a delinquent," "the bad guy," and "a problem," echoes the dubbed *Menace II Society* sample that begins the track "Bang Bang." What's more, the translated quote from *Menace* that serves as my epigram above, provides a social translation for Xiao and Mani as well, in effect saying: we are *le cauchemar de la France*—France's nightmare. The "we" that he is speaking both to and for is his racially diverse and economically marginalized postcolonial community in Paris's 19th *Arrondissement*. As Blackara communicates through their *Arriviste* ideology, their eschewal of French patrimony and paternalism, and their sense of community self-determination in Jaurés, they have nothing to lose and everything to gain.

Pour EUX je suis :
un moins que rien,
un voleur, un fainéant,
un délinquant, un sauvage,
un exclu, un lâche,
un détenu, le mal,
un ignorant, un imbécile,
un problème, un bon à rien,
UN ESCLAVE MODERNE
Mais quand JE me regarde dans mon miroir, je vois :
un père, un fils, un frère,
un battant, un génie,
l'avenir, un arriviste,
un bosseur, un penseur,
un visionnaire,
UN HOMME LIBRE
Ils nous jugent mais ...

hip-hop marianne: uncle sarko's nightmare

As I walked around Place de la Bastille, a few weeks after my interview with Xiao and Mani, I came across two overlapping posters affixed to a streetlight outside the Bastille FNAC record store [Fig. 4]. There were hundreds of music advertisements plastered to the signs, poles, and walls around the large music retailer, and these two posters in counterpoint, proved a poignant example of the overlapping discourses of hip-hop, minority identity, and Americanization in Paris during the spring of 2007.

The first image that caught my eye was an Uncle Sam figure pointing to the viewer with the classic tag line: "I Want You." On further inspection, however, the face of this symbol of U.S. patriotism par excellence was that of Nikolas Sarkozy. After seeing the poster at the Bastille, I began to notice it elsewhere on Parisian street corners—a caricature of the French Interior Minister's pro-American leanings that was designed to elicit fears about the country's cultural and economic self-determination and distributed across the city in advance of the National election. Nowhere else, however, was the polemical image plastered over an equally evocative re-imaging of French cultural *patrimoine*.

For here, under Uncle Sarko's mug, was the bust of a headscarved and headphoned Marianne—the personification of the French Republic and symbol of French patriotism.

figure 7.4: overlapping posters on a place de la bastille street light. top: iconic personification of the us "uncle sam" refigured with sarkozy s face. bottom: poster advertising the hip-hop compilation cd: ecoute la rue marianne (listen to the street marianne). the cover art features the iconic personification of france "marianne" in a headscarf and wearing headphones.

In this formulation, the artwork, title, and musical contents of the politically progressive album—*Ecoute La Rue Marianne* [Listen to the Street Marianne]—work together to implore the French establishment to listen to the diverse postcolonial viewpoints of lower class residents of Parisian 'hoods and the surrounding *banlieues*. Importantly, the French Socialist Party, which is most likely responsible for the Uncle Sarko image, has had a problematic relationship with the anti-assimilationist politics of French hip-hop. Regardless of whether the political operative who posted the anti-Sarkozy material over the hip-hop advertisement intended to obscure the mild defamation of French universalist republican values, or to highlight the irony of these two images in counterpoint, the photo captures a moment that is a quite literal snapshot of Parisian cultural politics in the run-up to the 2007 election. Together, the advertisements were a caricatured microcosm of the fears on both sides of France's culture wars. Uncle Sarko vs. MC Marianne Ali, if you will.

In closing, I would like to return once more to Blackara's idea of "*le cauchemar*." Xiao and Mani portray themselves as the nightmare of French society not only because they are anathema to the political Right's fantasy of an ethnically pure nation, but also because they complicate the political Left's dream of a race

native tongues: an african hip-hop reader

free society. As the form of cultural politics that these rappers employ indicates, this polarized vision for solving France's "race problem" posits two unacceptable and indeed untenable options: 1.) deport everyone of immigrant origins from France or 2.) require that all citizens assimilate into a post-racial (i.e. white) French culture. Importantly, both are in fact "race free" dreams. Eschewing both of these unfeasible ideals, these self-defined minority rappers choose "to maintain their race identity until... the ideal of human brotherhood has become a practical possibility."[25]

In their music Blackara make it abundantly clear that this possibility has not yet come to pass, but in hip-hop music and community they find the most readily available means to work towards that end. While Xiao and Mani present a gangsta-modeled, albeit highly nuanced, vision of hip-hop, the degree of variance between forms of racialized hip-hop politics in France today is indicative of the available space within articulations of minority identity. In the oppositional models of an array of African American cultural forms they locate a politics best suited to their realities and work with those frameworks to make the music their own and to create their own "new ethnicities."[26]

Furthermore, as the medium of hip-hop continues to capture the imaginations of minority youth, the electronic media through which rap music is disseminated will, perhaps ironically, continue to provide postcolonial subjects a position of power at the center of debates about the future of France. Perhaps then, *un cauchemar*—a nightmare—is just what is needed in order to wake the nation up from its dreams of a race free France and start working towards the structural equality that would enable such a possibility.

notes

1. The original line, untranslated is: "Now O-Dog was the craziest nigga alive. America's nightmare: young, black, and didn't give a fuck." *Menace II Society*, dir. Albert Hughes (New Line, 1993). This chapter is drawn from a larger study entitled *Musical African Americanization: European Hip-hop and Minority Identity* that is currently in preparation.

2. *Marché Noir* airs every Thursday at Midnight on 106.3 FM, Paris. Previously aired programs, videos, and other information are available at www.marchenoir.biz, last accessed November 12, 2007.

3. All photographs were taken by the author with the permission of the artists. Special thanks to Xiao, Mani, Swift, Tarik, Boramy, Khosa, and the other Marché Noir regulars for taking me under their wing in Paris and to Pizko MC for introducing me to the cipher.

4. Cheryl Keyes, *Rap Music and Street Consciousness* (Urbana, Ill.: University of Illinois Press, 2002), 124.

5. Blackara MySpace page, http://myspace.com/blackara, last accessed 3 November 2007.

6. *Menace II Society*, dir. Albert Hughes.

7. All translations of lyrics and interviews are my own unless otherwise noted.

8. W. E. B. Du Bois, *The Souls of Black Folk*, Ed. David W. Blight and Robert Gooding-Williams (New York: Bedford Books, 1997).

9. Du Bois, "The Color Line Belts the World," in *W. E. B. Du Bois: A Reader*, ed. David Levering Lewis (New York: H. Holt, 1995), 42. See also Robin D. G. Kelley's "'But a Local Phase of a World

Problem': Black History's Global Vision 1883-1950," *The Journal of American History*, Vol. 86, No. 3 (Dec. 1999), 1045-1077.

10. Paul Gilroy, *Small Acts* (New York: Serpent's Tail, 1993), 12-13.

11. Ralph Ellison, "What America Would Be Like Without Blacks," *Time Magazine* (6 April 1970).

12. For an account of the symbolic weight of gold in South African hip-hop see: Gavin Steingo, "The Politicization of Kwaito: From the 'Party Politic' to Party Politics," *Black Music Research Journal* 27, No. 1 (Spring 2007), 23-44.

13. Countless colonial and postcolonial scholars have examined this process, most notably Walter Rodney in his *How Europe Underdeveloped Africa* (Washington, D.C.: Howard University Press, 1982).

14. 50 Cent, *Get Rich or Die Tryin'* (Interscope 2003).

15. *The Village*, dir. M. Night Shyamalan (Touchstone, 2004).

16. Du Bois, "The Conservation of Races," in *The Souls of Black Folk*, 237.

17. Blackara, "Bang Bang," Myspace.com/blackara. Last accessed 15 September 2008.

18. John Williams's *Theme to Jaws* is, of course, the most remarked upon example of this most basic of musical signifiers.

19. Tejumola Olaniyan, "The Cosmopolitan Nativist: Fela Anikulapo-Kuti and the Antinomies of Postcolonial Modernity," *Research in African Literatures* 32, no. 2 (Summer 2001), 76-89.

20. Olaniyan, "The Cosmopolitan Nativist," 77.

21. Tejumola Olaniyan, *Arrest the Music: Fela and His Rebel Art and Politics* (Bloomington: Indiana University Press, 2004), 25.

22. De La Soul, "In the Woods" on *Buhloon Mind State* (Rhino 1993).

23. Ingrid Monson, *Saying Something: Jazz Improvisation and Interaction* (Chicago: University of Chicago Press, 1996), 2.

24. Monson, *Saying Something*, 1-2.

25. Du Bois, "The Conservation of Races," in *The Souls of Black Folk*, 237.

26. See Stuart Hall, "Old and New Identities, Old and New Ethnicities" in *Culture, Globalization and the World System: Contemporary Conditions for the Representation of Identity* (Binghamton: State University of New York, 1991).

references

50 Cent. *Get Rich or Die Tryin'*. Interscope 2003.

Blackara, "Bang Bang," Myspace.com/blackara. Last accessed 15 September 2010.

De La Soul. "In the Woods" on *Buhloon Mind State*. Rhino 1993.

Du Bois, W. E. B.. "The Color Line Belts the World," in *W. E. B. Du Bois: A Reader*, ed. David Levering Lewis. New York: H. Holt, 1995.

Du Bois. "The Conservation of Races," in *The Souls of Black Folk*.

Du Bois. *The Souls of Black Folk*, eds. David W. Blight and Robert Gooding-Williams. New York: Bedford Books, 1997.

Ellison, Ralph. "What America Would Be Like Without Blacks," *Time Magazine* (6 April 1970).

Gilroy, Paul. *Small Acts*. New York: Serpent's Tail, 1993.

Hall, Stuart. "Old and New Identities, Old and New Ethnicities" in *Culture, Globalization and the World System: Contemporary Conditions for the Representation of Identity*. Binghamton: State University of New York, 1991

Keyes, Cheryl. *Rap Music and Street Consciousness*. Urbana, Ill.: University of Illinois Press, 2002.

Kelley, Robin D. G.. "'But a Local Phase of a World Problem': Black History's Global Vision 1883-1950," *The Journal of American History*, Vol. 86, No. 3 (Dec. 1999).

Menace II Society. Dir. Albert Hughes. New Line, 1993.

Marché Noir Website. www.marchenoir.biz. Last accessed November 12, 2007.

Monson, Ingrid. *Saying Something: Jazz Improvisation and Interaction*. Chicago: University of Chicago Press, 1996.

Olaniyan, Tejumola. "The Cosmopolitan Nativist: Fela Anikulapo-Kuti and the Antinomies of Postcolonial Modernity," *Research in African Literatures* 32, no. 2 (Summer 2001).

Olaniyan, Tejumola. *Arrest the Music: Fela and His Rebel Art and Politics*. Bloomington: Indiana University Press, 2004.

Rodney, Walter. *How Europe Underdeveloped Africa*. Washington, D.C.: Howard University Press, 1982.

Steingo, Gavin. "The Politicization of Kwaito: From the 'Party Politic' to Party Politics," *Black Music Research Journal* 27, No. 1 (Spring 2007).

The Village. Dir. M. Night Shyamalan. Touchstone, 2004.

PART III

---

the rap-up: conversations
and interviews

CHAPTER 8
putting two heads together:
a cross-generational conversation about hip-hop in south africa

SHAHEEN ARIEFDIEN AND MARLON BURGESS

The following conversation represents a snapshot of an on-going discussion between two Cape Town-born hip-hop heads invested in nurturing a respectful dialogue across a generational divide. Hesitant to use the old/new-school binaries, we are aware that the term *generation* is rather slippery.[1] In the context of South African hip-hop, the idea of generation varies between a notion of musical periods/trends in the U.S. and the socio-political history of South Africa. For the purpose of this discussion, we span the ten years (1970–1980) between the time of our births which also coincides with the major transitions that propelled South Africa from apartheid to a neo-liberal state. We also periodize our experiences in relation to important moments and shifts in global hip-hop – instances that, for the most part, are in conversation[2] with the U.S. hip-hop tradition. We feel that this approach is important, especially in a volume on African hip-hop, because too often there is the desire to view hip-hop traditions outside of the U.S. – and particularly in Africa – as isolated. Rejecting the expectation of an isolated "African" hip-hop tradition as well as exotifications of black performers, we situate South African hip-hop within moments of U.S. hip-hop history with a sense of ownership because we participated in debates, upholding of traditions (the five elements), promotion and popularization. Situated at the southernmost tip of the continent, Cape Town has functioned for centuries now as a nexus for diasporic communities.

shaheen ariefdien, born 1970, cape town

I was introduced to hip-hop in the early 1980s. Like many students of my generation, in high school I increasingly became involved in student activism. I incorporated hip-hop into activities and campaigns as a means to invoke attention, interest and commitment to the anti-apartheid cause. In 1988, together with DJ Ready D, I co-founded the hip-hop crew, Prophets of da City (POC). This gave me the opportunity to be involved with a number of hip-hop and youth-related projects that took me to different regions in South Africa and abroad. Although I co-produced six albums with POC and toured extensively, I became frustrated with the music industry, locally and globally. After I left POC, around 2000, I pursued academia to hone the skills I thought would help me accomplish my own political and creative goals. During my undergraduate degree at the University of Cape Town, I got involved in a number of youth-related projects that fused hip-hop, grassroots media and academia. My work in these areas continues. The scope of this discussion will not focus on my experiences as a member of POC because that is covered elsewhere (Ariefdien, forthcoming).

marlon burgess, born 1980, cape town

I first came in contact with hip-hop in the early 1990s, and more actively in the mid-90s. Although I was always rhyming and singing during high school, it was only after graduation that I was exposed to rhyming specifically, for a larger audience, thanks to a community radio show hosted by Ariefdien, DJ Big Dre and others.[3] This show not only introduced me to a larger audience of hip-hop heads across the country, but also helped me become aware of a powerful link between hip-hop and the kind of community activism that can attract attention on a national level. I decided to complement my artistic pursuits and community organizing with academic skills. From the University of Cape Town to New York University, I am constantly learning to balance these efforts.

in collaboration

Since our first meeting on the airwaves in 2000, we have been involved in various projects that were sometimes connected to Cape Town's Bush Radio – "Mother of Community Radio." In the following conversation we merge some of our artistic, political and scholarly interests, knowing fully that there is no clear separation. These are our experiences and not the voice of a homogenous Capetonian hip-hop community. Given South Africa's preoccupation with racial and ethnic categorizations, we anticipate that being classified coloured[4] and our ambivalence/resistance to those labels does contribute to how we frame our perspectives.

We draw largely from personal experiences, observations, feedback, input from respected peers and also from literature. Instead of providing a linear discussion that attempts to be exhaustive of any particular topic, we offer theme-driven glimpses into the most salient moments of an ongoing conversation – a kind of stop-motion, animation-like montage.

As artists and practitioners, we are invested in the aesthetic quality of performance. As members of various communities that try to use hip-hop for positive change, we have extra passion for the potential and limitations of hip-hop as a tool for justice, however that is imagined. The following might not overtly address all these considerations, but it does inform and bring to light some of the overlapping concerns and issues. We must explicitly acknowledge that race and class influence our perspective just as much as gender, which is elusive in spite of a large body of scholarship about it. Evidently this amount of scholarship has not ensured basic rights for girls and women.

making contact: how i found hip-hop

An opening dialogue in which we reflect on how we came to hip-hop and how wider socio-political factors in the country embedded us at large.

Shaheen: After the cinematic releases of *Beat Street* (1984) and *Breakin'* (1984), the initial fad of breakin' fizzled out by the mid-80s. Getting hold of hip-hop music and information from wider Africa and overseas became extremely difficult. At that time the airwaves mirrored the racialized segregation grid that was an outcome of more than four decades of the Group Areas Act (Act No. 41 of 1950). We thus had little exposure to black South African musicians, not to mention international ones beyond the top 20 pop charts. Being a hip-hop head back then meant that international boycotts, divestment, and sanctions that I supported and internal censorship laws restricted one's journey of seeking music and information. In spite of these constraints, we managed to develop research and networking skills that made it possible to obtain what we felt we needed from relationships with overseas pen-pals or friends and family in exile/abroad. In addition to finding some imported records at local record stores, we also depended on alternative distribution networks: i.e., bootleggers. In Cape Town there was a matinee club, The Base, where deejays like Rozanno and Ready D played hip-hop sets every

Saturday afternoon. A common struggle against local and global oppression and a love for the artistic elements we identified with when we "discovered" those earlier hip-hop songs and movies fueled our passions. After the end of the Boycott, Divestment, and Sanctions (BDS) campaign in 1994, the flow of information opened up drastically even though the mediascapes were less multi-directional than often imagined.

My first question may have an obvious answer now that everything from television commercials to sitcoms has incorporated aspects of hip-hop, but what was your experience in encountering hip-hop in a time when it was quite ubiquitous, compared to the 1980s?

Marlon: One of my earliest involvements with hip-hop was not through the mainstream media, but rather seeing a local crew, Black Noise, who gave a b-boy workshop when I was in high school in 1995. Even though the airwaves were opening up, there was still a lack of representations of hip-hop on national television. It was quite difficult to sustain interest in breakin' and finding peers, mentors or materials from which to learn. This is because growing up in Kensington[6] meant that, to a large degree, we were isolated from the Cape Flats where hip-hop was happening more visibly. Kensington's isolation was a legacy of apartheid's displacement policies still felt to this day. Apart from the Beastie Crew (Kensington/Maitland-based b-boys), hip-hop was harder to recognize there. Mitchell's Plain however, was so prolific that an ongoing debate ensued about this area being the South African equivalent to the South Bronx of the late 1970s. Various elements developed more rapidly there and one could see it publicly in the street. While aerosol art and deejaying interested me a lot, it was too expensive to get into. Emceeing, however, could be done anywhere and at anytime so we practiced that consistently with our friends. Interestingly enough, I remember kids in primary school reciting one of your songs, *Dala Flet* (1989)[7] from memory. It became somewhat of a standard and yet I don't remember it being called rap because it felt so indigenous given that it was in Afrikaans. Similarly, we had not yet heard of the cipher concept but we were doing it.

Shaheen: Yes, creating ciphers during the 1980s was an unintentional political act because during the state of emergency they were often regarded as "illegal gatherings," thus making us vulnerable to police harassment at times. The same was true for breakin' and, even more so, graf. What influenced your journey?

Marlon: Coinciding with the transition in the mid-1990s, many of us were learning lyrics from G-Funk emcees because that was what we were seeing on music videos. N.W.A's *Straight Outta*

Compton (1988) continued to have impact and a spate of Hollywood gangsta films like *Boyz n the Hood* (1991) and *Menace II Society* (1993) bolstered the popularity of albums like Dr Dre's *The Chronic* (1992). Cassettes played a major role in spreading music. In fact I usually didn't hear a full album, but instead got mix-tapes with different cuts from various albums.

Shaheen: The same was true for the 1980s. Cassettes were the primary distribution method across the Cape Flats. I know of heads who found it strange to listen to the original album and CD versions of songs because their ears were so accustomed to listening to really bad quality dubbings. Another fascinating difference is how G-funk resonated with you guys because many of the heads whom I grew up with viewed that period quite suspiciously. G-funk's popularity climaxed at the same time as major media consolidation and monopolization in the United States so that the effects of these policies rippled to South Africa. In my opinion, this resulted in rather formulaic releases and media programming and I think G-funk became the poster-child for what we saw as hip-hop's move from barrio to boardroom. Many of us associated G-funk with a moment in hip-hop when greater marginalization of other elements such as deejaying, graf, and breakin' occurred. We also noticed a decline in politically conscious releases and a particular interpretation of skill requirements shifted the benchmark for what a good emcee was. Therefore, G-Funk represented a loss for many of us. I recall that we dissed talented local South African crews like Nasty Weather, mostly because they represented a G-funk sound and also because they viewed G as short for "Gam,"[8] a derogatory term for coloureds. In addition to the fact that we viewed colouredness as a colonial inheritance, an endorsement of alcohol and drug abuse was equivalent to letting the enemy win in light of South Africa's history with the "dop system."[9] It's really important now to have this conversation with you because I may have easily dismissed much of it in the past, but now I'm really interested to know what it was about G-funk hip-hop that appealed to you?

Marlon: Well, for one, the story-telling appealed to all kinds of listeners, not just hip-hop heads. We could relate to the gangster content in particular because it verbalized what many of us saw and thought while growing up. Our role models were infamous, mythical gang leaders like Franky Duiwel, Bobbie Mongrel or the Staggie twins. We correlated those role models to the messages in the music so that personas like Snoop, Kurupt, Tupac, or film characters like O-Dog[10] were both fascinating and familiar to us. It wasn't always a simple glorification however, because just as we did with local gang culture, we often had fun parodying G-Funk because of how it depicted excesses that bordered on the comical. G-funk was abundant as it was all over film, print media and music.

The feel of Dr Dre's production gelled with the often stereotypical, laid-back atmosphere of Cape Town. The unexpected juxtaposition of violent images over smooth, funk-oriented beats corresponded well with certain aspects of our life-style. These paradoxical combinations of the laid-back atmosphere right next to brutal realities of disenfranchised, dis/relocated and systematically impoverished township residents created both tragic and oddly comical disjuncture. G-funk may also have had a resonance because it drew so much from George Clinton's P-Funk – Parliament and Funkadelic – which was a force in shaping the artistic tastes of my parent's generation and a formative period in my own childhood.

Eventually I encountered many other types of music and I grew to think critically of G-Funk. There were two memorable moments that changed my opinion about it. Firstly, a particular phase of "conscious" hip-hop became a buzz again with the emergence and rediscovery of artists like De La Soul[11], Kweli and Mos Def (Black Star)[12], Common[13], The Roots[14], Lauren Hill[15] and some others. Secondly, Nas's *Illmatic* (1994)[16] and the soundscapes created by the likes of A Tribe Called Quest required a more nuanced re-evaluation of street poetics. These examples brought home the extent to which flow, poetry, and other technical aspects outweighed violent images, and catapulted them to the foreground.

While I can see your peer-group's point of view on G-funk, I, on the other hand, did not experience it as a robbing of hip-hop because until then I had not really seen hip-hop up close and had no conceptualization of its entirety. To me the music videos were only the rap/story-telling aspect of it. Of course I saw all the elements happening in different places and at different times, but not all in the same setting. It was only later that I attended park jams, mostly in Mitchell's Plain, and saw all of the elements celebrated simultaneously. The feeling was quite overwhelming, a little bit like meeting your long-lost family member, and it was this experience that deepened my interest and love for the culture.

"a provocative plan can bring a knot to my hand." how i began rhyming

Literature on South African hip-hop has generally overemphasized the social meaning in lyrical content at the expense of artistic value. Our conversation moves on to what influenced us artistically as well as how we translated these influences to our writing processes.

Marlon: Coming into contact with a combination of street poetry and technical sophistication got me excited about writing lyrics. Although I had been playing around with little raps before, seeing the music video to Wu-Tang's *Triumph* (1997)[17] inspired me to write my own song. Although their song was not even the best example of technical sophistication, there was something about the epic nature of its imagery, the relentlessness of rapid verses with no chorus, and the non-linear style of the crew's lyrics in general that made me comprehend the limitlessness of the art-form and it actualized my ability and desire to experiment with it.

What reinforced this desire to express local styles and concepts was also the fact that the mainstream continued to severely marginalize working-class coloured and black aesthetics even though the country touted a rainbow-nation-with-eleven-official-languages rhetoric. When I came across community radio, where people celebrated the way we spoke and who we *were*, it was my first experience of public affirmation. The perpetual pretense of middle-class contentment in media all around me stood in strong contrast to the presenters of the shows, who verbalized the need for critical thinking in a linguistic style that I could have heard on my own street corner. This vastly expanded my imagination of what was possible in the world. Tuning into the hip-hop show *Headwarmers* forever changed the way I interpret the function of hip-hop and music more generally. The show streamed homegrown hip-hop as well as American music, but it was grimy, politically edgy and the commentary on the music conveyed an unapologetic Cape Flats/Township sensibility. The audience that called the *Headwarmers* show almost always spoke/rhymed in local ways and were broadcast across the Cape. This communal conversation made me more serious about writing and bringing to light locally pertinent topics. At first, I exclusively focused on creating imagery with my lyrics. Then competition culture gained critical mass as rhyme spitters from all over the province vied for the weekly top honors. A number of internal criteria had to be met for the majority to consider you a more complete emcee. I got attuned to multi-syllables, inner/outer rhymes, harmonic rhythmic patterns, similes, metaphors and creative narrative variations.

The music you played exposed me to a whole new universe of aesthetic choices. It makes me wonder whether the playlist consisted of the deejays' personal tastes. If so, how did the variety of taste relate to your own writing?

Shaheen: I had commitment to community radio in Cape Town because of the importance it played in making music and ideas available that were generally not heard elsewhere. The music Big Dre and I played reflected our own aesthetic preferences. Even before I joined the regular on-air team, a general U.S. east coast aesthetic dominated the playlists and we certainly didn't play any G-funk. To be clear, our decision not to play G-funk had nothing to do with U.S. east-coast west-coast politics.[18] This is not to say that youth in our communities were impermeable to those politics.[19] The music we played legitimized a certain canon and intellectually galvanized a particular school of thought. I would say that our choices of what to broadcast gained contours through our aesthetic orientations and the way political sensibilities were, in part, responses to what we felt was a corporate colonization of culture.

During those early years, heads were not generally interested in mastering only one element. I was b-boying and I had a little breakin' crew with my cousins though I was quite wack. I dabbled in graf, and again, I had neither the skills nor the patience. In lieu of wrecking my aunt's record player while attempting to scratch, deejaying simply ceased to be an option because it was too expensive. On the other hand, I memorized and regularly recited verses from *Rapper's Delight* (1979) and songs from the *Beat Street* and *Breakin'* soundtracks. Although Cape Town introduced me to hip-hop, I did not pen my own verses until my family moved to Ciskei, one of the country's ten Bantustans.[20] In the Western Cape, I had dabbled with four and eight bar verses to pass time when I was bored in class. When we moved to Ciskei, writing verses connected me to Cape Town and it was a way for me to vent my frustrations, fantasies and fears.

Back then I studied Melle Mel's story-telling abilities, followed by LL Cool J because he projected an incredibly inspiring audacity in his delivery. LL was something like a blueprint emcee for many of us. I remember one local emcee, Teddy Converse who even tried to look like LL. Troop and Kangol wasn't available in South Africa at the time, so Converse became Teddy's trademark gear. My process started out with mono-syllabic rhymes that later developed into more complex uses of punch line/

simile/metaphor. Sometimes the punch line would have some political reference, but that was not essential during battle raps. It was pretty standard during the mid-1980s to engage in battles and it came easy to me because I had devised a formula.

A major shift came when I encountered Eric B and Rakim's *Paid in Full* (1987).[21] Rakim's debut reminded me of a bebop-like shift from the past. I use the bebop analogy, because, like bebop musicians, Rakim's frustrations with conventional techniques of the time opened an opportunity for experimentation with complicated, hardly replicable rhythms and melodies that pushed the art into unchartered directions. Before Rakim, delivery was usually staccato and the emcee's tonality had an aggressive tendency. He changed many of the rules and developed a range of innovations of delivery, content, and form, thus taking emceeing to a new level.

At that point the challenge was the expression of clear ideas and concepts with interesting rhyme sounds. For example, I'd come up with a line like *"I throw bad flows at those that go mad fo' that pro-black vocab."* This displays a measured two-syllable rhyme technique that excited me at the time and made me push my own creative boundaries. There surely were many influential emcees after Rakim, including Ice Cube, Freestyle Fellowship, Nas, and Pharaoh Monche to name a few. I would compare my level of development in those days to South African emcees like Roxy, Ready D, Marchant, and I.N.T.R.I.B.E. because they were also pushing the limits.

Abdullah Ibrahim's and Hotep Idris Galeta's compositions taught me to consider the economy of words. I had started out cramming as many rhymed syllables as possible into a line, but their music inspired me to space things out a bit and concentrate on key emotions. I could say that U.S. emcees influenced me lyrically whereas I got my stylistic cues from UK-based emcees and crews like Hijack, MC Mello, London Posse, and Silver Bullet.

When we started producing our own tracks, the production style was like a lot of hardcore British hip-hop. During the mid-80s to early 1990s, Britain had a flourishing hip-hop scene and the energy was contagious. Their music was generally more aggressive, less conventional in melody and slightly more up-tempo, which served us well because we always had b-boys in the crew.

I think another resemblance to UK hip-hop was that we did not manage to mix and master the songs as warm and big[22] and yet as clear as many U.S. hip-hop albums. It is hard to find any U.S. album (from pop to rock) that does not incorporate a hip-hop sensibility in the "phatness" of the way the songs are mixed. While lots of writing on hip-hop focuses on how it has shaped other musical styles, I think there is a dearth of literature that appreciates mixing and mastering.

Marlon: Tell me more about the equipment.

Shaheen: I would argue that experience and creativity with which you use whatever gear you've got is as important as the sophistication of your equipment. Due to the BDS campaign against apartheid, only Roland musical equipment was available in South Africa. At the time, Black Noise owned a TR-808 drum machine and a few crews, including us (POC), had TR-909s. We had a Roland S-10 sampler, but its frequency settings and sample times (0.4 second per bank on 4 patches) were quite annoying. We had to be inventive to get a gritty sound and fit whatever we wanted to sample into 0.4 second. Ready D owned a Lenco turntable that needed a coin to balance the stylus, but it had 78 and 16 rpm settings. This meant we could sample a record at 78 rpm, then trigger it on a lower octave. Sometimes we managed to get a bar's worth of sample. We tried to do on this machine what U.S. producers were doing on SP-1200s and AKAI samplers. We worked in an 8-track home studio as we didn't have access to SSL studios. When we did mix a song in a "proper" studio, we'd constantly fight with engineers who had been trained to get rid of the frequencies we wanted to highlight. In fact, when the test pressings of our very first release were handed to us, it sounded muffled and nothing like the mastered version we had sent to the pressing plant. We found out that the engineer at the plant didn't know what scratching was, so he tweaked the equalization to get rid of those frequencies. This obviously altered the whole song while he was under the impression he had deleted an annoying "noise."

Marlon: These days you can find cracked software virtually everywhere in the township and it is much easier to come by than it used to be under apartheid, where the only hardware you got was really low-end products. Do you think that technology levels the playing field between producers?

Shaheen: I think technology makes music-production more accessible. There are lots of interesting projects happening that, using technology, challenge all kinds of boundaries, including geographical ones. The internet and affordable or bootlegged software made it possible for groups to form that consisted of members from different regions of the world. Rogue State Alliance, for example, has South African and Swiss heads in it. Nevertheless, only a few South Africans have access to top of the line technology and you cannot ignore the disparity of the conditions around which the technology is used. Technological utopianism has a tendency to overlook how technology is implicated in social, political and economic processes. So I don't think there is any automatic leveling of a playing field. Coming back to your point, I think South African producer/engineers who have exhausted the possibilities of Cubase, for instance, still aim to get the sound quality that is warm, clear and big as, say, a Jay Z album audio mix-down. That kind of sound quality is what many still aspire to and this quest isn't unique to South Africa of course.

Marlon: Ok, but how is it that U.S. producers set the standard for sound quality as if it's a Holy Grail that you can't afford to steer away from or reinterpret when we've practically been militant about innovation in every other aspect of hip-hop?

Shaheen: I would be curious to hear someone rework hip-hop styled mixing, but I must admit that I love that boom bap sound. There are different phases in hip-hop history as well as different phases in an individual's journey that determine(d) how to interpret ways of doing/being hip-hop as "authentic." Some regard emulation as part of staying true to some universal hip-hop tradition, even if it crystallized in the U.S.. Another way of looking at "staying true" is that the incorporation of local elements guarantees distinction between Cape Town and California for instance. In this view, alterity drives originality and identity, but it all depends on how we imagine hip-hop's trajectory. Many heads at home have vested interest in what's happening in hip-hop elsewhere. For them the "Holy Grail" issue is not a matter of cultural imperialism. When folks choose to identify with trends that happen elsewhere, they don't necessarily compromise core values. I agree that practices like hip-hop are processes and products of history that are culturally constructed, essentialized and reified. They are also relational, contingent, if not interdependent, and often produced to maintain forms of hegemony. However, I think a lot of preoccupation with "'reworking'" and the apprehension for copying the U.S. comes from the fact that many of us generally take issue with American imperialism, especially as it plays out in foreign policy, militarization, and corporate recklessness. One of my concerns is the way hip-hop may be implicated in the more imperialistic aspects of a globalizing world.

It is undisputable what role the U.S. played in launch-padding hip-hop, but it's a fact that influences from all around the world have shaped hip-hop. They continue to do so. The Jamaican sound systems have not only influenced hip-hop deejaying, but, in my opinion, their emphasis on the lower frequencies made a significant difference to the studio mixing process as well. Also, in this era of digital music-making and the ensuing sonic sterility, it sounds as if hip-hop engineers are attempting to re-create the warmth that was heard on the songs the producer's sample.

I actually think it is more of an audio engineering issue than a music production one. I'm not necessarily referring to individual stylistic approaches to production or sonic textures (as in sample-based methods, the exclusive use of live instruments or mostly synth-based productions), but rather the general placement of the bass and drums in relation to the rest of the track and the way equalization, compressors and outboard gear are used. This, after all, is what sonically links and defines this heterogeneous genre to a large degree. I have noticed this general approach in hip-hop productions from Thailand to Tanzania and Luanda to London. Regardless of the local musical influences that might be incorporated into a song, there are enduring characteristics that are universal to most of these music productions. The same logic applies to the other elements as well. Wherever one goes, musicians draw from local references in verses while experimenting with flows and delivery. However, we still use rhyme schemes, punch-lines, and poetic devices that an international audience can recognize and respond to. In the same line of thought, I've seen dancers incorporate gumboot dancing and other traditional South African movements into b-girling/b-boying, but in the end their choreography still revolves around conventional break moves.

Coming back to the topic of music and fusion, I'd say that when we formed POC and took our time to experiment, we sampled South African music as a way to express how we imagined the sound of a South African style. We played around with 6/8 timing, we sampled marimbas, kudu horns, and so on, but we still layered it with hip-hop drum sounds. We'd use the voice of, say, Mandela or Mzwake in the way that U.S. crews used Malcolm X or Farrakhan. However, we did not refer to the music as afro-hop to claim some kind of uniqueness to what we were doing – it was still hip-hop.

word! language and power

Even though language has been used as a tool for oppression as well as resistance since the earliest colonial period, the Soweto student uprisings and the massacre of June 16th, 1976[23] brought it to the world's attention for the first time how a language policy dispute ended in a massacre. In this part of the conversation we discuss how hip-hop has challenged and/or reinforced deep-running anxieties related to the history of our languages.

Shaheen: Anyone who has ever faced a language barrier knows that language marks difference. In South Africa we face language barriers daily and it's fascinating to see how language – one of the most contested terrains – plays out in hip-hop both socially and artistically. Under apartheid, coloured schools were generally divided into English and Afrikaans. Whether justified or not, an assumption settled into place that English was spoken by middle-class kids while Afrikaans was spoken by the children of working-class families. However, in coloured township areas where most Afrikaans speakers live, English speakers were constantly harassed for wanting to be/act white. In schools dominated by English speakers, on the other hand, Afrikaans speakers faced chastisement if their second language skills were not good enough. The irony was that many Afrikaans speakers, like myself, would almost always rap in English, more precisely "Black American English." It was only after forming POC and experimenting even more that rhyming in Cape Flats Afrikaans not only became a possibility, but also a discovery of unique rhythm and rawness that suits hip-hop in surprising ways. The power and value of *Dala Flet* was that we were celebrating a "dialect" that the majority of the South African middle and upper classes still look down on.

Marlon: Yes, even referring to it as "dialect" re-enacts a post-colonial hangover from the racist power game that dominated South Africa for hundreds of years. The misconception that the Afrikaans spoken by Africans is a bastardized off-shoot of a pure European language is widespread but nevertheless historically inaccurate. It's often overlooked that Afrikaans formed very much like a creole between Dutch settler groups, several

African languages, Arabic, Malay and some English. As the settlers retreated into the interior[24] to avoid relinquishing control over the enslaved labor force, they not only adopted indigenous knowledge about land and agriculture, but also language.[25] In fact, before Malay Islamic scholars first wrote Afrikaans in the Arabic script, the average Afrikaans speaker was actually illiterate. These Islamic scholars also promoted anti-colonial education in Afrikaans.[26] I continue to run into non-South Africans with the perception that Afrikaans is the "Boer-language." I am certain that this misperception has something to do with the lack of representation on our behalf.

Shaheen: Good point. To add insult to injury, many economic elites and political activists alike have demonized and vilified the way we speak. It came into association with all the negative stereotypes about poor people, especially poor people of color. Another reason why we could identify with U.S. hip-hop was its emergence from a context that established language as a marker of race/class hierarchy.

Marlon: The need to upset this hierarchy was actually the primary aspect that motivated me to get into emceeing. My emcee-name was *Caco*, which is an acronym for Cape Coloured. My rationale behind it was that the category had been constructed in an oppressive setting. It defined people without their consent. However, as constructed as the origins of the "coloured" category are, you now have a "community" that self-identifies with it. My idea attempted to create a positive trajectory, fully conscious of the history, but determined to reconstruct it in the present while neutralizing its negative impact. I eventually found out that reclaiming the term "Cape Coloured" did not preclude the colonial divide-and-rule strategy. Inadvertently, the problematic coloured-nationalist sentiment that began to circulate at the time compromised my intention. As we speak, it continues to gain strength in response to unequal redistribution of resources and the selective application of affirmative action, which benefits a small black and coloured elite. This kind of economic exclusion partners with cultural exclusion as working-class coloureds still struggle for access to dignified mainstream representation. The lack of representation of working-class people from our communities was very frustrating. There was no media whatsoever that dealt with our community in a respectful manner. This was especially disheartening in the era immediately after the first democratic election when everyone, not only in the country, but around the world, celebrated this "miracle" transition and yet we were still completely invisible to the public psyche. The fact that we were either invisible or reduced to the image of minstrels compelled me and my peers to rectify our image through hip-hop. I did feel like we were contributing to an already established field, resonating with the likes of POC, Brasse Vannie Kaap, and others.

You are right about language's way of signaling difference and social status in South Africa. Hip-hop and lyricism became very attractive and powerful resources for challenging the status quo. The late Mr. Devious, Burnie (of Godessa), Isaac Mutant, and later Jaak and Jitsvinger have also made invaluable contributions to enlivening this debate. In keeping with this work, the first topic I was inspired to write about was this linguistic marginalization of *our* Afrikaans. Looking closer, there were two issues I wanted to discuss. One was the way many English-speaking blacks and coloureds promoted middle-class agendas through their privileged access to the media. The second issue was that some local emcees used American accents, thus conforming to a performativity that did not have our self-esteem at interest.

I wanted to promote critical thinking about linguistic tendencies and choices among emcees. I wanted to get to the root of the embarrassment around rolling of the *r*, for example, known in formal linguistic terms as an alveolar trill. Though I recognized the need and legitimacy of code switching, I wanted to draw attention to the inferiority/superiority complexes of language choice.

Shaheen: I appreciate your sensitivity and the fact that you're politicizing "dialects," but I realize that we're talking about particular moments in our respective journeys. What you have said suggests that regardless of the content and the conditions in which composers produce songs, all is good as long as they use some locally spoken accent or language. We need to complicate this further because linguistic practices don't always correlate to political ideology.

Marlon: Point taken. Like I said, there is a contradiction in apprehending "all things American," expressing disdain for U.S. foreign policy and idealistically endorsing American speech at the same time. Ultimately, language is so contentious in South African hip-hop and South African society in general precisely because issues of purity and authenticity have been so central in the workings of colonization there.

keepin it realigion

The conversation proceeds to connect problems around authenticity to themes such as spirituality, validation systems and gender. Thinking through language inevitably requires us to grasp what classicism means in South Africa, always contingent, of course, with other forms of exclusion. The dialogue goes on to probe the extent to which hip-hop has excluded constituencies and also how some social formations have excluded hip-hop.

Marlon: Around 1999, Rastafarian cultures merged significantly with hip-hop in the scenes that I frequented. There were the matinees at Angels (Greenpoint) and the afternoon gigs at All Nations (Observatory). This co-existence and collaboration of sub-cultures strongly affected my intellectual and spiritual development.

Shaheen: What attracted you to Rasta?

Marlon: There was a logical overlap between Rastology and hip-hop. In 1994 I did not identify as hip-hop head in the same way that I do today because I did not sense a need for it. However, as the post-election disillusionment settled in and the gap between the haves and the have-nots widened by the day, the identification as hip-hop head functioned like an act of resistance to the hypocrisy within the glossy images promoted by rainbow-nation discourse. I explored various philosophies in an attempt to understand what can be done about the constraints and contradictions of increasingly unbearable race/class stratification. Rastafarianism stood out as a powerful vehicle for self-actualization in the context of pan-African subjecthood. Since Rasta rejects divisions among people of African descent, my coloured identity found relief in the Rastafari perspective on African solidarity, poverty, human rights, and dignity. Instead of feeling like a victim of a trickle-down system, Rastology urged me to think of poverty not as personal failure, but rather as an indicator of my refusal to participate in capitalist cut-throat relations with other humans.

Rastafarianism explained racial injustice from yet another viewpoint and it intersected with hip-hop organically. Rasta's definite respect and high regard for women (at least in rhetoric, if not always in action) contributed very positively to hip-hop environments that were prone to discriminatory, if not misogynist, dynamics between men and women. The emphasis on respectful forms of address ensured an interesting competition between the queen/king and sister/brother titles and the bitch/ho nigga/thug frames of reference. Though male counterparts still outnumbered female participants, women received keen and earnest attention in circles that incorporated Rastafarian sensibilities.

Rasta and hip-hop subcultures complemented each other in their prescriptions for public behavior in such a way that it became natural for heads from both camps to attend each other's events. Deejays would usually play dub and hip-hop at the same gig. The anti-establishment stance of both music styles did not exclusively compute into reactionary attitudes, but more importantly it promoted proactive measures of anti-alcohol, pro-health, and pro-family mentality. In addition to lifting race and class-consciousness, there was an emphasis on seeking knowledge, personal self-development, and striving toward self-reliance. The promotion of healthy lifestyles amounted to the most basic type of resistance to the oppressive system.

Shaheen: There are two things I'd like to comment on. Firstly, I think that the unified moment between Rasta and hip-hop was period-specific. The level of intensity that you speak of happened during the zenith of the so-called second "conscious" phase – the first phase being the Public Enemy and X-Clan moment. Rasta has been around so much longer than hip-hop as we know it today and, in some ways, is a living ancestor thereof. I believe that this unity (in terms of co-membership) was less pronounced during the 1980s and I'm sensing some decline currently. I know some Rastas who accuse hip-hop of having betrayed its spiritual and political ideal. Many feel that the "bling" mentality has colonized hip-hop to the point where it can't be saved anymore. Secondly, the valorization of a "Queen" is not unproblematic. The use of the term is also not only confined to Rastas. I find that it often gets used as a policing mechanism that enforces desired behaviors, especially around sexuality. The sharp bipolarity between "pure queen" and "filthy ho" leaves surprisingly little space for other subject positions. I understand the psychological role it plays in a white supremacist context, but terms like "queen" do not excite me automatically.

Marlon: I agree that this binary is dangerous and I can see how each individual would occupy the subject-position of "queen" or "king" differently. At the same time I see that the little grey space in between the extremes still allows for reinvention, contestation, and resistance. I try to be careful about defaulting into distinctly "western" feminist analysis. Their discourse often dismisses all prescriptions for behavior between genders as oppressive toward women. The debate about the veil is a good example because eurocentric value-judgments have dominated it until recently.

Shaheen: I know that academic analysis has a huge blind-spot for the post-colonial dilemma, but the bottom-line is that most belief systems do not work in women's favor. With regard to hip-hop we mustn't ignore that Christianity and Islam have influenced it in both positive and negative ways.

Marlon: What was your experience of the relationship between Islam and hip-hop in Cape Town?

Shaheen: I was raised Sunni Muslim. The first time I heard an overt reference to Islam in a hip-hop song was on Eric B and Rakim's *Paid in Full* and it affected me profoundly. In the 1980s I did not have a good understanding of what the Nation of Islam (NOI) was all about. I thought it was just a general shout-out to Muslims. Then I started noticing many emcees with Arabic sounding names and the Five Percenter vocabulary with its specific NYC lyrical styles came to my attention, making it extremely attractive to embrace Islam as a head. In fact, I dropped my former emcee name, DSA, for my given name, Shaheen. Looking at it more closely, however, identification with Islam in hip-hop often did not go beyond the superficial invocation of general references. These musical offerings vocalized a wide-spread respect for Africa and its contribution to world civilizations. However, even those who claimed love or allegiance to Africa often had contested relationships with Africans that reveal a considerable degree of internalized oppression. Our favorite emcees subscribed to Islamic strands of philosophy that originated in the U.S. and some of us endorsed them without even knowing what the specific teachings contained. During the early to mid-1990s, a local chapter of the NOI opened in Cape Town and almost every member was a hip-hop head. More than half were Sunni, but not everyone was practicing. NOI's brief popularity was also due to local organizers having direct connections to U.S. hip-hop artists. NOI's life-span in Cape Town was rather short, partly because of local in-fighting and the reality of a doctrine-clash between Capetonian orthodox Sunni Muslims[27] and the NOI's core beliefs, which went through several changes within a short period.

Marlon: I see. I find it interesting that Christian hip-hop has enjoyed popularity for quite some time, but it tends to sequester itself from the larger hip-hop scene. This is not surprising, given that one camp is wary of the other's intent to proselytize, while mainstream hip-hop, when seen in its totality, contains several elements that offend Christian customs and conventions around morality. This potential rift is also applicable to Islam-inspired hip-hop. In what you said about the NOI's relationship to Cape Town's orthodox Sunni I not only see a doctrine-clash, but also, again, that generational clash.

It's slightly trickier to put a finger on elements that root in indigenous African spiritual orientations. I'm constantly amazed by its submerged presence within and outside Africa. Whether it is in the form of proverbs or extensive philosophical treatises, the referencing of Africa's intellectual heritage introduces and nurtures a sensibility for distinctly African cosmologies. I say "cosmology" to distinguish our indigenous ontology from institutionalized belief systems, which came to Africa hand in hand with the colonial apparatus and often run the risk of turning into dogma.

The thing that is special about hip-hop is that it sometimes managed to create a forum in which the different faiths could reason through their differences while also affirming their common perspective on oppressive systems, the role of blackness, the value of the art-form, and other themes that pertain to everyone, regardless of religious affiliation.

An interesting twist to globalization is that empires often export their own counter-cultures. Once exported, they don't stay the same. Even if one did not fully or overtly identify with

Rastafari, NOI, or Pan-Africanism, the co-presence of such diverse beliefs under one hip-hop roof created a space for subject formation that was hardly available elsewhere. As someone who lives with the legacy of being coloured, I also have to say that this space invited the African in me to belong to a world-moment.

being down with growing up: the cross-generational discussion

Having illustrated cross-generational dialogue in this paper, the conversation now goes back to the topic of bridging several age sets before highlighting some concluding thoughts.

Shaheen: I don't think any "generation" ever speaks with one voice, but what do you think are the biggest problems some older heads have with younger cats?

Marlon: Well, first of all I'd have to re-state that I have hardly seen South Africa beyond the Cape. I can only speak to impressions and interactions I've had over the years. Older brothers and sisters have expressed to me a range of opinions about my generation's refusal to acknowledge what the previous generation accomplished in creating a culture that we benefit from so much. Funny – as I say brothers and sisters, I wonder at what point a brother turns into an uncle and a sister into an aunt. Ways in which we refer to one another can either bridge or compound the generation gap. One doesn't have to belong to the older generation in order to see how members of either have sold out to neoliberal values, commercialization, commodification, and misappropriation. Another communication problem stems from many older heads still having a missionary intentionality in how they wish to spread a particular take on culture. When their younger audience rejects parts of their arguments, feelings of resentment recycle in the community. It spirals into a tendency to accuse the new wave of followers for not knowing the local and international origins of hip-hop.

I can understand why the older generation would be invested in keeping a particular vision of hip-hop culture alive and how annoying it must be when younger heads take it for granted that hip-hop *is* alive. I also get the sense that older heads take entrepreneurship more seriously, possibly because of the emphasis on "do for self" back then. Several elders have indicated to me that parenting extends into a negotiation and even a policing of what their kids listen to. There is definitely a readiness to apply hip-hop as a tool for social change among older heads that I find strangely and sadly absent in my peers.

Shaheen: I think younger heads place a lot of importance into having their work acknowledged, gaining respect and not being treated as ignorant novices. Many view success in terms of monetary value; they feel that the old cats might have been socially relevant under apartheid, but that the priorities of a new South Africa call for fresh blood, fresh ideas, and individuals who can make some serious money. Another notion that I have come across is age limit; folks want you to clock out like a factory clock card when your time is up in their esteem. The flipside of underestimating the older cats is that they are indeed often out of touch with what young people are up against these days. This intergenerational dynamic is similar to what plays out between "rebellious teens" and "grown-ups." Occasionally older heads hog the spot-light, knowledge and resources; this is even more intensified where, using apartheid's categories, younger "black" heads feel that old school "coloured" heads do not make any serious attempts at reaching out and assisting. I think many of the latter feel that they are unable to benefit from black economic empowerment, which brings with it policies and programs that have arguably discriminated against coloureds. I think young white Afrikaner heads struggle to find their place within hip-hop. In addition to facing ostracization by their own group for selling out, many Afrikaners (in and outside hip-hop) don't know what to do with their white guilt. I guess it doesn't help that heads of color resent them for being the descendants of (former) oppressors.

In some of my observations, young English-speaking whites, leaning towards liberalism, display more entitlement when it comes to space and mic-sharing. They have yet to confront the way they benefit from and propagate white privilege. Interestingly, they claim the luxury of color-blindness and a notion of post-racial South Africa while directing all efforts to getting their skills published and acknowledged. Again, my statements are based on observations and experiences and I'm not suggesting that more nuanced articulations do not exist. I'm still concerned about the way hip-hop environments shut out women of color, maintaining a hostile space that discourages them from participating in hip-hop beyond being consumers. Also, within South Africa, Africans from other countries still face marginalization and, even though hip-hop has taken a stance against xenophobia, non-South Africans continue to work in precarious contexts.

I want to revisit some of the points you made about how artists derive authenticity from specific places of origin; from this we get uniqueness after all. Next to space, temporality also plays a vital role. This is not inimitable to hip-hop – the more you know about the origin of myths, the more cultural cachet you possess. In hip-hop this often translates into "being real." Make no mistake about it – one cannot acquire this knowledge automatically. The so-called first-generationers had to navigate many kinds of obstacles to get hold of information and music. With all the restrictions we faced under apartheid, we had to seek out and interpret what we heard, read and saw; then we had to re-work it and make it our own while dodging censorship-laws and other limitations to freedom of speech. For more than twenty years, deejays like Rozanno and Ready D invested an enormous amount of time, energy and money into sharing music with others. B-boys like Emile of Black Noise also play a crucial role in keeping b-boying/b-girling the most widely practiced hip-hop art form in Cape Town. I do, however, have strong objections against mythologizing or glorifying the past in a manner that claims cultural superiority simply because someone was born at a specific time. Even more irritating is, as you've suggested, the demonization of youngsters who have made sense of hip-hop in their own way. Regarding this, I have room for improvement too because I've also castigated "new comers who've been in hip-hop for a few summers" (1995).[28]

Just like literary analysis and art critique, the major pedagogical value inherent in hip-hop has to do with multiple interpretations. Hip-hop becomes a pivotal educational tool when the "teaching-method" pays respect to how younger generations adapt to and adopt the art form. For some reason, many older heads resist such hermeneutical endeavors even though it has served us well in the past. These tensions can be fruitful and healthy; tradition should not restrain or police where hip-hop has to go next. I remember judging a battle once where several young cats rejected the innovations we tried to add to the battles. In that case, we wanted to experiment with drawing topics out of a hat once we became aware that some emcees cheated by disguising written work for off-the-dome rhymes. Most of the younger emcees complained, "what the hell is this drawing topics out of a hat? That's not hip-hop." I realized that they were claiming some traditional take on hip-hop in order to control the collective artistic space. Interestingly the younger heads pulled the tradition card on this older head.

Having said all this, I don't think it's necessarily a generational issue because, after all, differing visions and versions of culture should get into contact through tension, friction and negotiation. There have always been different schools of thought and arguments about who or what is wack. These debates and the nature in which they occur often get negative portrayal, but I'd argue that these contestations are part of hip-hop's DNA and can be productive.

Marlon: I'm glad you brought up the issue of hogging spotlights. I have experienced being shut by older cats, but there have been other venues at which they embraced me warmly and showed sincere interest in my growth. This cultivated a sense of responsibility in me for passing my contribution on to others in the same way that I benefited from lessons learned. This kind of apprenticeship is so valuable to me; quite frankly, if it had not been for the work and help of Godessa,[8] I may not have gotten the chance to try out my first recording and grow as a lyricist. Having profited so decisively from a women's collective, I am especially impatient about the fact that women do not have this kind of access to "elders." Hip-hop culture often functions like fraternities of men that exclude women and I have no good ideas for a reversal of this entrenched dynamic and demographic. I think that this imbalance will continue to delay the development of hip-hop. If we get the issues around gender straightened out, the interaction of the various generations may very well fall into place. Once you touch this gender-button, it unravels into several issues that we cannot address in a single conversation, but that nevertheless need our attention desperately. Whether it's old or new school, both camps are male-dominated and have failed to deal with the heteronormative trap, for example. We have barely begun to confront homophobia in South African hip-hop and I can't wait for the time where a serious analysis of masculinity gains momentum.

Shaheen: I absolutely agree with you. We often reproduce the same hierarchies and exclusionary practices that we think we're fighting against. At some point youngsters will be their own "old school" and thus we're constantly preparing for future new schools. We have so much work ahead of us....

concluding thoughts

We have offered glimpses of an on-going conversation in which we touched on the intersections between art and politics by foregrounding how the personal blends into the political in South Africa's particular matrix of race/class/gender relations. We are passionate about hip-hop's potential and limitations when used as a tool for social justice or education. Rather than delving into the details of our own work, we set out to situate the relationship between art and politics in the trajectory of our own growth. The large themes of art, race, politics and gender are multiplicative and cannot conveniently be separated out. We hope that our conversation will contribute to the very small amount of respectful cross-generational dialogue.

notes

1. Jeff Chang's disclaimer on the word *generation* is pertinent to the way we are using it in this paper:

   > Generations are fictions. The act of determining a group of people by placing a beginning and ending date around them is a way to impose a narrative. They are interesting and necessary fictions because they allow claims to be staked around ideas. But generations are fictions nonetheless, often created simply to suit the needs of demographers, journalists, futurists, and marketers.

   Can't Stop Won't Stop: A History of the Hip Hop Generation (New York: St. Martin's Press, 2005) p 1.

2. We use "conversation" in a hermeneutical framework, recognizing that although the art of popular artists spoke to us and we spoke back through our art, communication did get lost owing to slanted distribution channels as well as skewed perceptions of Africa. In terms of hermeneutics and Bakhtin's dialogic imagination, however, this still constitutes a conversation even though

the strands of the conversation may not find each other through mutual audience or reciprocal peer-to-peer dialogue.

3. This weekly Friday evening program inherited its slot from "The Show", which aired from 1993 to 2000. Although many emcees and deejays were part of "The Show", Shamiel X Adams and Ashley Titus (MC Fat) pioneered hip-hop radio in South Africa. Eventually "The Show" reinvented itself as "The Headwarmers" and it still airs today.

4. For the sake of simplicity, we use "coloured," in its South African spelling, without endorsing it and without putting it into inverted commas throughout the paper. This dilemma of language choice only attests to the lack of a better word. We not only reject the reductionism of the coloured category, but also wish to point out its inherent instability. At various historical moments coloured people have identified as black, for example, in solidarity with the black consciousness movement. Alternately, coloured people have also elected to pass or cross over into the white category, either because their skin tone allowed it or because life held more opportunities or safety that way.

   We cannot do this complexity justice here, but for further reading consult: Adhikari, M. 2009 *Burdened by Race: Coloured Identities in Southern Africa.* Cape Town: Double Storey Publishers; Erasmus, Z. (ed.) 2001 *Coloured by History, Shaped by Place: New Perspectives on Coloured Identities in Cape Town.* Cape Town. Kwela Books. See also Remi Warner's chapter "Colouring the Cape Problem Space: A Hiphop Identity of Passions" in this publication.

5. Located 10km (6.2 miles) from Cape Town's central business district, Kensington is a township that was declared coloured after the 1950 Group Areas Act forcefully relocated people all over the country. Until then, Kensington was multicultural, but eventually black and white people were moved out of it, turning it into an exclusively coloured working-class and middle-class area.

6. "Dala Flet" is a song on Prophets of da City's debut album *Our World* (1989). It became the first ever hip-hop song in Cape Flats Afrikaans to be released on wax, cassette and cd.

7. The derogatory term "Gam" derives from Ham, son of Noah, in the Old Testament. It invokes the Hamitic curse, which destines

people of color to a life of shame and servitude to the Semitic and Japhetic races (Genesis 9: 24–27).

8. The dop system had its beginning during colonialism, but extended into apartheid. White-owned farms employed workers (usually black and coloured) in hideous conditions and paid them in alcohol rather than currency. This is partly responsible for a proliferation of alcoholism. Although the plight of workers has become more visible, the dop system unfortunately has not yet been made obsolete.

9. Larenz Tate plays Kevin "O-Dog" Anderson in *Menace II Society* (1993), directed by Allen and Albert Huges

10. De La Soul. *Stakes is High*. Tommy Boy Records. 1996.

11. Black Star, *Mos Def & Talib Kweli. Are Black Star*. Rawkus. 1998.

12. Common. *Resurrection*. Relativity Records. 1994; *One Day It'll All Make Sense*. Relativity Records. 1997; *Like Water for Chocolate*. MCA/Universal Records. 2000.

13. The Roots. *Do You want More*. DGC/Geffen/MCA Records. 1994; *Illadelph Half Life*. DGC/Geffen/MCA Records. 1996; *Things Fall Apart*. MCA Records. 1999.

14. Lauren Hill. *The Miseducation of Lauren Hill*. Ruffhouse/Columbia. 1998

15. Nas. *Illmatic*. Sony. 1994.

16. Wu-Tang Clan. Wu-Tang Forever. Loud/RCA/BMG. 1997

17. Although we identify the sound as "east-coast hip-hop," it isn't literally confined to the east-coast region of the U.S. Our playlists regularly included groups from the west coast like Freestyle Fellowship and Hieroglyphics who mastered the east-coast feel; at the same time we omitted the majority of Bad Boy Records releases (apart from some Notorious B.I.G. songs) although they were from New York.

18. Powerful street gangs formed in Cape Town calling themselves the Junior Mafias, named after New York emcee The Notorious B.I.G.'s group of the 1990s. 2-Pac murals also appeared as a marker of gang territory. However it was not only American influences that had this impact. Gangs named after British football teams Liverpool and Manchester United competed fiercely, mirroring the years-long rivalry between those soccer teams.

19. Bantustans were "independent homelands," set up by the apartheid regime to control or prevent the extent of black unification so that the most desirable land could be secured for the regime. It also functioned as a labour reserve.
20. Eric B and Rakim. *Paid In Full*. 4th and B'Way/Island. 1987
21. I use *big, phat* and *phatness* interchangeably. In pedestrian terms, phat is a mix that sounds large and contains bright high frequencies in combination with punchy, prominent low frequencies. The overall mix also contains multiple sonic textures that usually draws from sampled sounds that are either singular drum sounds or multi-layered full bar loops.
22. The Afrikaans Medium Decree of 1974 forced all black schools to use Afrikaans and English in a 50-50 mix as languages of instruction. Black students in Soweto set out to peacefully protest the legislative imposition of this decree and suffered a brutal massacre at the hands of the police. This led a wave of protest to sweep the entire country.
23. This process became known as the Great Trek which itself has been used to construct an Afrikaner national identity.
24. Mesthrie, R. *Language in South Africa* (Cambridge: Cambridge University Press, 2002).
25. Davids, A. *The Mosques of Bo-Kaap*. (Cape Town The South African Institute of Arabic & Islamic Research; 1989); "Words the Cape Slaves Made: A Socio-historical Study." *Studies in the History of Cape Town*, Vol.4. (Cape Town: African Studies/History, UCT, 1990).
26. For a more detailed discussion on this see Essof. S and D. Moshenberg. *Searching for South Africa*. (UKZN Press, forthcoming)
27. Ariefdien, in "Prophets of da City. Hardcore B-Boys" from *Universal Souljaz*. Nation Records. 1995
28. Godessa is a Cape Town-based hip-hop crew consisting of Eloise "EJ" Jones, Bernadette "Burni" Amansure and Shameema "Shame" Williams. The group formed in 2000 and has since made a stellar contribution to combining critical social commentary with potent musical innovations. Their debut album *Spillage* (2004) received critical acclaim.

bibliography

Adhikari, M. *Burdened by Race: Coloured Identities in Southern Africa.* (Cape Town: Double Storey Publishers, 2009).

Chang, J. *Can't Stop Won't Stop: A History of the Hip Hop Generation.* New York: St. Martin's Press, 2005) p 1.

Davids, A. *The Mosques of Bo-Kaap, Cape Town.* The South African Institute of Arabic & Islamic Research. 1980).

_____. "Words the Cape Slaves Made: A Socio-historical Study." *Studies in the History of Cape Town,* Vol.4. (Cape Town: African Studies/History, UCT, 1990).

Erasmus, Z. (ed.). *Coloured by History Shaped by Place: New Perspectives on Coloured Identities in Cape Town.* (Cape Town. Kwela Books 2001).

Essof, S., and D. Moshenberg. *Searching for South Africa.* (UKZN Press, forthcoming).

Mesthrie, R. *Language in South Africa* Cambridge: Cambridge University Press, 2002).

discography

Black Star. *Mos Def & Talib Kweli Are Black Star.* Rawkus. 1998

Common. *Resurrection.* Relativity Records. 1994

_____. *One Day It'll All Make Sense.* Relativity Records. 1997

_____. *Like Water for Chocolate.* MCA/Universal Records. 2000

De La Soul, *Stakes is High* Tommy Boy Records. 1996

Eric B and Rakim, *Paid In Full.* 4th and B'Way/Island. 1987

Nas. *Illmatic.* Sony. 1994

Prophets of da City. "Dala Flet" from *Our World.* Ku Shu Shu/Teal Trutone. 1991

Prophets of da City. "Hardcore B-Boys" from *Universal Souljaz.* Nation Records. 1995

The Roots. *Do You want More.* DGC/Geffen/MCA Records. 1994

_____. *Illadelph Half Life.* DGC/Geffen/MCA Records. 1996

_____. *Things Fall Apart.* MCA Records. 1999

Wu-Tang Clan. *Wu-Tang Forever.* Loud/RCA/BMG. 1997

CHAPTER 9
bongo flava, hip-hop and "local maasai flavors": interviews with x plastaz

KATRINA DALY THOMPSON

In 2006, I began working on a project examining the representation of ethnicity in Tanzanian youth music. In an earlier project examining the representation of ethnicity in Tanzanian comics from the late twentieth century, I had found that the Maasai bear the brunt of Tanzania's ethnic stereotyping (Thompson 2006). I was therefore intrigued by the more positive, but still highly stereotyped and problematic, image of the Maasai projected by the Tanzanian hip-hop group Xplastaz.[1] In addition to analyzing their lyrics and publicity materials, I interviewed three of the six living members of the group – siblings Gsan, Steve, and Diana Rutta – as well as their Dutch manager, Thomas Gesthuizen.

In large part due to Gesthuizen's assistance, Xplastaz has achieved far more international success than most Tanzanian artists, and puts out very high quality publicity materials. Their website, for example, includes a great deal of historical background on the group that I had access to before conducting these interviews. I refer the reader there. In addition, one page of the site includes a history of the group in Swahili written by one of the group's founding members, Nelson Rutta (a.k.a. Faza Nelly). To the great disappointment and sadness of the crew's fans, Faza was murdered on 27 March 2006. Thus the *Historia* 'history' page of the website is a unique source which provides a rare glimpse into his views of the group's beginnings, the role of hip-hop in Tanzania, and the crew's future plans. I translate his text here:

> The group Xplastaz is represented by three artists, Nelson Chrizostom Rutta a.k.a. Faza a.k.a. Rufnelly, Abdala Farouk Minja aka Ziggy-Lah and Godson Chrizostom Rutta a.k.a. Gson.
>
> There is also a Maasai, [and] this one decorates their music by putting flavors of Maasai origin. He joined this group after being seen to be very skilled in singing Maasai songs in [his] village Monduli Juu. He is called Yamat Ole Meipuko a.k.a. Merege […]. Another one is Simon Binara. He joined this group for a short time before going to Belgium where he continues musical activities.
>
> All of them were born in the city of Arusha. Faza aka Ruffnelly was born in 1976 in Mount Meru Hospital, and he was raised in Arusha and studied in Kijenge primary school. After finishing his primary education he got the opportunity to continue with studies in secondary school, [at] Arusha Secondary School, which is in the city of Arusha, and finished his studies in 1996.[2] He didn't get an opportunity to be able to continue with Form Six studies and [so] continued to do odd jobs as well as this style of rap music.
>
> Gson is Ruf's cousin [*ndugu*].[3] He also went to primary school at Kijenge and continued with Form One at Arusha Secondary School in the city of Arusha. When he finished Form Four he continued working in the arts and research on the origins of various African things, especially those of the Maasai, and tourism work.

Ziggy was born in the city of Arusha and later studied in primary school at Manyara Range in Manyara, Arusha. When he finished he went to complete his studies in a secondary school in Minja in the Kilimanjaro region. He didn't get an opportunity to continue and [so] he went to the city of Dar es Salaam and later Tanga and around 1993 he returned to Arusha town where he met up with his friends Gson and Nelly.

[...]⁴

We began to perform in various entertainment clubs like Cave Disco, By Night Disco, Metropole Disco and Chik King a.i.c.c.⁵ in Arusha town, as well as in entertainment halls.

Before beginning this group, each one of us was a self-reliant artist (solo artist). We knew each other from meeting all the time in disco halls, shows, and various places that were allowing youth who loved rap music to meet up. Later Ziggy, who was known as Dr Abby, went to Dar es Salam, continuing with his studies. At that time Ruf, who was well known by the name of R'nell, was continuing with his studies in Arusha town with Gson.

Later, in 1993 we – Ruffnelly and Ziggy – met up again and that's when we founded the group known as 2 Rough G'z and that very day we successfully wrote the song "Bamiza" which launched us in the world [lit: 'skies'] of music here in Tanzania and outside of the country.

In 1996 we decided to change [our] name and call ourselves Xplastaz after discovering that that name [2 Rough G'z] would not hold much interest in the society in the future.

The same year, we met with a reporter, Peter, from Holland, who arrived in Arusha to do research about the motivation behind rap music with Mr 2, Diplomatz and 4 Crews Flava from Dar. We joined up with other artists at Mawingu Club and did a show with cooperation and love, with us as their hosts. A promoter liked the work and after the show, we talked with him and after an interview, we gave him our addresses and [he] promised us he would give the message to his friend Thomas Gesthuizen who sent us a first letter a few months later. We continued to correspond until 1997, when Thomas came to the country and successfully arrived in Arusha town and, working with DJ Mudd-G of Arusha, recorded our first song, "Bamiza." This song is in fact what gave us a name and fame in the world of music and publicized us both in and out of the country and got us gigs in various discos and entertainment halls.

In 1998 we recorded another song which was known as "Wacha[ga] piga chata." In 1999 we were lucky to be in a documentary that was made in conjunction with various local artists, under the direction of Martin a.k.a Mongo Star and the whole leadership of the Madunia company from Holland. And that helped to publicize us outside and inside of the country. In 2000, we shot the music video for "Bamiza," which was edited in Holland under Thomas' supervision. This video became of great interest and a conversation topic for those who saw it through various radio [TV?] stations locally and outside of the country.

Because of the perseverance, cooperation and close communication of our sponsors and various people locally and outside of the country, at the beginning of 2001 we got together with other artists from Holland and South Africa: EJ, Devious, 2 Tall and Skate the Great, as well as other local artists. We did various seminars in the Simba Grill hall of the Kilimanjaro Hotel, and a show which was put on in the hall of FM Club. And later we recorded two tracks, "Round Table" and "Life in a Day," which also involved the young artists Fortune Tellers from Arusha and

native tongues: an african hip-hop reader

Hashim a.k.a. Dogo and some others, under producers Pfank, the local Master J, and 2Tall from Holland.

We have been lucky to record a whole album with thirteen songs that went by the name of "Ushanta"[6] which was finished up in Holland, under the editing of producers Halfan a.k.a. Pfunk and Raymond a.k.a. Kid Sundance with the sponsorship of the Madunia company, which is in Holland.

We have also successfully made another video of the song "Ushanta" under the direction of Thomas Gesthuizen a.k.a. Juma4.

We got an invitation to go to Holland and Belgium to do a show with Festival Mundial in various cities in those countries and successfully promoted ourselves in Europe as well as promoting our country in various sectors such as culture, tourism, investment and Swahili hip-hop. Some visitors have already come to the country and others are planning to come in order to encourage and raise up the quality of hip-hop music.

Belgium, Holland and all of Europe are very different than our country Tanzania in terms of development, the economy, and a great many other things. We got to meet MCs and people of various other types. The lifestyle, weather and time are all very different.

What we learned the most is to see the way artists there have so much professional cooperation, in meetings and frequent informal gatherings, talking about the problems they face, powerfully defending their rights and sending their complaints to the relevant channels and getting help. Their unity has made artists valued and made music into a profession that sustains their every day lives, profiting from music.

In the experience of preparing a show and performing before a crowd of more than 100,000 people as well as the experience of talking with reporters

from various news agencies, we have also successfully promoted our country in various sectors such
as tourism, politics, investment and religion.

For now we have finished the contracts and
various agreements and soon we expect to put out a
cd-single and our album with thirteen songs, which
will be on the market soon. That album goes by the
name "Ushanta" along with a video and our website
which is know as www.xplastaz.com.

We also have a plan to put out a video with
the song "Ushanta" which will be heard and seen
on various radio and TV stations soon. That album
includes various local artists like Hashim a.k.a Dogo,
Fortune Tellers, and so on.

As the days go by, Tanzanians become more
and more educated through hip-hop music and the
whole society seems to receive it [i.e. the music] well
because of listening to Bongoflava a lot.

Our songs really touch the feelings of listeners
because they have an important message that talks
about things that surround the society, such as: politics, religion, war, family, education and culture and
the way the whole word is going.

As artists and the mirror of society, we have a
lot of problems, such as problems getting money
to go into the studio, and basic needs because of
many artists coming from poor families, being seen
as hoodlums in the society, and being outcast from
their families because of being seen as hoodlums in
the society. The government doesn't like to be close
to artists and it doesn't care about us.

Another issue that troubles us Tanzanian artists
is copyright. The government has been ignoring it
and closing its eyes to the issue of copyrights and this
law seems not to be working the way it should.

That's why we are so oppressed in the sale of our
work and in festivals and shows that we put on.

We artists in Tanzania don't have unity, cooperation, love and unity. This contributes to the [suppres-
sion of] talents of emerging artists. Artists fighting at
live shows and causing this music to be looked down
upon by people of a certain age and class status. This
has made some artists write and sing songs that don't
have a message for society. Also it has caused artists
to build up hatred between artists and producers,
because some artists speak rudely with provocation,
hatred, arguing, and [thereby] create a class of MCs
which wants to spoil the progress of hip-hop locally.
[Further problems include:] Producers having false
promises, arrogance and lies for some artists; and
sometimes causing some of the radio stations to dis-
criminate against the work of some artists; in some
places and various disco halls and hip-hop shows,
bringing arguments between artists and fans.

Our plan is to extend our prowess in the art of
music because it [i.e. doing so] shows success.

We want to be more successful musically and to
learn more so that later we can be good producers
and help others who are emerging and help our families so that the society accepts [the fact] that music is
a profession. Each one of us in the Xplastaz crew has
the hope of recording his own unique album.

Music is a profession like any other, not hooligan-
ism like some parents [who] think that hip-hop musicians are hoodlums and rapists, thieves, alcoholics.

Hip-hop is not thievery nor is it wasting your
life; hip-hop educates, entertains and stirs up change
because [but?] a salary is difficult.

We love our music because even outside [of Tan-
zania] it is loved.

Let us not put down other's work.

Let's have good cooperation because that is what
will bring progress in our world of music because we
artists are the mirror of society.

In my initial reading of Faza Nelly's Swahili history of the group I was particularly struck by the first two paragraphs, in which he describes the group as having only three members (himself, Ziggy and Gsan) with Diana and Steve described as a separate group (Fortune Tellers) and Yamat not as a full-fledged member of the group but rather as "decorating" their music ('huyu huupamba music wao kwa kuweka vionjo vya asili ya Kimasai'). Thus, many of my questions in the subsequent interviews concern Xplastaz's relationship with Yamat, the Maasai artist who inspired the name of the group's first album, *Maasai Hip-hop*. In other publications I have addressed in more detail the issue of how Yamat in particular, and the Maasai and "tradition" more generally, are used to differentiate the crew from other musicians both locally and abroad (Thompson 2008).

The full interviews, however, delve into several other issues that will be of interest to fans and scholars of African hip-hop, especially when read alongside Faza Nelly's words translated above. These include: the role and influence of U.S. hip-hop on African artists; competition between groups and collaboration among group members; the hip-hop economy (monetary prizes, payment for concerts, album sales, and bribery among DJs); the role of (largely foreign) music festivals in the promotion and personal growth of musicians; the need for improved training of those in the music industry and for increased access to quality equipment; the relationship between "traditional" and emerging musics; and, indeed, the uses of the concept "tradition" in this context.

Those interested in Tanzanian hip-hop in particular will find value in the artists' commentary on what constitutes Bongo Flava vis-à-vis (conscious) hip-hop. The term "Bongo Flava" derives from the Swahili words *bongo* 'brains,' a slang term for Dar es Salaam referring to the street smarts required to live there, and *fleva* 'flavor.' Gradually *Bongo* has come to mean all of Tanzania, so "Bongo Flava" is music with a Tanzanian flavor, especially musical styles recently imported from the West such as hip-hop, R&B, reggae and so on, which have been "Tanzaniafied" in various ways, including linguistically, topically, and instrumentally. It is often used synonymously with the label *muziki wa kizazi kipya* 'music of the new generation,' a label which emphasizes its status as a youth music rather than its genres, which are diverse. In fact, in the interview below Gsan uses this label to refer specifically to hip-hop, while rejecting the association with Bongo Flava. Thus, while many Bongo Flava listeners and scholars include hip-hop within Bongo Flava, or use the terms interchangeably (e.g. Englert 2003; Reuster-Jahn 2007; Stroeken 2005a; Stroeken 2005b), it is telling to listen to this crew's critique of what they see as a misnaming of Tanzanian hip-hop as well as a selling out of political concerns.

I present the interviews here in the order in which I conducted them, first with Gsan via email in early August 2006, then with Steve and Diana in person at the Via Via Club in Arusha in late August 2006, and finally with Thomas via email in January 2007. Gsan's and Thomas's responses to my questions are unedited except for obvious typographical errors. Thomas and I corresponded several times, so I have rearranged some of my questions so as not to interrupt the flow of our "conversation" as we returned to earlier topics in the disjointed way that email requires. In the interview with Gsan, I sent him my questions in English but asked him to respond in whatever language he felt more comfortable with, and he chose to respond in Swahili. Hence my questions are in English but I provide both the original and translation of his answers. Steve, Diana and I spoke in Swahili while I made a video recording of our conversation, which I transcribed with the help of a UCLA graduate student, Michelle Oberman. In the Swahili transcripts I have indicated occasional codemixing with English using italics. All translations from Swahili into English are my own, and I accept full responsibility for any errors therein. All of the interviewees gave their informed consent to be interviewed and to have their comments published under their true names. As I have written elsewhere, and as I discuss with Diana and Steve below, for logistical reasons I was unable to interview Yamat. The (absence of) his voice remains critical to my interrogation of Maasai representation, and I hope to add his words to the mix in the future.

godson rutta (a.k.a. gsan), august 2006

KDT: How did you get involved in hip-hop music?

Gsan: Kabla ya kuwa wanamuziki ktk hii fani ya hip-hop, tulikuwa tukipenda miziki ya kila aina kwani tulishawahi kuwa underground dancers wa miziki iliyokuwa ikipendwa na jamii.

Tulitokea kuupenda sana music wa hiphop kutokana na hisia, mizuka na ujumbe mzito unaoweza kuifikia jamii kwa urahisi na haraka zaidi. Na Hii ilikuwa baada ya rap kuanza kuutingisha ulimwengu wa muziki na kutokea kupendwa na vijana wengi baada ya kuingia nchini Tanzania.

Tulipenda kusikiliza nyimbo za vikundi mbalimbali kutoka Marekani kama vile, Mc Hammer, NWA, Leaders of the new school, Cold Crush, Wu Tang, Lords of the underground, Onyx, Naughty by Nature nk. Baadaye tulianza kusikia nyimbo za Saleh Jabir, alizozibadilisha kutoka katika Kiingereza kwenda katika Kiswahili na baadaye tuliwasikia wasanii wengine kama Mr 2 nk.

Hapo ndipo tulipopata hisia na gadhabu ya kuanza kutunga na kuandika nyimbo zetu ktk Kiswahili.

Gsan: Before being musicians in this hip-hop style, we were liking all kinds of musics because we had already been underground dancers for musics that were popular then.

We came to love hiphop music because of the feelings, visions and weighty messages that can reach society more easily and quickly. And this was after rap began shaking up the music world and came to be very popular with many youth after it entered Tanzania.

We liked listening to the songs of various groups from the United States like MC Hammer, NWA, Leaders of the New School, Cold Crush, Wu Tang, Lords of the Underground, Onyx, Naughty by Nature, and so on. Later we began listening to the songs of Saleh Jabir, who changed them from English to Swahili and later we listened to other artists like Mr II and so on.

That was when we got the feeling and the rage to start composing and writing our own songs in Swahili.[7]

KDT: Describe your relationship to Maasai culture.

Gsan: Kwanza kabisa mmasai ni mmoja tu ndani ya kundi ambaye ni Yamat Ole Meibuko a.k.a Merege. Halafu Godson C. Rutta a.k.a Gsan, Nelson C. Buchard a.k.a Mzee wa hisia kali FAZA, Stephen C. Rutta a.k.a KDT: Kamaa na Diana C. Rutta a.k.a Dinee. Kikabila ni wahaya kutoka Mkoa wa Kagera Bukoba japokuwa wote tumezaliwa mkoani Arusha. Na Abdalah F. Minja a.k.a Ziggy kikabila ni Mpare kutoka mkoa wa Kilimanjaro na yeye pia kazaliwa Arusha.

Uhusiano kati ya kundi la Xplastaz na utamaduni wa kimasai umesababishwa na sisi wote kuzaliwa na kuishi mkoani Arusha pia ni upande wa muziki na sio mambo mengine. Na zaidi wamasai ni wengi mkoani Arusha kuliko mikoa mingine nchini Tanzania.

Gsan: First of all a Maasai is just one in our group, who is Yamat Ole Meibuko, a.k.a. Merege. Then Godson C. Rutta a.ka. Gsan, Nelson C. Buchard, a.k.a. the Elder of Strong Feelings FAZA [Father], Stephen C. Rutta a.k.a. Kamaa, and Diana C. Rutta a.k.a. Dinee. Ethnically, they/we are Haya from the region of Kagera, Bukoba, although all of us were born in the Arusha region. And Abdalah F. Minja a.k.a. Ziggy ethnically is a Pare from the Kilimanjaro region and he also was born in Arusha.

The relationship between the Xplastaz group and Maasai culture is caused by all of us being born in the Arusha region and is in terms of music and not other things. And moreover, the Maasai are more numerous in the Arusha region than in other regions in Tanzania.

KDT: What do you think are the most important facets of Maasai culture?

Gsan: Kitu muhimu katika utamaduni wa kimasai ningependa kusema ni 'Umoja' tofauti na makabila mengine nchini Tanzania.

Gsan: Something very important in Maasai culture I'd like to say is 'Unity,' different from other ethnic groups in Tanzania.

KDT: How does Maasai culture influence your music?

Gsan: Siku zote muziki ni muziki tu popote pale duniani haijalishi ni wa aina gani. Ila Nyimbo nyingi za kimasai huwa wanaimba kama vile wana rap ambapo imekuwa rahisi sana kuchanganya muziki wao na muziki wa Hip-hop. Kama utapata nafasi ya kusikiliza vizuri nyimbo za kimasai utaelewa ninachokisema. Zaidi wamasai wa kijijini sio hawa wa mjini.

Gsan: All the time music is just music wherever you are in the world; it doesn't matter what kind it is. Though many Maasai songs they sing them like they're rapping so it has been very easy to mix their music with Hip-hop music. If you get a chance to listen well to Maasai songs you will understand what I'm saying. Rural Maasai especially not these ones in the city.

**bongo flava, hip-hop and "local maasai flavors":
interviews with x plastaz**

KDT: How are the Maasai viewed by other ethnic groups within Tanzania?

Gsan: Unajua maisha ya Mjini yako tofauti sana na maisha ya kijijini ama porini. Na mmasai anapokuja mjini anakuwa tayari yuko nje ya mazingira aliyozaliwa na kukulia yaani maisha aliyoyazoea ya kuchunga N'gombe, Mbuzi na Kondoo. Hivyo linapokuja suala la kutafuta kazi mjini inakuwa vigumu sana kupata kazi tofauti na kazi ya ulinzi.

Kwahiyo makabila mengine nchini Tanzania zaidi mjini yanafikiri wamasai ni washamba na hawakusoma. Ila asilimia kubwa ya makabila yanaheshimu mila na utamaduni wa kimasai kwa sababu makabila mengi yameshindwa kudumisha utamaduni wao ipasavyo, Wengi wanataka utamaduni wa TV. Pia kuna wamasai waliyokwenda shule lakini baada ya kumaliza masomo baadhi yao huwa wanakiuka baadhi ya miiko ya kimasai kama vile, kula Samaki, Nguruwe, Kuku na kadhalika. Ama kuvaa tena mavazi ya kimasai kwa kuhofia kuonekana washamba labda wanapokuwa kijijini.

Gsan: You know urban life is very different from rural or bush life. And when a Maasai comes to the city he is already out of the environment in which he was born and grew up, that is the life that he was used to, of herding cows, goats, and sheep. So when the issue of looking for work in a city comes up it's very difficult to get a job other than in security.

Therefore other ethnic groups in Tanzania especially in the city think that the Maasai are backwards and that they didn't go to school. But a large percent of ethnic groups respect Maasai customs and culture because many ethnic groups have failed to preserve their culture as they should. Many want the culture shown on TV. Also there are Maasai who went to school but after finishing their studies some of them avoid some of the prohibitions of the Maasai like eating fish, pork, chicken and so on. Or wearing Maasai clothing again because of fear of looking like bumpkins when they are in the village.

KDT: Why do you rap in Swahili rather than your first language?

Gsan: Kiswahili ndiyo lugha yangu ya kwanza kuongea kabla sijajua kuongea kihaya, kimasai, kiingereza nk. na ndio maana ninatumia Kiswahili. Na Yamat kimasai ni lugha yake ya kwanza na ndio maana anaimba kwa lugha ya kimasai. Yamati alianza kujifunza Kiswahili na kiingereza mwaka 2001.

Gsan: Swahili is my first language to speak before I knew how to speak Haya, Maa, English, etc. And that's why I use Swahili. And Yamat, Maa is his first language and that's why he sings in Maa. Yamat began learning Swahili and English in 2001

KDT: Do you consider your music 'Maasai hip-hop'? Why or why not?

Gsan: Ni kweli kwamba muziki wetu tumechanganya na muziki wa kimasai lakini haina maana ya kwamba mziki wetu kwa ujumla unaitwa hivyo. Ni albamu pekee ndiyo inayoitwa 'Maasai hip-hop" na muziki wetu kwa ujumla ni 'AFRICAN HIP-HOP' na sio 'Bongo flava'

Kwahiyo usishangae katika albam ya pili ikaitwa Hadzabe hip-hop ama jina lingine lolote ambalo hijawahi kulisikia maishani. Ni kwamba tunapenda sana kuchanganya muziki wetu na muziki asili ya tamaduni mbalimbali.

Tulianza na kabila la kimasai kwa sababu lililokuwa karibu na sisi na ni kabila ambalo tumeishi nalo kwa muda mrefu tangu tumezaliwa.

Gsan: It's true that we have mixed our music with Maasai music but that doesn't mean that our music in general is called that. It's only an album that is called "Maasai hip-hop" and our music in general is "AFRICAN HIP-HOP" and not 'Bongo flava'

So don't be surprised in our second album if it's called Hadzabe hip-hop or any other name which you've never heard in your life. It's that we love to mix our music with the traditional music of various cultures.

We began with the Maasai ethnic group because it was near us and it's an ethnic group that we have lived with for a long time, since we were born.

KDT: What is different about performing in Tanzania versus internationally?

Gsan: Tofauti iliyoko ni kubwa sana zaidi linapokuja suala la lugha. Tunapokuwa nchi zingine watu hufurahia sana muziki lakini hawaelewi lugha tunayoitumia. Na tunapokuwa Tanzania Wanafurahia sana muziki na pia wanaelewa na kuzungumza lugha tunayoitumia. Kwa hiyo tunapokuwa nchi za nje inabidi tutumie nguvu za ziada ili kuwafurahisha na kuwaridhisha mashabiki wetu. Pia nchi za nje wana vyombo vya muziki vyenye ubora wa hali ya juu kuliko vya nyumbani Tanzania.

Gsan: The difference which is there is huge, especially when question of language comes up. When we are in other countries people enjoy our music very much but they don't understand the language we use. And when we are in Tanzania they enjoy our music very much and they also understand and speak the language we use. So when we are in foreign countries we have to use extra energy in order to please and satisfy our fans. Also in foreign countries they have musical instruments with a much higher quality than those at home in Tanzania.

KDT: What kind of response have you had from Tanzanian hip-hop listeners? And international listeners?

Gsan: Wasikilizaji wa muziki huu wa kizazi kipya 'HIP-HOP' Tanzania wanaupokea muziki wetu kwa furaha kubwa na kwa nia moja ya kwamba sisi ni wasema ukweli na sio uongo.

Kuna vikundi vingi ambavyo vinafanya kazi zao kama utani na pia kuimba kuhusu vitu ambavyo havipo ndani ya jamii ya mtanzania na hiyo ndiyo Bongo flava. Nyimbo nyingi ni flava tu hakuna ujumbe wa maana. "Wanaimba kufuata mauzo na sio ukweli wa mawazo"

Sasa hivi tatizo kubwa lililoko nchini Tanzania na Afrika ya mashariki kwa ujumla ni usambazaji wa kazi za wasanii. Kampuni nyingi za usambazaji zinafaidika sana kuliko wasanii wenyewe na wasanii hawajui wameuza nakala ngapi za cd zao kutokana na haki miliki haifanyi kazi ipasavyo. Kwa mfano, hata iki-tokea msanii kajua kampuni iliyoiba muziki wake inakuwa ni vigumu msanii kusimama kizimbani na kushinda kesi kwa sababu ya rushwa. Kampuni ina fedha kuliko msanii.

Pia watangazaji wa redio za FM na TV wamekuwa na tabia ya kutaka rushwa kutoka kwa wasanii kwa ajili ya kupiga nyimbo zao. Ila sisi kama Xplastaz tumegoma na tutaendelea kugoma milele hatutakubali kutoa rushwa kwa sababu hatupendi kuendekeza tabia kama hiyo kwani 'RUSHWA NI ADUI WA HAKI.'

Gsan: The listeners of this music of the new generation 'hip-hop' in Tanzanian receive our music with great pleasure and with one thing in mind: that we are tellers of the truth and not of lies.

There are many groups that do their work like it's a joke and also sing about things that are not in the culture of the Tanzanian and that is Bongoflava. Many songs are songs flavor; theirs is no meaningful message. "The sing according to sales and not the truth of thoughtfulness."

Right now a big problem in Tanzania and in East Africa in general is the distribution of artists' work. Many distribution companies are profiting a lot more than the artists themselves and the artists don't know how many copies of their CDs they have sold because copyright doesn't work the way it should. For example, even if it happens that an artist knows the company that stole his or her music it's very difficult for the artist to stand up in court and win the case because of bribes. The company has more money than the artist.

Also FM radio and TV announcers have had the habit of wanting bribes from artists in order to play their songs. But we, as Xplastaz, we have refused and we will continue to refuse forever; we will not agree to pay bribes because we don't want to encourage a practice like that because 'BRIBERY IS THE ENEMY OF RIGHT.'

KDT: Why do you think Westerners are so interested in Maasai people and their culture?

Gsan: Nadhani Watu wengi wa nchi za Magharibi wanapenda sana kuona vitu ambavyo hawajawahi kuviona na havipo katika mazingira yao ya kila siku mbali na wamasai na utamaduni wao.

Mila na utamaduni wa kimasai ni wa kipekee na uko tofauti sana kulingana na makabila mengine mbalimbali kote duniani. Na sio nchi za magharibi tu zenye hamu ya kuujua utamaduni wa kimasai bali hata wazawa wa Tanzania na nchi zingine za Afrika zinatamani kuujua utamaduni wa kimasai.

Gsan: I think many people in Western countries love to see things which they've never seen and which are not in their everyday environment, not just the Maasai and their culture.

The customs and culture of the Maasai are unique and very different compared to various other cultures the world over. And is not just Western countries with the desire to know Maasai culture but those born in Tanzanian and other African countries; they want to know Maasai culture.

KDT: I've heard that young people often pretend to be Maasai to gain entrance into the tourist economy. Have you observed this? What do you think of this practice?

Gsan: Utalii umechangia sana kuwepo kwa tatizo kama hili. Na tatizo hili lilianzia kwa wamasai wa Ngorongoro kwa sababu ndipo kuna watalii wengi kuliko sehemu nyingine wanazoishi wamasai.

Maderava wa makampuni ya utalii walikuwa wakiwapeleka wageni kupiga picha za wamasai, nyumba na mifugo yao kama vile nao ni mojawapo ya wanyama wanayoishi Ngorongoro. Na maderava hao Walikuwa wakilipwa na wageni kwa kufanya hivyo. Mwisho wake wamasai wakagundua kwamba maderava wanalipwa na wageni, kwahiyo na wao wakaanza kugoma na kukataa kabisa kupigwa picha bila sababu maalumu au malipo.

Gsan: Tourism has contributed a lot to the existence of problems like this. And this problem started with the Maasai of Ngorongoro because that's where there are more tourists than in other areas where the Maasai live.

Tour company drivers were sending visitors to take photos of the Maasai, their homes, and their cattle, as if they are one of the animals living in the Ngorongoro. And those drivers were being paid by visitors to do that. In the end the Maasai discovered that the drivers are paid by visitors, so that began to object and to refuse completely to be photographed without a good reason or a payment.

Hapo ndipo ikabidi madereva kuwa wanawabembeleza wamasai wakubali kupigwa picha na kuwaahidi ya kwamba watawalipa. Mwisho wamasai wakakubali tena kuendelea kupigwa picha ila kwa malipo maalumu. Baada ya hapo tabia ikazua mazoea na ndio maana utakuta baadhi ya vijana wamasai wa mjini wanafanya hivyo ili kupata pesa. Sijui wa kumlaumu ni nani! WAGENI, MADEREVA au WAMASAI?

Then and there the drivers had to persuade the Maasai to agree to be photographed and to promise them that they will be paid. In the end the Maasai agreed again to continue to be photographed but with a special payment. After that the practice became normal and that's why you will see some young urban Maasai do that in order to get money. I don't know whom to blame! The visitors, the drivers, or the Maasai?

diana rutta (a.k.a. dineh) and steve rutta, august 2006

KDT: Mnaweza kuanza na kueleza historia yenu tu, majina yenu na ... ? Sijui. Utambulisho tena tu.

Diana: Sawa. Um, mimi naitwa Diana Rutta. Memba ya X Plastaz. Mmm, tulianza muziki mwaka tisini na saba baada ya kuona *mabratha* wanafanya muziki na sisi tukapenda. *So*, wakaamua tu kututungia *verses*. Tukajaribu na tukaweza. Tukaungana nao tisini na saba mpaka saa hivi tupo nao. Tumeshasafiri sehemu mbalimbali.

Steve: Mimi naitwa Steve Rutta. Nilianza muziki tisini na saba. Na nilikuwa pamoja na sista. Kwa hiyo, tulianza kama kikundi cha Fortune Tellers kwa sisi wawili. X Plastaz ni kaka zetu. Baada ya kufanyafanya *concert-concert*, baadaye tukaja tukawa X Plastaz.

KDT: Can you begin by just explaining your history, your names and ... ? I don't know. Just introductions again.

Diana: Okay. Um, I'm called Diana Rutta. I'm a member of X Plastaz. Mmm, we began [doing] music in '97 after seeing [our] brothers doing music and we liked it. So, they just decided to compose some verses for us. We tried and we were able [to rap]. We joined up with them in '97 and up to now we're with them. We've already travelled various places.

Steve: I'm called Steve Rutta. I began [doing] music in '97. And I was with [my] sister [Diana]. So, we began as the group Fortune Tellers, the two of us. X Plastaz are our brothers. After doing lots of concerts, later we came to be X Plastaz.

KDT: Nyinyi mlikuwa na miaka mingapi mwaka wa tisini na saba?

Diana: Nilikuwa na miaka–. Nilikuwa na miaka tisa.

KDT: Ah, aisei.

Steve: Nilikuwa na miaka saba? La.

Diana: Tisa au kumi. Nilikuwa na miaka kumi.

Steve: Nilikuwa na miaka nane.

KDT: Aisei! Mtoto mdogo.

Diana: Kweli.

KDT: Sasa nyinyi bado mko shuleni?

Diana: Eh. Ya, tupo shuleni.

KDT: Kama darasa gani?

Diana: Mimi nasoma komputa, IT.

Steve: Mimi ndo naingia pre-Form 1. Ni mwaka huu naingia pre-Form 1.

KDT: Mlianza kuvutiwa vipi na muziki wa aina hii?

Diana: Kwa kweli kwangu mimi, nilikuwa naona kaka wanaimba vile, na mie nikawa najaribu najaribu, nachukua *verses* za watu. Naiga kuimba nini nini. Ndo akaamua yeye mwenyewe, Gsan, kunitungia *verse* aka.. Nakumbuka niliweza kutumia [?] ya Davina. Baada ya hapo kwa kuwa kulikuwa na mashindano yakiendelea Christ Hall *so* walinipeleka, na namshukuru Mungu nilishinda.

KDT: How old were you in '97?

Diana: I was …[*She pauses to remember.*] I was nine years old.

KDT: Oh, wow.

Steve: Was I seven? No.

Diana: Nine or ten. I was ten years old.

Steve: I was eight years old.

KDT: Wow! A small child.

Diana: True.

KDT: Now are you still in school?

Diana: Yup. Yeah, we're in school.

KDT: Like what grade?

Diana: I'm studying computers, IT.[8]

Steve: I'm entering Pre-Form 1. This year I'm entering Pre-Form One.[9]

KDT: How did you start to get interested in this type of music?

Diana: Actually in my case, I was watching how [our] brothers sing, and I started trying all the time; I would take other's verses. I would imitate them singing this and that. Then Gsan decided to compose a verse for me himself, and he … I remember I was using [a song] of Davina's. After that there was a competition going on at Christ Hall so they sent me, and I thank God I won.

Steve: Mimi hapa nafikiri zaidi. Kipindi hiyo Mr. II alikuwa, kipindi hiyo aliitwa 2 Proud. Kwa hiyo, kipindi hiyo zile nyimbo zake, nini, nilikuwa nazipenda sana. Kwa hiyo kila Jumapili tulikuwa tunaenda Mawingu. Siku moja nika… tukaandikisha jina. Kwa hiyo, nikachana pale bila *brother* kujua lakini. Tulivyomaliza, nilituzwa siku hiyo vizuri. Nilichana vizuri. Kwa hiyo, nilivyomaliza pale, baada ya kwenda nyumbani, *bro* akaniambia niko vizuri na vile vile. Akaanza kunitungia.

KDT: Kwa hiyo mwanzowe …

Diana: Tulikuwa Fortune Tellers, tukawa X Plastaz.

KDT: Kwa hivyo, Gsan na wengine walikuwa wameshajiita X Plastaz kabla ya nyinyi kuingia?

Diana and Steve: Ya, ndiyo.

KDT: Walikuwa wameshamwalika Yamat au bado?

Diana: Walikuwa hawajamwalika Yamat bado. Yamat alialikwa mwaka 2001. Mwaka tunajiandaa kwenda Netherlands kwa mara ya kwanza, mwezi wa pili.

KDT: Ninyi mlianza kuvutiwa zaidi na muziki wa Tanzania au mlikuwa umeshasikia sana hip-hop ya Marekani?

Diana: Ya, tulikuwa tulishasikia *hiphop* ya nje.

Steve: I'm still thinking. At that time there was Mr. II, at that time he was called 2 Proud.[10] So, at that time, those songs of his, and so on, I loved them. So every Sunday we would go to Mawingu.[11] One day, I … we signed up. So, I rapped there, but without [our] brothers' knowing. When we finished, I was honored well that day. I rapped well. So when we finished there, after going home, [my] bro told me that I'm good and so on. He began composing for me.

KDT: So in the beginning …

Diana: We were the Fortune Tellers; then we were [part of] X Plastaz.[12]

KDT: So Gsan and the others were had already called themselves X Plastaz before you entered?

Diana and Steve: Yeah, yes.

KDT: Had they already invited Yamat, or not yet?

Diana: They hadn't invited Yamat yet. Yamat was invited in 2001, the year we were preparing to go to the Netherlands for the first time, in February.

KDT: Did you begin by being interested in Tanzanian music or had you already listened to a lot of American hip-hop?

Diana: Yeah, we had already heard foreign hip-hop.

KDT: Mliposhindana, kwenye mash-indano hayo mliyoshinda, zawadi zilikuwa kama vitu gani?

Diana: Kwa kweli, sana sana zawadi zilikuwa ni pesa tu.

Steve: Pesa. Begi.

Diana: Pesa tu. Begi. Tshirts. Caps.

KDT: Mlipataje nafasi hiyo ya kwenda Netherlands?

Diana: Tuna meneja yetu ambaye anaitwa Thomas. Alikuja Tanzania mwaka tisini na saba. Alipokuja tisini na saba alikutana na X Plastaz. Alikutana na X Plastaz wana*perform* Mawingu Club. Alikutana X Plastaz akawasikiliza wanavyo*perform*, akapenda, akachukua *contacts* zao. Akawaambia atarudi Tanzania kuwasaidia. Akaja akarudi mwaka elfu mbili. Aliporudi mwaka elfu mbili, tukakaa naye. Tulifanya *concert* mwaka 2001 Dar es Salaam. Kulikuwa na Mr. 2, Dola Soul, Inspecta Haroun, Profesa Jay, wasanii wengi wengi. Baada ya hapo tuli*perform* Dar es Salaam, akaondoka. Na baadhi ya vipande vipande amevichukua. Akaenda Festival Mundial. Hapana, alikutana na Madunia. Akaonyesha vile vipande vipande. Festival Mundial ikawa inaandaliwa. *So*, wakatualika. Wakatupenda walituita, mwaka 2001 mwezi wa pili.

KDT: Mlienda kwa muda gani?

Diana: Tulikaa *one month*.

KDT: Ilikuwaje?

KDT: When you competed, in those competitions that you won, what were the prizes like?

Diana: Actually, most of the time the prizes were just money.

Steve: Money; bags.

Diana: Just money, bags, t-shirts, caps.

KDT: How did you get the opportunity to go to the Netherlands?

Diana: We have our manager who is called Thomas [Gesthuizen]. He came to Tanzania in '97. When he came in '97 he met X Plastaz. He met X Plastaz performing at Mawingu Club. He met X Plastaz and he heard them perform, he liked it, he took their contact information. He told them that he would return to Tanzania to help them. He came back in 2000. When he came back in 2000, we stayed with him. We did a concert in 2001 in Dar es Salaam. There were Mr. II, Dola Soul, Inspecta Haroun, Profesa Jay, [and] lots of other artists. After we performed in Dar es Salaam, and then he left. And he took some of our raps with him. He went to Festival Mundial.[13] No, he met with Madunia.[14] He showed off those raps. Festival Mundial was being set up. So they invited us. They liked us, [so] they sent for us, in February 2001.

KDT: For how long did you go?

Diana: We stayed one month.

KDT: How was it?

Diana: Ilikuwa nzuri sana.

Steve: Ilikuwa nzuri.

Diana: Sana! Ilikuwa ndo *trip* yetu ya kwanza kwenda Europe. So tuli*enjoy* sana.

KDT: Mmeenda tena baada ya hapo?

Diana: Ya, mwaka 2002 tulienda tena ambapo tulienda Coulour Cafe Belgium. Na mwaka 2003 tukaenda tena. Tulienda Netherlands, Uingereza ... Ya. Na 2005 tulienda Brazili, Norway, Sweden, Netherlands tena. Na Mwaka huu pia tumeshaenda Gabon.

KDT: Ehe, nilisoma hivyo. Na Gabon ilikuwaje?

Steve: Ilikuwa nzuri.

Diana: Gabon ilikuwa nzuri ijapo watu hawajui *English*. Ni Kifaransa peke yake. Lakini, unajua, *music is music*. Hata kama mtu haelewi, anaweza aka*feel*. Walitupokea vizuri.

KDT: Je, sema, kuna tofauti zo zote baina ya maonyesho ambayo mnafanya hapa Tanzania na maonyesho ambayo mnafanya nje?

Diana: Ya, tofauti ipo kubwa sana. Sana!

KDT: Nielezee.

Diana: It was very nice.

Steve: It was nice.

Diana: Very! It was our first trip to Europe. So we enjoyed ourselves a lot.

KDT: Have you gone again after that?

Diana: Yeah, in 2002 we went again when we went to Coulour Café in Belgium.[15] And then in 2003 we went again. We went to the Netherlands, England ... Yeah. And in 2005 we went to Brazil, Norway, Sweden, and again to the Netherlands. And this year [2006] we have already been to Gabon.

KDT: Yeah, I read that. And how was Gabon?

Steve: It was nice.

Diana: Gabon was nice except that people don't know English. It's only French. But, you know, music is music. Even if a person doesn't understand, he can feel it. They received us very well.

KDT: Tell me, are there are any differences between the shows you do here in Tanzania and the shows you do outside [of the country]?

Diana: Yeah, the difference is very big. Very!

KDT: Explain it to me.

Diana: Sababu kule watu, *I mean*, kule watu wanaielewa. *I mean,* wana*concentrate* sana au wako wana*experience*. Siyo kama huku. Unajua huku mtu anaweza kukuona unaimba nini, akaona, "A! Anafanya nini pale?!" Unaona, eh? Ni kama anakudharaudharau lakini kule ni [tofauti]. Halafu kuna *support*. Siyo kama huku Tanzania. Tanzania ni watu wachache sana wanao*support*.

KDT: Kwa nini?

Diana: Wengine wanachukulia muziki wa hip-hop ni wa kihuni. That's why *support* inakuwa ni ndogo sana.

KDT: Lakini ni hivyo Marekani pia.

Diana: Kweli?

KDT: Ndiyo. Wazee wengi wanafikiri hip-hop ni ya kihuni tu.

Diana: Because there, people, I mean, there, people understand it. I mean, they really concentrate or they are there experiencing it. Not like here. You know here a person can see you singing and think, "A! What is she doing there?!" You see, eh? It's like he's looking down on you, but there it's different. Moreover, there's support. Not like here in Tanzania. In Tanzania there are very few people who support [music].

KDT: Why is that?

Diana: Some think hip-hop is hoodlum music. That's why support is so little.

KDT: But it's like that in the United States as well.

Diana: Really?

KDT: Yes. Many older people think hip-hop is for hoodlums.

[Diana and Steve laugh.]

KDT: Lakini katika jinsi nyinyi mna-vyocheza kwenye maonyesho, kuna tofauti zo zote huko na huku?

Diana: Kwa kweli tofauti zipo. Kimavazi. Kwa sababu sisi tukifanya *performance* hatuvai kama wasanii wa huko wanavyovaa: kama *bling bling,* iko "50 cent," sijui nini. No. Tuko tukivaa kiasili.

Steve: Ya kiasili.

Diana: Nguo zetu kiasili.

KDT: Kama nini?

KDT: But in the way that you perform in shows, is there any difference there and here?

Diana: Actually there are differences. In clothing. Because when we do a performance we don't dress like artists over there dress: like bling bling that says "50 cent" or things like that. No. We're just dressing traditionally.

Steve: Traditionally.

Diana: Our traditional clothes.

KDT: Like what?

Diana: Kama Maasai wanavyovaa: *Batiks*, kanga, shanga.

KDT: Lakini mkicheza huku Tanzania hamvai hivyo?

Diana: Hata Tanzania tunavaa hivyo. Ndo maana tunaitwa Maasai hip-hop.

KDT: Ungesema muziki wenu kwa jumla ni Maasai hip-hop?

Diana: Ya, ni Maasai hip-hop.

KDT: Vipi "Bongoflava"? Mnatumia jina hilo?

Diana: Kwa kweli, hapana.

KDT: Kwa nini?

Diana: Hatutumii "Bongoflava." Sisi tunaimba *hardcore hip-hop*. Maasai hip-hop.

KDT: Kuna tofauti gani baina ya hip-hop na Bongoflava?

Diana: Kwa kweli, tofauti ipo. Kama watu wa Bongoflava wanapoimba: starehe, wanawake, *clubs*, *party*, nini nini. Vitu kama hivyo. Unaona? Lakini sisi tunaimba tofauti na wao: kuhusu maisha, historia ya mitaani, wanawake, ugonjwa wa ukimwi, vitu tofauti tofauti, madawa ya kulevya. Ya, siyo sawa na wasanii wa Bongoflava.

KDT: Mmewahi kusikia hip-hop nyingine za Kiafrika?

Diana: Ya, tumeshawahi kusikia. Hip-hop ya Senegal tumeisikia.

Steve: Mali.

Diana: Like the Maasai wear: batiks, kangas, beads.

KDT: But if you perform here in Tanzania you don't dress like that?

Diana: Even in Tanzania we dress like that. That's why we are called Maasai hip-hop.

KDT: Would you say that your music in general is Maasai hip-hop?

Diana: Yeah, it's Maasai hip-hop.

KDT: What about "Bongoflava"? Do you use that name.

Diana: Actually, no.

KDT: Why?

Diana: We don't use "Bongoflava." We sing hardcore hip-hop. Maasai hip-hop.

KDT: What's the difference between hip-hop and Bongoflava?

Diana: Actually, there is a difference. Like the Bongoflava people when they sing: entertainment, women, clubs, parties, and so on. Things like that. You see? But we sing differently than them: about life, street history, women, AIDS, lots of different things, drugs. Yeah, not like Bongoflava artists.

KDT: Have you ever heard other African hip-hop?

Diana: Yeah, we've heard it. We've heard hip-hop from Senegal.

Steve: Mali.

Diana: Mali. Na Benin, ya. Na Gabon. Na nyingine nyingi tu.

KDT: Unaonaje muziki wenu katika uwanja huo mkubwa wa hip-hop ya Kiafrika?

Diana: Kweli muziki wetu, yaani unakubalika. Kweli, ya. Kwa sababu mara nyingi sana tunapokutana na wasanii wa Afrika -- sehemu tofauti tofauti -- wengi wao wanakuwa watumia Kifaransa. Kwa hivyo wanaelewana. Sisi tunakuwa tuna-tumia Kiswahili. Lakini tunaweza kukabiliana nao. Ya.

KDT: Kuna wanamuziki wengine wa Kitanzania ambao wamepata nafasi nyingi za kusafiri kama nyinyi?

Steve: Mr. 2.

Diana: Ya, *some of them*, kama Mr. 2

Steve: Dola Soul.

Diana: Dola Soul, ambaye saa hizi yuko Marekani.

Steve: Sijui, lakini nasikia amesharudi.

Diana: Oh. Na kina Mandojo, lakini wao walikuwa *made a trip* moja kwa moja. Si kama sisi.

KDT: Mnaona sababu zo zote ambazo nyinyi mmebahatika kuliko wengine?

Diana: Mali, and Benin, yeah. And Gabon. And lots of others.

KDT: How do you see your music in that larger field of African hip-hop?

Diana: Truly our music, I mean, it's been accepted. Truly, yeah. Because many times when we meet with African artists – in various places – many of them are using French. So they understand each other. We are using Swahili. Yet we can approach each other. Yeah.

KDT: Are there other Tanzanian musicians who have had many oppor-tunities to travel like you?

Steve: Mr. II.

Diana: Yeah, some of them, like Mr. II.

Steve: Dola Soul.

Diana: Dola Soul, who is in the United States these days.

Steve: I don't know, but I hear he's already come back.

Diana. Oh. And Mandojo and those guys, but they just made one trip each. Not like us.

KDT: Do you see any reasons why you have been luckier than others?

Diana: [Laughs] Sababu naweza nikasema labda kwa sababu tunaimba Maasai hip-hop. Muziki ambao tumechanganya na mambo ya kiasili. Mm-hmm. *That's right.* Kwa hiyo, yaani tuna Tofauti ladha tofauti na watu wa Bongoflava, ndo maana. Ya.

Diana: A reason I can say is maybe because we sing Maasai hip-hop. Music that we have mixed with traditional stuff. Mm-hmm. That's right. So, in other words we have a different flavor, different from Bongoflava people; that's why. Yeah.

KDT: Kiswahili ni lugha yenu ya kwanza au ya pili?

KDT: Is Swahili your first language or your second?

Diana: Katika?

Diana: In?

KDT: Katika maisha yenu, mlijifunza Kiswahili kwanza au lugha nyingine?

KDT: In your lives, did you learn Swahili first, or another language?

Diana and Steve: Kiswahili.

Diana and Steve: Swahili.

KDT: Kwa hiyo nyumbani wazazi wenu walisema Kiswahili tu?

KDT: So at home your parents only spoke Swahili?

Diana and Steve: Mm-hmm.

Diana and Steve: Mm-hmm.

KDT: Mmewahi kujifunza lugha nyingine?

KDT: Have you ever learned another language?

Diana: Nilijaribu kujifunza Kiholanzi, lakini nilishindwa. Ya, Kidachi. Kiko kigumu sana.

Diana: I tried to learn the language of Holland, but I couldn't. Yeah, Dutch. It's very difficult.

Steve: Nilifunza Ki*spanish.*

Steve: I learned Spanish.

KDT: Ki*spanish.* Lakini lugha nyingine za Kitanzania?

KDT: Spanish. But [what about] other Tanzanian languages?

Diana: Pia lugha yetu sisi. Ijapo hatuijui sana kwa sababu hatukuzaliwa kijijini.

Diana: Plus our own language. Although we don't know it well because we weren't born in the village.

KDT: Ambayo ni Kihaya?

KDT: That is Haya?

Diana and Steve: Kihaya, ya.

Diana and Steve: Haya, yeah.

KDT: Mmeanza kujifunza Kimaasai?

KDT: Have you begun learning Maa?

[Both laugh.]

Diana: Kweli, bado.

Diana: Actually, not yet.

Steve: Bado.

Steve: Not yet.

Diana: Bado. Gsan ndo yeye kuongea Kimasai.

Diana: Not yet. It's only Gsan who speaks Maa.

KDT: Yamat ameanza... amejifunza Kiswahili?

KDT: Has Yamat begun ... has he learned Swahili?

Diana: Yamat amejifunza Kiswahili mwaka 2001.

Diana: Yamat learned Swahili in 2001.

KDT: Na Kiingereza pia?

KDT: And English as well?

Diana: Kiingereza pia.

Diana: English as well.

KDT: Mnaweza kuzungumza zaidi kidogo juu ya athari za Umaasai kwenye muziki wenu? Mmesema mnavaa nguo za Kimaasai mara nyingine. Na athari nyingine zo zote?

KDT: Can you tell me a little bit about the effects of Maasainess on your music? You've said that you wear Maasai clothing sometimes. Are there any other effects?

Diana: Kuna ku*paint*. Tunakuwa tuna*paint* mwili. *Faces*, tuna*paint*.

Diana: There is painting. We often paint the body. We paint [our] faces.

KDT: Mnafikiri mnapocheza nje ya Tanzania, wasikilizaji wanafikiri nyinyi nyote ni Wamaasai?

KDT: Do you think that when you perform outside of Tanzania, your audience thinks that all of you are Maasai?

Diana: [laughing] Ya, wengi wanasema sisi ni Wamaasai. Wengi wanatuita sisi Maasai, lakini siyo. Maasai ni mmoja tu katika kundi la X Plastaz.

Diana: Yeah, lots of them say that we are Maasai. Lots of them call us Maasai, but no. A Maasai is just one in the group X Plastaz.

KDT: Wakifikiri hivyo mnawasahihisha?

KDT: If they think that do you correct them?

Diana and Steve: Ya, tunawasahihisha.

Diana and Steve: Yeah, we correct them.

Steve: Mm-hmm.

Steve: Mm-hmm.

Diana: Lazima tuwaambie kwamba Maasai ni mmoja tu katika *group*.

Diana: We must tell them that a Maasai is just one in the group.

KDT: Ulisema Watanzania wengine wanadharau muziki ya hip-hop.

KDT: You said that some Tanzanians look down on hip-hop music.

[Diana nods emphatically.]

KDT: Umeona pia kwamba wengine wanawadharau Wamasai? Au siyo?

Diana: Wamasai? Ya, wako wengine wanaodharau Wamaasai. Kwa sababu kuna wengine wanaotuuliza, "Kwa nini mmeweka Maasai hivi katika group lenu?" Sisi tunajibu, "kwa sababu tunataka tuwe tofauti na watu wengine." Kitu kama hicho. Hatutaki kufanana. [Laughs]

KDT: Unaona ule Umaasai ndani ya muziki wenu umekusaidia nje ya Tanzania?

Diana: Ya.

Steve: Umesaidia sana.

Diana: Kuitangaza Tanzania.

KDT: Labda ndani ya Tanzania ni tofauti?

Diana: Ndani ya Tanzania pia, umetusaidia.

KDT: Kweli? Kujitofautisha?

Diana: Kujitofautisha na magroup mengine.

KDT: Mnaweza kuongea kidogo juu ya athari za utandawazi? Kwanza, katika maisha yenu au Tanzania, na pia katika muziki wenu. Umeona utandawazi ukoje Tanzania?

Diana: Kwa kweli, nimeona ni mzuri. Unatusaidia. Kwa sababu ... *Can you repeat?*

KDT: Tuseme kwanza, nikisema "utandawazi," maana yake ni nini kwenu? Katika maisha yenu au katika Tanzania? Umeona ishara gani?

KDT: Have you also seen that some look down on the Maasai? Or not?

Diana: On the Maasai? Yeah, there are some who look down on the Maasai. Because there are some who ask us, "Why have put a Maasai like this in your group?" We answer, "because we want to be different from other people." Like that. We don't want to be similar.

KDT: Do you think that Maasainess in your music has helped you outside of Tanzania?

Diana: Yeah.

Steve: It has helped a lot.

Diana: To advertise Tanzania.

KDT: Is it maybe different inside of Tanzania?

Diana: Inside Tanzania too, it has helped us.

KDT: Really? To differentiate yourselves?

Diana: To differentiate ourselves from other groups.

KDT: Can you talk a little bit about the effects of globalization? First, in your lives or in Tanzania, and also in your music. What have seen globalization is like in Tanzania?

Diana: Actually, I see it as good. It helps us. Because ... Can you repeat?

KDT: Let's say, first, if I say "globalization," what does it mean to you? In your lives or in Tanzania? What effects have you seen?

Diana: Ishara za utandawazi? Hebu niambie utandawazi ni nini? Globalization? Ya! [Laughs] Kiswahili kigumu! Ya, umesaidia.

KDT: Umesaidia kwa njia gani?

Diana: Kama vile, kutuletea maendeleo.

Steve: Umetusaidia katika mambo yetu mengi.

Diana: Kama *website*.

KDT: Nyinyi mlifanya tovuti hiyo au–?

Diana: Thomas alifanya tovuti, kwani anasaidiana na sisi.

KDT: Nilipotaja "utandawazi" nilikuwa nikifikiri athari za muziki wa nje ya Tanzania na mambo kama hayo. Umeona athari hizo? Kwa mfano, athari za muziki wa hip-hop ya Kimarekani. Ilipoingia Tanzania, watu walianza kuiga lakini sasa wameibadilisha.

Diana: Ya, waliiga: kuvaa, kuimba, *Lifestyle* wanavyoishi. Walijaribu kuishi kama Wamarekani, lakini kwa sasa wanapunguza. Ni wachache wanaofanya hivyo.

KDT: Nilipomhoji Gsan, aliniambia kwamba, kabla ya kucheza muziki wenu, mlikuwa "underground dancers" au yeye alikuwa "underground dancer," lakini sijafahamu maana ya kuwa "underground dancer."

Steve: Yeye alikuwa *underground dancer.*

Diana: The effects of globalization? Hey, tell me, what is "utandawazi"? Globalization? Yeah! Swahili is hard! Yeah, it has helped.

KDT: How has it helped?

Diana: Like bringing progress.

Steve: It has helped us a lot with our stuff.

Diana: Like [the X Plastaz] website.

KDT: Did you do that website or …?

Diana: Thomas did the website, because he helps us out.

KDT: When I mentioned "globalization" I was thinking about the effects of music from outside of Tanzania and things like that. Have you seen such effects? For example, the effects of American hip-hop music. When it entered Tanzania, people began it imitate it but now they've changed it.

Diana: Yeah, they imitated the dressing, the singing, [and] the lifestyle they live. They tried to live like Americans, but now they're doing that less. It's only a few who do that now.

KDT: When I interviewed Gsan, he told me that, before playing your music, you were "underground dancers," or he was an "underground dancer," but I haven't yet understood the meaning of being an "underground dancer."

Steve: He was an underground dancer.

Diana: Yeye mwenyewe alikuwa underground dancer. Kwa sababu X Plastaz mara ya kwanza alikuwepo marehemu Faza Nelly na Ziggy ambao walijiita "Two Rough Gs." Baadaye, na Gsan alikuwa *underground dancer*, wakaja wakajiunga wote.

KDT: Lakini maana ya "underground dancer" ni nini?

Diana: Yeye ni kama ... Anacheza ...

Steve: Alikuwa kwanza anachezacheza. Ni mtu wa kucheza. Mfano, leo imeandaliwa *concert* ya kuvaa kizamani. Mtu ambaye atavaa kizamani na kucheza kizamani atashinda. Ndo hivyo. Alikuwa ana*design* nguo zake. Anavaa vile kizamani na kucheza. Alikuwa anashinda lakini alikuwa ni *underground*. Kipindi hicho bado alikuwa hajaingia.

KDT: Alikuwa hajajulikana.

Steve: Alikuwa hajaingia kundi la X Plastaz.

KDT: Lakini nyinyi hamkufanya hivyo pia?

Diana: Hapana sisi hatukufanya. [Laughs.] Tulikuwa bado wadogo sana. Tulikuwa bado hatujaingia kwenye muziki.

KDT: Nyinyi kama kundi la X Plastaz mna mipango gani ya baadaye? Mtaendalea kutunga *album*?

Diana: He himself was an underground dancer. Because X Plastaz ... At first there was the late Faza Nelly and Ziggy who called themselves "Two Rough Gs." Later – and Gsan was an underground dancer – they ended up joining together.

KDT: But what does "underground dancer" mean?

Diana: He's like ... He dances ...

Steve: He was first dancing all the time. It's someone who dances. For example, today a concert for dressing traditionally[16] has been prepared. The person who will dress traditionally and dance in traditionally will win. Like that. He was designing his clothes. He was dressing traditionally like that and dancing. He often won but he was underground. At that time he had not yet entered.

KDT: He wasn't yet known.

Steve: He hadn't yet entered the group X Plastaz.

KDT: But you two didn't do that too?

Diana: No, we didn't. We were still very little. We still hadn't entered music.

KDT: What future plans do you as X Plastaz have? Will you continue making albums?

Diana: Ya. Kwa sasa, tuna album, tunaandaa album ya pili ambayo tulishafanya wimbo nne. Tuna mpango wa kuimalizia.

KDT: Mnapocheza, mnalipwa vizuri?

Diana: Inategemea na sehemu tunapo*perform.*

Steve: Kama sehemu ni kubwa, malipo yanaongezeka lakini kama sehemu ni ndogo, inategemea na idadi ya watu.

Diana: Na inategemea na wasanii watakao*perform.* Kama ni wasanii wakubwa wakubwa, ndiyo utalipwa hela ya juu kidogo. Na kama ni underground underground, hamt-alipwa sana.

KDT: Mnaposafiri nje mnalipwa vizuri?

Diana: Ya, kwa kweli tunaweza kusema tunalipwa vizuri, lakini siyo sana.

Steve: Angalau siyo sana

Diana: Tunalipwa vizuri lakini siyo sana. Na tunaenda kwa sababu tunataka kubadilisha, I mean, kujifunza mambo mengine mbali na Tanzania. Siyo kusema tukienda kuperform kule tunapata hela nyingi zaidi kuliko Tanzania, no. Kwa sababu tunaweza tukafanya *concert* hapa hapa tukapata hela ambayo tunapata *abroad.* So, inategemea tu. Na uandaaji.

KDT: Lakini wanakulipia angalau safari za kuenda.

Diana: Yeah. For now, we have an album; we're preparing a second album for which we've already done four songs. We have a plan to finish it.

KDT: When you perform, are you well paid?

Diana: It depends on the place where we are performing.

Steve: If the place is big, the payment increases, but if the place is small, it depends on the number of people.

Diana: And it depends on the artists who will perform. If they are really big artists, yes, you will be paid a slightly higher rate. And if they are underground artists, you won't be paid much.

KDT: When you travel outside of the country are you paid well?

Diana: Yeah, actually we can say we are paid well, but not a lot.

Steve: Better but not a lot.

Diana: We are paid well but not a lot. And we go because we want to alter …. I mean: to learn some things far from Tanzania. That's not to say if we go to perform there we get a lot more money than [we do] in Tanzania, no. Because we can do a concert right here and get the same money that we get abroad. So, it just depends. On the preparation.

KDT: But they pay you at least for your travel expenses.

Diana: Ya, wanalipia safari za kuenda, kila kitu.

Steve: Yaani, kila kitu.

KDT: Na mnajifunza nini huko?

Diana: Tulijifunza mengi: kuishi na watu wapya, jinsi ya kukutana na wasanii wengine. Mm-hmm.

KDT: Mlijifunza vyo vyote kimuziki kutoka wanamuziki wa nje?

Steve: Mfano, labda–. Mfano … wako juu zaidi, wako juu sana.

KDT: Nani? Waholanzi?

Steve: Waholanzi, na watu wengine ambao tulikutana nao. Wana*base* sana katika *music*. Tofauti na hapa.

Diana: Wanaheshimu kazi ya muziki. Siyo kama hapa.

KDT: Labda ni kwa sababu mnakutana na wanamuziki wengine mnafikiri watu wa huko wanaheshimu muziki. Nadhani mkikutana na watu wa kawaida mtaona wengi wanadharau hip-hop kama watu wa hapa. Nafikiri duniani ni kama muziki wa vijana. Watu wanaozeeka wanaidharau kiasi.

Diana: Yeah, they pay for travel, everything.

Steve: In other words, everything.

KDT And what do you learn there?

Diana: We learned a lot: living with new people, how to meet with other artists. Mm-hmm.

KDT: Did you learn anything musically from foreign musicians?

Steve: For example, maybe … For example … They are more professional; they are very professional.

KDT: Who? People in Holland?

Steve: People in Holland, and other people whom we met. They are really based in music. Different from here.

Diana: They respect musical work. Not like here.

Katrina: Maybe it's because you are meeting other musicians that you think people there respect music. I think if you meet average people you will see that many look down on hip-hop like people here do. I think throughout the world it's like youth music. Those who've gotten older look down on it a bit.

Diana: Ni kweli. Halafu kitu kingine kwa hapa Tanzania watu wakienda *concert*, wanakuwa hawako *serious*. Kwa sababu nje, kabla ya ku*perform* lazima ufanye *sound check*. Lakini hapa hapa Tanzania hamna vitu kama hivyo. Ni kwamba ninyi mmeitwa tu kwenye *stage* tu, basi mnaimba. Hawajali kama sauti yako ni mbaya au mmekaa vizuri. Ni vigumu sana. Hata kwenye mashindano, inakuwa ngumu sana. Inakuwa ngumu sana kumpata mshindi kihalali. Kwa sababu wanakuwa hawajafanya *sound check*, hawajajiandaa. Wanaweka *speaker* tu, *mic*, *mix*: "*Okay*, imba sasa."

Steve: Wala hata siyo *beats*. Unamkuta mtu mwingine anatumia *playback*.

Diana: Ya, *playback*. Unaona?

Steve: Siyo vizuri.

Diana: Siyo vizuri. Watu wengine wa huku Tanzania wanatumia *playback*.

KDT: *Playback* ni nini?

Diana: Anaimba juu ya nyimbo yake.

Steve: Ni juu ya nyimbo yake. Siyo kwamba anaimba *live*.

Diana: Anaweka *CD*.

KDT: Hata Wamarekani wanafanya hivyo.

Diana: Huku Tanzania ni wengi sana.

Steve: Tanzania ni wengi.

Diana: It's true. Then another thing here in Tanzania is that if people go to a concert, they're not serious. Because outside [of Tanzania], before performing you must do a sound check. But right here in Tanzania there's nothing like that. You are just called to the stage, and you just sing. They don't care if your voice is bad or if you have situated yourself well. It's very difficult. Even in competitions, it's very difficult. It's very difficult to get a legitimate winner. Because they're not doing sound checks, they haven't prepared themselves. They just put on the speaker, the mic, [and] the mix: "Okay, sing now."

Steve: Not even beats. You can find someone using playback.

Diana: Yeah, playback. You see?

Steve: It's not good.

Diana: It's not good. Some people here in Tanzania use playback.

KDT: What is "playback:?

Diana: He or she sings over his or her song.

Steve: It's over his or her song. It's not that he or she is singing live.

Diana: He or she puts on a CD.

KDT: Even Americans do that.

Diana: Here in Tanzania it's a lot of them.

Steve: In Tanzania it's a lot.

Diana: *Especially* nanii Dar es Salaam.

Steve: Wabongoflava wengi.

Diana: Wabongoflava, ya.

KDT: Ni kawaida sana Marekani. Hata wanamuziki wa juu, kama Madonna na kadhalika utasikia wasikilizaje wanalalamika kwamba anafanya hivyo.

Steve: Lakini ukiimba *live*, ukiimba ile kitu *live*, yaani hata wewe mwenyewe unajisikia vizuri.

Diana: Ya, *you can feel it.*

Steve: Hata wewe mwenyewe, una*feel* ule muziki. Hata washabiki wenyewe wana*feel*. Wanaona kwamba wewe una uwezo wa kurekodi nyimbo ikatoka vizuri. Na una uwezo pia wa ku*perform live* na uka*perform* vizuri. Siyo ile una-*perform playback* na watu hawajui, "Vipi? Kipaji chako, je, kikoje? Na unajitangazaje?"

Diana: Kwa hapa Tanzania ni wengi.

KDT: Mnaweza kuniambia zaidi kuhusu kufanya kazi na Yamat? Naona ni vigumu kuwasiliana naye kwa simu. Mnakutana lini na vipi? Mnafanya mazoezi vipi?

Diana: Mara nyingi anakuja Monduli mjini, kwa sababu Monduli mjini kuna *network*. Anakujaga, mara nyingi anakujaga Ijumaa kwa sababu kuna mnara pale. Anawasiliana na sisi. Anatuuliza, "Kuna mpya yo yote?" Tunamwambia "Kuna mpya" na anakuja.

Diana: Especially, um, in Dar es Salaam.

Steve: A lot of the Bongoflava people.

Diana: The Bongoflava people, yeah.

KDT: It's very common in the United States. Even very professional musicians, like Madonna and so on, you will hear listeners complaining that she does that.

Steve: But if you sing live, if you sing that thing live, I mean, even you yourself will feel good.

Diana: Yeah, you can feel it.

Steve: Even yourself, you feel the music. Even the fans themselves feel it. They see that you have the ability to record a song and will come out well. And you also have the ability to perform live and to perform well. Not that you perform playback and people don't know [and therefore ask], "What's up? What's your talent like? And how are you advertising yourself?"

Diana: Here in Tanzania it's a lot of them.

KDT: Can you tell me more about working with Yamat? It seems difficult to get in touch with him by phone. When and how do you meet up? How do you practice?

Diana: Lots of times he comes into urban Monduli, because in urban Monduli there is a cell phone network.[17] He comes often, lots of times he comes on Fridays because there is a cell phone tower there. He gets in touch with us. He asks, "is there anything new?" We tell him, "There is something new," and he comes.

KDT: Yeye mwenyewe anatunga nini?

Diana: Yeye mwenyewe anatunga *rhymes* zake za Kimaasai.

KDT: Maana yao inaendana na maneno mengine ya Kiswahili katika nyimbo zenu?

Diana: Ya, kwa sababu kabla hatujatunga wimbo, tunakaa tunaitana, tunaambizana, "Leo tunataka kutunga wimbo. Unahusu nini? Kwa hivyo, wewe utatunga *verse* yako, mimi *verse* yangu, yeye *verse* yake, na Yamat *verse* yake Kimaasai.

Steve: Baadaye tunaanza kurekebishana: "Hapa ufanye hivi, fanya hivi, fanya hivi. Imetokaje? Je, imetoka vizuri, au?"

KDT: Lakini kama nyinyi hamfahamu Kimaasai, mnajuaje kama sehemu zake zimetokea vizuri?

KDT: What does he compose, for his part?

Diana: For his part he composes his Maasai rhymes.

KDT: Does their meaning go along with the other Swahili words in your songs?

Diana: Yeah, because before we have composed a song, we sit, we convene a meeting, we tell each other, "Today we want to compose a song. What is it about? So, you compose your verse, I'll do my verse, he his verse, and Yamat his verse in Maa."

Steve: Later we begin correcting each other: "Here do this, do this, do this. How has it come out? Has it come out well, or ...?"

KDT: But if you don't understand Maa, how do you know if his parts have come out well?

[Diana laughs.]

Steve: Gsan anamrekebisha.

Diana: Kwa sababu Gsan anajua Kimaasai. Lakini kwa sisi ni ngumu sana kumrekebisha.

KDT: Gsan alijifunzaje...?

Diana: Alijifunza Kimaasai alipoenda kumchukua Yamat.

Steve: Kuna kipindi alipenda kuendaga. Haipiti mwezi bila kuenda Umaasaini.

Diana: Ndo kitu alichopenda ndo maana akajifunza.

KDT: Nyinyi mmewahi kuishi Umaasaini pia?

Steve: Gsan corrects him.

Diana: Because Gsan knows Maa. But for us it's very difficult to correct him.

KDT: How did Gsan learn ...?"

Diana: He learned Maa when he went to get Yamat.

Steve: There was a time when he liked to go all the time. A month would not go by without him going to Maasailand.

Diana: It's something that he liked so he learned [it].

KDT: Have you two ever lived in Maasailand too?

Diana: [laughing] Kweli, hatujawahi.

Diana: Actually, we never have.

Steve: Tunatembelea tu.

Steve: We just visit.

Diana: Tumeenda kutembea tu halafu kurudi. Kama kulala siku moja siku mbili, tunarudi.

Diana: We have gone to just look around and then come back. Like sleeping [there] one or two days, and then we come back.

KDT: Haya, maswali yangu yame-kwisha. Kuna cho chote ambacho nyinyi mnataka kusema?

KDT: Okay, my questions are finished. Is there anything you want to say?

Diana: Kweli mimi natia moyo wasanii wengine tupendane, tush-irikiane, tupeane ushauri.

Diana: Truly, I encourage other artists: Let's like each other, let's work together, let's give each other advice.

Steve: Na vilevile, tuwe *serious* katika kazi zetu.

Steve: And, too, let's be serious in our work.

Diana: Tusidharau kazi ya mtu fulani.

Diana: Let's not look down upon anyone's work.

KDT: Asanteni sana.

KDT: Thank you both so much.

Diana: Asante na wewe. Karibu.

Diana: Thank you, too. You're welcome.

thomas gesthuizen, january 2007

KDT: How did you get involved in hip-hop music in general, and Tanzanian hip-hop specifically?

Thomas: Hip-hop: through my cousin who was a hip-hop fan and dj since about 1985. He first gave me some underground tapes around 1987 and I have been listening ever after. In 1991 I first visited Tanzania (at the age of 17) and during my next visit in 1993 I found that there was local hip-hop which interested me a lot also because I was studying African studies/linguistics and taking Swahili courses [at Leiden University]. In 1994 I bought my first Tanzanian rap tapes and a year later I learnt about rap in other African countries (Senegal and South Africa). In 1997 I started a website to promote the music of Tanzanian artists that

I had come to know, and [music] of other groups. That site grew out to be Africanhiphop.com and it still exists. By the way I also bought every Tanzanian rap cassette that came out from 1992 to 2000; that's about 100 tapes and I still have them.

KDT: Tell me about how you first met Xplastaz and why you were interested in their work.

Thomas: I met em through another student of anthropology [Peter-Jan Haas] who had borrowed my idea to write a thesis about hip-hop in Tanzania; we kept in touch and he went to do research for his MA thesis shortly before I went out there, in summer 1997. So he posted me contacts and info, and he bumped into X Plastaz as they were the Arusha opening act for a touring group of Dar es Salaam-based, well-known emcees. He told me that X Plastaz were really much better, more energetic and raw than the Dar performers. Also they had painted their hair and put plasters on their faces ('X Plastaz'). They got the crowd on their hand. So I started to write [i.e. correspond] with them (in Swahili) and when I finally popped up at their haircutting saloon in Arusha town, they didn't want to believe it was me who had been writing because I was white. But I stayed in Arusha for a while and we actually went out to the Maasai steppe together to visit a village that I had been to before, on holidays. That's the start of the whole Maasai angle. We went to the local club (Mawingu, which was run by the same people who now run Clouds radio in Dar) and recorded their track 'Bamiza' using my portable minidisc, which at the time was an absolute novelty there – digital sound recording of a local group! In 1998 I sent a few people in Dar a cd-r with a collection of American and Tanzanian songs; Bamiza was on there, and one of them actually sold his cd-r to the Indian music pirates who pressed up copies and sold em all over E. Africa! But thanks to him, Bamiza became a radio hit.

KDT: Tell me more about your visit to Maasailand and how Yamat got involved with the group.

Thomas: My 2nd time in Tanzania I was on holidays with my father and we ran into a French woman living there, who urged us to take a tour with her low budget travel company, into a small and very remote village called Sukuro (near Terat, 60 km south of Arusha). She used to take tourists there who were then hosted by the local chairman and his family who lived in a boma and who showed people around. The remoteness, the hospitality and the culture impressed me a lot so I wanted to visit again in 1997 when I was with X Plastaz.

So we took a trip out there on the back of a landrover and just went – and to X Plastaz it must have been an adventure cos they had never been out there but they took it like it was an everyday trip. So at night around the fire in the boma we heard the women and kids singing and that was the 1st time for the three of em (Nelly, Ziggy and Gsan) to witness Maasai culture from nearby.

In the next 2 years all of em did some part-time work in tourism and on one of those trips into the bush, Gsan met Yamat. He heard that Yamat was the champion singer of his area, he had one some local competitions among his age mates. So he linked up with him and even though Yamat didn't speak Swahili and Gsan didn't speak much Maasai, they communicated through music. So Gsan asked him to see if he could sing over hip-hop beats, and Yamat tried and it worked out. So he got to spend some time in Arusha with Gsan and learned to speak Swahili and to write. By 2000 or so, he was officially a part of the group and in 2001 he came out to perform in Holland.

KDT: When you helped them get tours to the Netherlands and elsewhere, how were those trips funded? (I.e. did ticket sales cover those costs?)

Thomas: Initially by invitations from organizations who approached me, such as Festival Mundial and later on (2003) a Belgian NGO and a lady in UK who ran a cultural organization. Usually they would pay for the tickets, visa and then sometimes we would get paid for the concerts, too.

In 2005 we partly paid for the ticket ourselves.

KDT: What role(s) do you currently play with regard to Xplastaz?

Thomas: They started to call me manager at some point but I had been doing everything except for making music or rapping. That includes promotion, marketing, management tasks such as arranging tours and getting album deals or arrange for their tracks to be used on compilations; also directing, shooting and editing videos such as the latest one Nini Dhambi kwa Mwenye Dhiki which we shot on the active volcano Ol Doinyo Lengai and which only cost us the fee for renting a Landrover, still it's played on MTV Africa. So the whole X Plastaz project is really do-for-self and low budget. We tend to think that we can set an example for others.

KDT: How would you compare or contrast Xplastaz to other popular Tanzanian music?

Thomas: X Plastaz are definitely influenced by the Tanzanian tradition of pop music, for example in the way they use messages to uplift society.

But they are also rebellious in a way that seems to be (or to have become) typical of Arusha hip-hop, and in that they are trendsetters. Arusha hip-hop is based in a different tradition of hip-hop than what is happening in Dar.

X Plastaz grew up with hip-hop acts like Das EFX, M.O.P. and the Def Squad whose musical style and dress refer to their getto backgrounds. Also X Plastaz have dared to use traditional

Tanzanian music in their rap songs, which not a lot of groups have dared.

Also they have been able to gain experience with foreign audiences and media, which added to their difference from the average Tanzanian rap group.

KDT: How would you define the term "Bongoflava"? Are Xplastaz part of "Bongoflava"?

Thomas: Bongo flava to me is a media term (invented by a dj at Clouds radio) for describing post-2000, radio friendly Tanzanian rap music. X Plastaz and a number of other groups have chosen not to call their music Bongo flava because they disagree with the direction that rap has taken on Tanzanian radio and television. At some point they were pressed into the same direction by radio deejays: use more anecdotes in their lyrics, childish stories and not focus so much on serious matters and problems.

Refusing to use the term has become more difficult because many people are not aware of the gap between the conscious hip-hop tradition and the poppy rap that is called Bongo flava, most young people and also labels and media abroad tend to call ALL Tanzanian hip-hop 'Bongo flava'.

KDT: Are their other Tanzanian artists you would consider "conscious hip-hop"?

Thomas: Yes, for example Hashim (Dar es Salaam), Hardcore Unit (Arusha), Kalamashaka (from Nairobi Kenya but also active in TZ), a couple of other Arusha artists like Stopparhymes, High Voltage, Nako 2 Nako... Also from the old school: Mr2 (aka 2Proud aka Sugu), Deplowmatz and Dola Soul who is a solo artist from that group...

KDT: In some other parts of the world (Cuba, for example) artists make a distinction between "underground" and "commercial" hiphop – where "underground" is used in the way (I think) you're using "conscious" in Tanzania. Do you think these distinctions useful in Tanzania? (Or are there other terms you would use? (Or heard used by Tanzanians?)

Thomas: In Tanzania some people misinterpret 'underground' as 'amateur' or 'not professional' as opposed to the artists who can live off their work or those who are heard on the media. But I think some people in Tanzania do use the word 'underground' and even the plural 'ma underground' to refer to those artists who are not embedded in a commercial structure. Also see this video which I shot in Arusha in 2004, I think the guys use the word 'underground': http://www.africanhiphop.com/index.php?name=News&file=article&sid=140.

KDT: If you were describing Xplastaz to someone who hadn't heard their music, how would you describe it?

Thomas: An energetic blend of underground hip-hop, traditional Maasai chants, reggae, dancehall and other traditional Tanzanian music.

KDT: What is it like to attend an Xplastaz performance? Are there any differences between their performances in Tanzania versus those elsewhere?

Thomas: X Plastaz make sure that the audience becomes part of their show. It's like a party in which people are asked to chant and dance along and join the performers on stage. They often manage to steal the audience's hearts. They appeal to different needs/wants of the audience: most people are mesmerized by Yamat's chants but they also get a bit of the hardcore hip-hop energy and then there is a girl on stage rapping, which is not a very regular sight in a rap group. They tend to bring a foreign dj so that's also a different sight.

KDT: Who's the foreign DJ X Plastaz brings with them? You?

Thomas: I have deejayed a few times but usually we bring dj 360 (Bamba Nazar, half Dutch/Surinamese who spent part of his youth in the U.S. and who has produced for Freestyle Fellowship, the Outsidaz and some other big names in U.S. music, and he produced some X Plastaz tracks) or Kid Sundance (my cousin Raimond who has produced for X Plastaz but also worked with US hip-hop pioneer Busy Bee and with Declaime aka Dudley Perkins).

KDT: When did you create the Xplastaz website? And MySpace page? How have these impacted the group?

Thomas: X Plastaz site: not sure, probably around 1999/2000. Myspace: 2005.

The website has done a lot for the group, especially with regards to international bookings and getting an album deal. All professional contacts tend to have a look at the site. Also we have published major news on the site, which was then taken over by media, for example when Nelly died.

Myspace: currently gets more hits per day than the website, so that's a good promotional tool. Though in the professional field a Myspace page has limited value since it's harder to express the group's identity since you're a bit limited to the default Myspace layout.

KDT: Are you able to make a living with hip-hop related work? Or do you have other employment?

Thomas: No not at this time. We hope to get funding for Africanhiphop.com – we have set up a NGO called the African hip-hop foundation with board members and volunteers from South Africa, Uganda, Somalia, Benin and Holland. I work 4 days a week for a tv production company making TV for immigrant communities in the Netherlands, I am responsible for the website – see www.mtnl.nl <http://www.mtnl.nl> (website in Dutch). One day a week I spend on my own projects and I present a radio show called One Blood for Dutch national broadcaster Vpro – see http://3voor12.vpro.nl/programmas/afleveringen/32138468 (you can listen there). So the work for X Plastaz and African-hiphop.com is and has always been confined to my free time at night and in the weekend.

KDT: Have you worked as directly with any other groups as you have with X Plastaz?

Thomas: No. I would have liked to but my budget and my time didn't allow. Also I haven't met many artists who I found as inspiring and talented as X Plastaz.

KDT: What effect do you think hiphop is having on the Swahili language?

Thomas: I noticed that some youth have started to purposely mispronounce Swahili to sound as if an American is speaking Swahili. So they have a certain American twang even though Swahili is their mother tongue. A couple of rap artists can be heard rapping like that (I can't think of any name right now).

Also hip-hop has helped to introduce certain slang or very local words into mainstream use. Swahili is notorious for that... inventions can travel really fast especially when popular culture gives a helping hand.

Some examples: chuna mbuzi = when a lady seduces a guy and then robs him off his wealth (and leave him after that). This was originally a song by an artist called Makoya Man around 1997/8.

cheza mbali na kasheshe = stay away from trouble

mtoto wa geti kali = a child from the barbed wire fence = a girl who can't get out of the house without her parents giving her a hard time (and probably her family is well to do), this is from a song by Gangwe Mobb from around 2001.

KDT: Gsan (and other artists I interviewed) told me that Tanzanian DJs are asking for bribes in order to play their music on the radio but that X Plastaz has refused to pay and so is not getting much airplay. What has your experience of this been?

Thomas: In the past (before 2000 for sure), deejays would just play any good music. But as commercialism kicked in and a structure came into place which supported rap music on various levels (managers, distributors, specialized deejays and journalists) and there were more tracks than a radio dj could play, those deejays started to favour the artists who gave them some money or found other ways to keep them friends (take em out for a beer, hang out etc).

Now X Plastaz were in Arusha so it was harder for them to keep that relationship, also they were broke most of the time and had no local manager/promoter.

On the other hand they always came up with something new and innovative and so at least a couple of deejays would still play their tracks & videos. Examples: the tracks 'Bamiza' (released in 1999 with a video in 2000), 'Aha' (video shot in Maasai village), 'Msimu kwa msimu' (video shot in Holland with special effects), 'Nini dhambi kwa mwenye dhiki' (after Nelly died) etc.

These days some media are pretty open about the bribing system, they just have fixed prices for promoting tracks. For example Clouds would hype a track for a full month in exchange for a couple of 100.000's. Also deejay collectives would hype tracks in the discos around Tanzania.

KDT: What does the future hold for X Plastaz after Nelly's death?

The group has chosen to keep on working like before when Nelly was still alive. So, to record the 2nd album and to do more foreign and local Tanzanian concerts.

In the near future we want to shop the demo tracks for the 2nd album, also to try to get concerts in Europe in summer 2007 so that we can record here; also to release a mixtape with unreleased and new tracks (about 25 tracks selected so far), release some of those new tracks to the Tanzanian media in early 2007, and to record a music video for some of the new songs. We also want to work on a documentary about Nelly's life since I have hours and hours of video tapes of all the concerts and tours we did since 2001 (including Brazil, Scandinavia, London, Belgium, Holland), and even of his funeral and the tribute in Gabon in June 2006.

If we manage to realize at least a couple of these plans I'll be happy...

But in any case X Plastaz seem to have fans all over the world, some people just know one track from one of the Rough Guide compilations or they saw their videos on Youtube.

notes

1. I have followed Xplastaz members Gsan and Faza Nelly in writing the group's name as "Xplastaz," although the name is often written as "X Plastaz" in their English-language publicity materials.
2. National exams after primary school and after Form Four serve as bottlenecks in the Tanzanian educational system.
3. The Swahili word *ndugu* can mean 'sibling' or 'cousin', and many Swahili speakers do not distinguish between these two relationships.
4. I have left out the next four paragraphs because they are identical (word for word) with Gsan's response to my first question, below.
5. Arusha International Conference Center.
6. The album was renamed "Maasai Hip-hop" before its release.
7. See footnote 1. Gsan's response here appears to be cut from the Swahili history on the X plastaz web site, which was – according to Gesthuizen – written by Faza Nelly.
8. In other words, Diana has finished secondary school and is now studying at one of the small private businesses in Arusha (and other Tanzanian cities) offering specialized classes.

9. In the Tanzanian educational system, students go from Standard Seven (the final level in primary school), to Form One (the first level in secondary school). Although pre-Form One courses have been repeatedly banned by the Ministry of Education, many students take them at private schools in order to bridge the gap between the two curricula, the former of which is in Swahili and the latter in English.

10. Mr. II was one of the most popular early rappers in Tanzania. He began performing under the moniker 2 Proud in the early 1990s, then became Mr II, and is now known as SUGU.

11. Mawingu Club is a popular dance hall in Arusha.

12. "We" here refers to Diana and Steve, who rapped together as the Fortune Tellers, not to all the members of X Plastaz.

13. Festival Mundial is a yearly two-day Tilburg-based music and cultural festival dedicated to the development of individuals and groups from the developing world

14. Madunia Music is "a non-profit non-governmental organisation based in the Netherlands that promotes African music and supports local initiatives of African musicians" and is listed as X Plastaz's international manager on the group's web site and as Thomas Gesthuizen's affiliation on the group's MySpace page.

15. Coulour Café is a three-day world musical festival held annually in Brussels.

16. Interestingly, here Steve uses the word *kizamani* (lit.: 'in the old way') to mean "traditionally," while earlier he and Diana used *kiasili* (lit.: 'in the original way'), which suggests a slightly different attitude toward "tradition."

17. Monduli Mjini, or 'urban Monduli' is part of the Monduli district just West of Arusha.

webography

http://sugumusic.tripod.com/
http://www.festivalmundial.nl/
http://www.myspace.com/Xplastaz
http://www.Xplastaz.com

works cited

Englert, Birgit. 2003. Bongo Flava (Still) Hidden: 'Underground' Rap from Morogoro, Tanzania. *Stichproben* 3, no. 5: 73-93.

Reuster-Jahn, Uta. 2007. Let's go party! Discourse and Self-Portrayal in the Bongo Fleva-Song Mikasi. In *Swahili Forum*, 14:225-244. Vol. 14.

Stroeken, Koen. 2005a. This is not a haircut. Neoliberalism and revolt in Kiswahili rap. *Image & Narrative: Online Journal of the Visual Narrative*, no. 11: 13 September 2007.

_____. 2005b. Immunizing Strategies: Hip-Hop and Critique in Tanzania. *Africa: Journal of the International African Institute* 75, no. 4: 488-509.

Thompson, Katrina Daly. Rap, Cartoon and Rap Cartoon: Representations of the Maasai in Contemporary Tanzanian Popular Culture. In *Music, Performance, and African Identities*, ed. Toyin Falola and Tyler Fleming. Bloomington: Indiana University Press, in press.

_____. 2006. The Stereotype in Tanzania[n] Comics: Swahili and the Ethnic Other. *The International Journal of Comic Art* 8, no. 2 (Fall): 228-247.

_____. 2008. Keeping it real: reality and representation in Maasai Hip-Hop. *Journal of African Cultural Studies* 20, no. 1: 33-44.

PART IV

"who shot ya?"

african hip-hop in focus

CHAPTER 10
photos from
south africa

NOELLE THEARD

figure 10.1: dj salsa performs at the
hip-hop indaba in cape town.

figure 10.3: an emcee cypher forms outside the
red bull battle of the year in johannesburg.

native tongues: an african hip-hop reader

figure 10.2: emile xy?, south african hip-hop pioneer, performer, and activist, talks to youth at the hip-hop indaba in cape town.

figure 10.4: benny, one of the world's best b-boys battles at the hip-hop indaba in cape town.

figure 10.5: legendary south african graffiti
artist mak1one paints in johannesburg.

figure 10.6: renown south african emcee, tumi, records in his johannesburg studio.

figure 10.7: girls pose for a photo at
a sunday hip-hop jam in the guguletu
township in cape town.

native tongues: an african hip-hop reader

figure 10.8: speakers are stacked as youth listen to the emcees at a sunday hip-hop jam in the guguletu township in cape town.

CHAPTER 11
photos from
"here and there"

MAGEE MCILVAINE

figure 11.1: bboy abdul kinyenya from
kampala, uganda, and founding member
of breakdance project uganda.

figure 11.3: emcee battle at waga **hip hop** festival in **ouagadougou,** burkina faso

native **tongues: an african hip-hop** reader

figure 11.2: bboy abdul kinyenya from kampala, uganda, and founding member of breakdance project uganda.

figure 11.4: pioneers of burkinabe hip hop, faso kombat are one of the biggest groups in the country: david le combattant and malkolm of faso kombat.

figure 11.5: **outspoken the alpha intellect** (dialectric blue crew and magamba cultural activist network) of zimbabwe. **outspoken performing with his band** *the essence.*

figure 11.7: mic the 7th,
from burkina faso.

native tongues: an african hip-hop reader

figure 11.6: cape verdean hip hop artist and
activist shokanti (he is playing the djembe).

contributors

Catherine Appert is a Ph.D. candidate in Ethnomusicology at UCLA, where her dissertation examines the dynamic between traditional and popular cultural production as expressed and negotiated through hip hop performance in Dakar, Senegal, and among Senegalese immigrants in U.S. urban centers. Her research interests include African and Afro-diasporic popular music, globalization and popular culture, and the intersections of music and gender.

Shaheen Ariefdien was born in Cape Town, South Africa. He was a key member of the pioneering South African hip-hop group *Prophets of da City*. He has worked on a number of youth education projects focusing on the use of hip-hop as a tool for social justice in places such as South Africa, Norway, Holland, Angola, to name a few. Some of these projects included voter education campaigns, creative writing for imprisoned youth, and educational workshops. He recently completed his M.A. in social anthropology at York University in Toronto, Canada.

Marlon Burgess was born in Cape Town, South Africa and was raised in Kensington on the Cape Flats in the 1980s. As a conceptual artist he has performed in and around Cape Town since the late 1990s including sharing a stage with Linton Kwesi Johnson at the Urban Voices International Arts Festival in 2004. He is currently a doctoral student at New York University's Department of Social and Cultural Analysis writing about the music of the African Diaspora. He is also completing a music project with a collective out of the University of Cape Town (UCT) Workers Support Committee which stands in solidarity with workers struggles globally.

Murray Forman is an associate professor of Communication Studies at Northeastern University. He is the author of *The 'Hood Comes First: Race, Space, and Place in Rap and Hip-Hop* (Wesleyan University Press, 2002) and co-editor, with Mark Anthony Neal, of *That's the Joint!': The Hip-Hop Studies Reader* (Routledge, 2004; Second Edition, 2011). He is also the author of numerous articles on youth, race, popular music, television, and film.

Daniel Künzler earned his doctorate at the University of Zurich (Switzerland) and then spent two years in West Africa for research and teaching. He currently lectures on sociology, social policy, and social work at the University of Fribourg (Switzerland). His main research areas are education and popular culture in sub-Saharan Africa. Among other publications, he is the author of several articles on both rap music and videos as well as a book on soccer.

Jenny F. MBaye is currently finishing her PhD in Human Geography (urban cultural economy) at the Department of Geography and Environment at the London School of Economics and Political Science (LSE). Her research interests focus on music economy and cultural entrepreneurship in Francophone West Africa (Ouagadougou, Burkina Faso and Dakar, Senegal). She has a Graduate Diploma in Management of Cultural Organisation (HEC-Montreal), an MSc in International Studies specialised in Ethnomusicology (University of Montreal) and BA in Sociology (Concordia University). Besides, she regularly works as a consultant for the Bureau of Cultural Engineering and Mediation, *Accents Multiples* (Dakar, Senegal).

Magee McIlvaine is co-founder of Sol Productions, a nonprofit film production company that has produced groundbreaking films such as *Democracy in Dakar* and *Democracy in Paris*. His work has been featured in the New York Times, Washington Express, Spin Earth, XXL, Billboard, and The Nation. Magee currently serves as Creative Director of Nomadic Wax LLC, the world's premiere global youth movement building and content creator. He is also co-founder of the monthly event series VOICES in DC, which works to raise both funds and awareness for youth-led grassroots movements around the world. He works regularly with both diaspora youth and young organizers in Africa, establishing himself as one of the leading experts on youth-initiated organizing in urban Africa and the diaspora here in the U.S.

Caroline Mose is an Urban Anthropologist, having completed her BA in Kenya and a Masters Degree at the University of Oxford in the UK. She is currently finishing her PhD Thesis on Urban Popular Culture at the School of Oriental and African Studies in London. Her research interests include popular culture/urban popular culture, popular music and emergent forms of urban popular expression.

Harry Nii Koney Odamtten is a citizen of Ghana, West Africa and holds a dual PhD in African American and African Studies, and History from Michigan State University. With an interest in African and African Diaspora intellectual and social history, he is presently Assistant Professor of History at the University of Central Arkansas.

J. Griffith Rollefson is a Lecturer in Musicology and Ethnomusicology in the Conservatory of Music at Chapman University. He holds the PhD in Musicology from the University of Wisconsin-Madison and is a recent Research Fellow at the Freie Universität Berlin where he conducted fieldwork for a dissertation examining minority protest strategies in European hip hop. He is currently preparing the study for publication as *Musical African Americanization: European Hip Hop and Minority Identity.* His research on music, race, and postcoloniality has appeared in *Black Music Research Journal, Popular Music and Society,* and *Music Research Forum,* in the collection *Crosscurrents: European and American Music in Interaction 1900-2000,* in the *Encyclopedia of African American Music* and elsewhere.

P. Khalil Saucier is Director of Africana Studies and assistant professor of sociology at Rhode Island College. He specializes in identity formation, black popular culture, social thought, and race and ethnicity. His publications are featured in the *Journal of Popular Music Studies, Rethinking Marxism: A Journal of Economics, Culture, and Society, American Communication Journal, Fashion Theory, Encyclopedia of African American Music,* and others. He has co-authored *Historical Dictionary of the Republic of Cape Verde,* 4th edition with Richard A. Lobban Jr. (2007).

Noelle Theard is a Miami-based freelance photographer and educator. She holds an M.A. in African Diaspora Studies from Florida International University, a B.A. in Journalism from the University of Texas at Austin, and a certificate in advanced studies from the Spéos Photography Institute in Paris, France. Her photographic work on hip-hop culture has taken her to South America, South Africa, and Europe. She is also co-director of FotoKonbit, a non-profit organization created to engage and empower Haitians to tell their own stories and document their communities through photography.

Katrina Daly Thompson is an Assistant Professor in the Department of Applied Linguistics at UCLA. She specializes in African languages and identities with a focus on ethnicity, gender and sexuality in Zimbabwean and Tanzanian discourse.

Remi Warner holds a PhD in social anthropology and teaches at York University in Canada. His research explores the politics and poetics of race and place, and the impact of the globalization of Black popular culture on youth identity in post-apartheid South Africa. He has also published on hip-hop in Canada.

index

Breakin' 133, 221, 223, 224, 228

Cape Flats 105-107, 115, 117,
    121, 124, 127, 129-133, 223,
    224, 234
Capitalism 15
Cipher (cipha) 180-183, 208, 223
Civil society 41, 43, 79, 149
code switching 236
collabos 78, 92
colonialism 120, 189, 205
coloured 106, 107, 115, 118-128,
    220, 224, 227, 234-236, 238,
    242, 243, 251
commercialization 69, 70, 76,
    79, 242
commodification 242
corruption 28, 39, 40, 42, 61, 80
cosmopolitan 116, 150, 202, 203
cosmopolitanism 203
cultural imperialism 112, 127,
    203, 232
cultural production 3, 6, 11,
    15-17, 108
    Culture 3, 4, 11-13, 16, 24,
    69, 71, 72, 75, 79, 80, 85-87,
    89, 91, 93, 147, 243, 246
culture 3, 4, 6, 10-13, 16, 23-25,
    52, 54, 63, 69, 71, 72, 75, 79,
    80, 85-87, 89, 91-93, 105,
    107, 113, 115-117, 120-125,
    134, 147-151, 153, 156, 157,
    159, 167, 169, 182, 185, 188-
    191, 195, 198, 200, 202, 204,
    206, 211, 212, 225-228, 235,

237, 238, 242, 243, 245, 246,
    257, 258, 263-267, 288, 293

democracy 38, 39, 58, 60, 61, 64,
    74, 157, 158
democratic 31, 38, 43, 52, 53, 62,
    64, 125, 156, 157, 180, 236
development 8, 25, 26, 31, 32,
    43, 58, 64, 79, 86, 93, 108-
    110, 113, 117, 127, 128, 130,
    131, 147, 152, 153, 188, 229,
    237, 239, 246, 257
diaspora 4, 13-15, 17, 77, 118,
    148
discourse 4-6, 15-17, 41, 43,
    52-54, 56, 58, 61, 64, 69, 70,
    79, 83, 119, 122, 128, 159,
    161, 182, 188, 203, 205, 210,
    238, 240
discursive practices 5, 54, 61
DJ (deejay) 7, 8, 14, 23, 27, 34, 44,
    56, 57, 87, 89, 106, 107, 110,
    115, 116, 121, 123, 131, 133,
    152, 159, 180, 182-184, 187,
    208, 219, 220, 223, 224, 227,
    228, 232, 239, 244, 256, 260,
    286, 290-292, 294, 301, 314
Du Bois, W.E.B. 186, 187, 190, 203

economic 3, 15-17, 24, 27, 31,
    32, 34, 35, 43, 52-54, 62, 63,
    76-78, 86, 93, 106, 112, 114,
    116, 117, 119, 128, 131-133,
    187, 193, 195, 202, 209, 210,
    231, 235, 236, 243

native tongues: an african hip-hop reader

native tongues: an african hip-hop reader

Social change 10, 43, 60, 61, 64, 243
Social justice 64
Social problems 79
Sub-culture 237
Sugar Hill Gang 110
Swahili 78, 82, 254, 257, 260-262, 264, 275-277, 279, 285-288, 293

Tata Pound 31, 39, 40, 42, 43, 57
Text 4-7, 9-11, 13-17, 25-27, 34, 51, 52, 54, 56, 63, 89, 93, 109, 114, 119-121, 124, 125, 127, 132, 133, 150, 155, 161, 166, 183, 185, 186, 188, 189, 198, 208, 218, 233, 235, 238, 239, 244, 254, 260
Tinny 148, 149, 152, 158-165, 167
township 27, 107, 111, 113, 115, 119, 123, 225, 227, 231, 234, 306, 307
tradition 3-10, 14, 16, 32, 34, 52, 53, 62, 79, 92, 93, 110, 123, 124, 126, 152, 153, 159, 168, 202, 203, 207, 218, 219, 232, 233, 245, 260, 265, 273, 280, 289-291
Traditional music 6-8, 110, 265
Transatlantic 11, 13, 16, 17
Transcultural 52, 54, 150, 151
Translocal 52, 54, 57-60, 63, 64, 133
Transnational 4, 6, 11-16, 112, 116

urban 10, 15, 16, 24, 27, 28, 34, 52-55, 58-61, 63, 64, 70, 85, 86, 93, 112, 113, 115, 118, 127-131, 133, 264, 268, 284

West Africa 10, 36, 42, 43, 51-54, 56-60, 63, 64, 148, 149, 151, 156, 158
Wolof 10-12, 59
women 23, 27, 34, 35, 61, 83, 84, 150, 151, 161, 163, 181, 200-204, 221, 238, 240, 244, 246, 274, 288

X, Malcolm 188, 191, 196, 205, 233
X-Plastaz 253, 268, 270, 271, 277, 279, 280, 287-295

Yeleen 25, 28, 30, 32-39, 41-43, 57
youth 3-7, 10, 11, 13-17, 23, 26, 29, 36, 44, 52-54, 57-61, 63, 64, 92, 105, 106, 108, 113, 115, 117-119, 122, 124, 133, 147, 149, 151, 153, 155, 156, 159, 163, 166, 169, 182, 213, 219, 228, 253, 255, 261, 262, 282, 292, 293, 303, 307